12 <u>95</u>.

Essays in Literature

Series editors:

NANCY ARMSTRONG

LEONARD TENNENHOUSE

The

IDEOLOGY OF CONDUCT

The
IDEOLOGY OF CONDUCT

ESSAYS ON LITERATURE
and the
HISTORY OF SEXUALITY

Edited by

NANCY ARMSTRONG

LEONARD TENNENHOUSE

Methuen
New York and London

First published in 1987 by
Methuen & Co.
in association with Methuen, Inc.
29 West 35th Street, New York NY 10001

Published in Great Britain by
Methuen & Co. Ltd
11 New Fetter Lane, London EC4P 4EE

© 1987 Nancy Armstrong and Leonard Tennenhouse

Photoset by Rowland Phototypesetting Ltd
Bury St Edmunds, Suffolk
Printed in Great Britain by Richard Clay Ltd,
Bungay, Suffolk

Library of Congress Cataloging in Publication Data
The Ideology of conduct.
(Essays in literature and society)
Bibliography: p.
Includes index.
1. Women – Sexual behaviour – History.   2. Sex role
in literature – History.   3. Women in literature –
History.   1. Armstrong, Nancy.   11. Tennenhouse,
Leonard, 1942–   . III. Series.
HQ29.I34 1987   306.7'088042   86-28446
ISBN 0-416-38600-8 (pbk.)
ISBN 0-416-38590-7

British Library Cataloguing in Publication Data
The Ideology of conduct: essays on literature
and the history of sexuality. – (Essays
in literature and society)
1. Sex in literature
I. Armstrong, Nancy   II. Tennenhouse,
Leonard   III. Series
809'.93353   PN56.S5
ISBN 0-416-38590-7
ISBN 0-416-38600-8 Pbk

For

Sarah Johnson Armstrong
and
Judy Greenbaum Armstrong

Contents

The literature of conduct, the conduct of literature, and the politics of desire: an introduction

NANCY ARMSTRONG
LEONARD TENNENHOUSE

> For, the clearer our conceptions in art and science become, the more they will assimilate themselves to the conceptions of duty in conduct, will become practically stringent like rules of conduct, and will invite the same sort of language in dealing with them.   (Matthew Arnold, *Literature and Dogma*)

This collection of essays grew out of our recognition of a very simple truth: the literature of conduct and the conduct of the writing known as literature share the same history. Both literature and conduct books, especially those written for women, are integral and instrumental to the history of desire. The essays in this volume demonstrate that conduct books for women, in particular, strive to reproduce, if not always to revise, the culturally approved forms of desire. Anthropologists generally agree that cultures systematically designate a certain kind of woman as the object of desire. The exchange of such women not only determines kinship relations among families or tribes but also determines the economic and political organization characterizing the group within which such an exchange of women takes place. If it is true that in other cultures the rules that govern kinship relations also regulate the political economy, and that kinship relations are in this respect one and the same as political relations, then we must also assume that whatever it is that makes certain objects of sexual exchange more valuable than others also provides the basis of political authority. Granting this, one must ask if our own culture does not yield to the same logic we identify in others: do we not have kinship rules as precise and elaborate as those we attribute to other cultures? Do these rules not reproduce a specific political order, one in which we play the roles of both subject and instrument? Do we not have a characteristic technology of desire which ensures the reproduction of prevailing kinship relations? When we speak of the woman we desire or the woman we desire to be, do we not appear to be speaking about what is most basic and natural in ourselves? And is it not this very knowledge of ourselves as the subjects and objects of desire that we have been taught to discover in literature?

It is the intention of this collection of essays to show that such expressions of desire in fact constitute ideology in its most basic and powerful form, namely, one that culture designates as nature itself. Of the means which European culture has developed to create and regulate desire, conduct books for women and certain other forms of writing now known as literature offer us the clearest examples. To us, it seems all too obvious that if sexual relations can uphold specific forms of political authority in other cultures, they must have the power to do so in ours; the terms and dynamics of sexual desire must be a political language in modern cultures too.[1] From this hypothesis follow certain implications for the study of literature. First, literature concerned with women and the vicissitudes of sexual love is no less political than literature that deals with men and the official institutions of state. Because redefinitions of desire often revise the basis of political power, or human nature itself, one might say that changes in the understanding of desire, the practice of courtship, and the organization of the family are culturally antecedent to changes in the official institutions of state. Second, where this relationship between personal and public experience can be shown to hold true, we must see representations of desire, neither as reflections nor as consequences of political power, but as a form of political power in their own right.

Because the relationship between sex and politics is an ancient and ongoing one, we have asked scholars working in various periods of literary history to read literature in relation to the literature of female conduct. As we will argue, these essays together demonstrate that the production of specific forms of desire has created and maintained specific forms of political authority, and that sexual desire therefore cannot be left out of political history. It seems clear to us that most critical approaches to literature cannot describe the role literature has played in the history of desire. For if critics do care to consider literature historically, they generally do so in reference to a world determined by economic and political relationships among men. In pursuing the relation between literature and conduct books, we have tried to resist this tendency. We have chosen to consider history as all those symbolic practices, among which writing is one, that make up the social reality at a given moment in time. Within such a framework, we can observe the terms of desire change from one age to the next. We can see the notion of gender undergo transformation. And we may conclude that literature played different – but nonetheless important – roles in effecting such changes.

Yet, despite remarkable parallels between the literature of conduct and the conduct of literature, literary histories rarely if ever contain references to the literature of female conduct, and even more rarely are conduct books for women allowed to contribute to our notion of cultural history. A glance at the subject holdings of any well-stocked library reveals numerous titles devoted to social and economic history as well as to the traditional history of ideas, and there are always a handful of titles concerned with the history of the family. Moreover, a closer look at the same catalogue uncovers other kinds of histories, what we usually mean by cultural histories, not only histories of literature and the sister arts, but also histories of folk practices and those forms of expression known as popular culture. Yet a search of any reputable research library will reveal that much the same conditions now prevail as reigned in Virginia Woolf's day when she made her historic trip to the British Museum and found no useful information under "women," nothing, at least, to help her explain the relationship between women and fiction. And even the most careful examination of the library will reveal few subject headings of the sort to which conduct books for women might belong. Still fewer headings link women and the cultural materials over which they hold sway with the events of traditional histories. Indeed, it is often difficult to locate conduct books for women in a library's catalogue unless they happen to be written by someone –

Lord Halifax or Mary Wollstonecraft, for example – known for writing in a more prestigious mode. By way of contrast to the fate of conduct books for women, Castiglione's *Book of the Courtier*, Guazzo's *Civil Conversations*, as well as advice in the form of "letters to a son" from Sir Henry Sidney to Lord Chesterfield have been regularly mined for historical insights. The conclusion to be drawn from this discrepancy is a rather obvious one. History has felt obliged to account for the qualities that represent the male of the dominant class as a desirable person to be, for such information seems to contribute directly to our understanding of political life – real and imagined – from the Middle Ages to the present day.

To generalize, then, about the way information is used if it concerns women and sexuality rather than men and political life, we have to say that information about women, as Woolf discovered decades ago, is still used primarily to essentialize women, to fix their natures, and in this way to remove them from the theater of political events that nature has apparently designated for men. But even though this writing has not been considered as history, an unbroken tradition of such instruction books for women extends from the Middle Ages to the present day. At one time, this writing took the form of devotional manuals for the wives and daughters of the aristocracy as well as courtesy books for would-be court ladies. To these, a later period added domestic economies for women who maintained the household through their own labor, as well as pamphlets on marriage and domestic life that represented a dissenting view. These coexisted with books that set the standards for polite demeanor to which the prosperous merchant's wife or the daughter of a gentry family was supposed to aspire. And still later authors took up the matter of the manners and morals of the woman who ensured her husband an orderly home and an emotionally gratifying family life. That literary scholars and historians have seldom turned to this kind of writing for historical insight seems all the more astonishing when one considers that during the eighteenth century the publication of conduct books for women actually surpassed in quantity and variety those directed at men. And to this day female conduct books in their many guises flood a highly competitive marketplace where they provide a major source of revenue for the publishing industry. We ourselves have seen this writing appear in a variety of formats from beauty guides and exercise booklets to etiquette manuals and glamor books.

Introduction

If information that sought to refine a woman's judgment, taste, demeanor, speech, and dress once existed in such abundance that it eventually changed the way literate people understood themselves in relation to others, representations of women have no less power today. With the development of the mass media such representations saturate the culture as never before. Not only does the billboard blond and television mini-series heroine reach out to virtually every social group including even the very rich and the very poor, but also the forms of desire authorized by these objects of desire allow little room for variation according to the ethnicity, region, class, or even nationality of individual consumers. Rather than formulating and disseminating an emergent ideology, the gendered world of information we inhabit today reproduces and maintains the dominant view.

Through all their historical permutations, books telling women how to become desirable have held to the single objective of specifying what a woman should desire to be if she wishes to attract a socially approved male and keep him happy. Conduct books for women may seem to strive simply for a more desirable woman. But in determining what kind of woman a woman should desire to be, these books also determine what kind of woman men should find desirable. Thus the genre implies two distinct aspects of desire, a desired object, and a subject who desires that object. While this form, like the two sexes themselves, appears constant through time, the content fillings – or what qualities make the female desirable, and what kind of male is supposed to desire her in this way – change along with those other cultural practices which are most important to maintaining political order. In tracing the history of desire, we will therefore be tracing a political process marked by moments where the object and subject of desire undergo transformation. We will be telling the story of the language of kinship relations and its appropriation by aspiring classes, the story, in other words, of the hegemony that brought the middle classes into power and made the world we inhabit today.

Early modern culture determined kinship relations largely by birth and title. The rules of kinship established who was and who was not included in the empowered group. Rules governing other sexual relations existed among professional people, merchants, and tradespeople, as well as the laboring classes. But even those who opposed political authority that was based on genealogy and distributed according to blood understood they had to acquire power through access to the nobility or imitation of it. A considerable body of medieval texts including Arthurian romances, dream visions, and other kinds of extended fictional narratives represented the aristocratic ideal of sexual conduct. These stories identified noble birth as the natural basis for kinship relations. The source of desirability resided in the woman's noble heritage, just as the compulsion to desire and the capacity to woo such a woman sprang from the aristocratic blood of the male. These stories mystified the element of blood by representing it as the ultimate source of sexual desire. But, as Kathleen Ashley argues, the emergence of an alternative way of figuring sexual desire can be discerned in the conduct books of the same period. During the high Middle Ages, the books that aimed at producing desirable women reiterated the common view that "good wymmen" are those who seek spiritual salvation by living the contemplative life. This principle was supposed to render a woman piteous, meek, and sweet tempered and, on this basis, desirable as a wife. During the late Middle Ages, however, one can see the bourgeoisie using the female to understand their interests as distinct from and even in opposition to those of the aristocracy. Thus, as Ashley demonstrates, female conduct books that were aimed at the non-aristocratic reader revised the values that patristic commentary formerly attributed to Mary Magdalene and Martha. Mary's contemplative posture in relation to Christ was no longer preferred to Martha's more active show of hospitality. Ashley shows how the inclusion of material from these conduct books eventually transformed episodes in the religious drama from a "mirror of Salvation" for the community into a secular form that established middle-class social models for the women in the audience. From this, she concludes that conduct books for women "seem to characterize the ideology of the newly powerful bourgeoisie in the late medieval and early Renaissance period."

It is reasonable to assume that an aristocratic model of kinship relations dominated the early modern period stretching between medieval romance and the appearance of fiction in which the contours of modern love can be discerned. But we must quickly note some basic changes in the Renaissance model from the one that Ashley describes. First of all, during the reign of Elizabeth I, the majority of English writers of poetry, prose fiction, and drama came from the middle ranks. The authors of Renaissance love lyrics might be as close to the aristocracy as Philip Sidney or as far from that élite social group as Christopher Marlowe, but despite the social barriers removing them from the community of illustrious blood, the authors of Petrarchan verse, sonnet sequences, narrative poems on topics of love, and prose romances celebrated the same object of desire. To a man, they found the aristocratic woman more valuable precisely because she was unavailable to men of their lower rank. This literature of love created a double bind where the poet situated himself, as desiring subject, in an alienated relationship to the object that his poetry defined as supremely desirable. While literary criticism has long been preoccupied with this form of male desire, only recently have critics and scholars begun to consider how female desire was understood in the Renaissance.

In her study of Renaissance conduct books for women, Ann R. Jones shows how the prevailing model of sexual desire placed the court lady in a double bind of a somewhat different nature. Jones draws her examples from fifteenth- and sixteenth-century Italian manuals, but the situation she describes holds true for other parts of Europe as well, including England. On the one hand, Jones explains, court ladies were expected to be visible, affable, endearing to men of their rank or higher, and, on the other hand, the desirable woman had to be modest in demeanor and emotionally reticent. It is not difficult to see how this double bind arose from and maintained political relations where power was concentrated in a secular oligarchy whose membership was largely determined by birth. As bearer of the blood, a female member of such an élite group was regarded as a living icon; her lavish dress and skillful speech was supposed to display her father's wealth and title. Her function, in Jones's words, was "to be a member of the chorus prompting men to bravery in tournaments and eloquence in conversation." But while as an object she was supposed to make aristocratic power seem consumately desirable, it was also necessary that an aristocratic woman appear chaste. Because she quite literally embodied the power of blood, this woman had to behave in a way that kept the community of blood closed, pure, and superior. The ritual punishment of desirous aristocratic women upon the Jacobean stage implies a situation where the ideal woman exerted extraordinary power as the object of desire, especially over men of aspiring social groups. But because the mere presence of female desire – as in Desdemona, the Duchess of Malfi, or Cleopatra – inevitably disrupted the power that flowed through her

7

to ensure the continuity from one generation of the nobility to the next, the ideal woman had to be totally devoid of sexual desire herself.

Contemporaneous with such female courtesy literature in England were instruction books that clearly spoke from a minority position by addressing a readership we might now loosely term as Puritan.[2] Their definition of the female role as object and subject of desire advanced the belief that political power should be based on moral superiority. At issue in the way that sexual relations were represented, according to Jacques Donzelot, "was the transition from a government of families to a government through the family."[3] Sexual relations so often provided the terms of argument during the early modern period that no representation of the household could be considered politically neutral. To contest the notion of a state that depended upon inherited power, Puritan treatises on marriage and household governance represented the family as a self-enclosed social unit in whose affairs the state could not intervene. Against genealogy the treatises posited domesticity. But in claiming sovereignty for the father over his home, it can be argued, they were not really proposing a new form of political organization. According to Kathleen M. Davis, the Puritan doctrine of equality insisted only upon the difference of sexual roles in which the female was certainly subordinate to the male, and not upon the equality of the woman in kind. "The result of this partnership," Davis explains, "was a definition of mutual and complementary duties and characteristics." Gender was clearly understood in oppositional terms that resemble a more modern world organized around gender distinctions. This can be seen in a chart compiled by John Dod and Robert Cleaver for their widely read Puritan manual on household government:[4]

Husband	*Wife*
Get goods	Gather them together and save them
Travel, seek a living	Keep the house
Get money and provisions	Do not vainly spend it
Deal with many men	Talk with few
Be "entertaining"	Be solitary and withdrawn
Be skillful in talk	Boast of silence
Be a giver	Be a saver

Introduction

| Apparel yourself as you may | Apparel yourself as it becomes you |
| Dispatch all things out of outdoors | Oversee and give order within |

According to handbooks such as these, the household consisted of a male and a female who were structurally identical in that they were represented as active and passive versions of the same attributes. In such a configuration, the female did not represent a different way of organizing social reality. By representing the family in terms of an opposition of complementary genders, Puritan tracts enclosed the domestic unit. It was clear that these authors wanted to cut it off from the genealogical tree of state and, as such, use it to represent an independent and self-generated source of power, but their moment in history had not arrived. The hegemonic potential of the model had yet to be realized at that point in time.

Unlike Puritan authors, middle-class reformers of nineteenth-century England could look back on a substantial body of writing that authorized such a political alternative. This writing produced a new kind of woman, a domestic woman, and established her as the most desirable woman to marry. It was she, and not her aristocratic counterpart, who ensured a man the sanctity and gratification of private life. Before the middle-class household could provide a common ideal for individuals from competing interest groups, Nancy Armstrong argues, the household must have been understood as a place that was governed by an essentially female form of power, power different from that of the male and yet a positive force in its own right. Although certainly subject to political force, the domestic woman exercised a form of power that appeared to have no political force at all, because that power seemed passive. It appeared to originate in the desiring subject, or male, rather than in the female object of desire. This power was the power of domestic surveillance. The husband who met the standard listed above passed into oblivion well before the aristocratic male ceased to dominate British political consciousness, but the domestic woman enjoyed an entirely different fate. In the centuries intervening between the Puritan revolution and the early nineteenth century, she was inscribed with values that addressed a whole range of competing interest groups, and through her these groups gained authority over domestic relations and personal life. In this way, furthermore, various interest groups aligned themselves against the old aristocracy and established the need for the kind of surveillance upon which modern institutions are based.

Indeed, the last two decades of the seventeenth century saw an explosion of writing that proposed to educate the daughters of numerous aspiring social groups.[5] These modern conduct books proffer an educational program on grounds that it will make these women desirable to men of a superior quality, in fact more desirable than women who have only their own rank and fortune to recommend them. With remarkable predictability, these books propose a curriculum they claim is capable of producing a woman whose value resides chiefly in her femaleness rather than in traditional signs of status, a woman possessing psychological depth rather than a physically attractive surface, one who, in other words, excels in the qualities that differentiate her from the male rather than in terms of her father's wealth and title. As femaleness was successfully redefined in these terms, the woman exalted by an aristocratic tradition of letters ceased to appear so desirable. In becoming the other side of a new sexual coin, the aristocratic woman in turn represented surface instead of depth, embodied material rather than moral values, and displayed idle sensuality where there should be constant vigilance and tireless concern for the well-being of others. The conduct-book doctrine of gender implied that such a woman was not truly female.

We are claiming, in effect, that a major historical change occurred in the early eighteenth century: the production of a new object of desire that – for the first time in history – represented the interests of those in the middle ranks of society. Defoe's conduct books come out of a tradition that harks back to Puritan marriage manuals but goes one better than them. Carol Houlihan Flynn explains how this literature translates the terms of a dissenting tradition into those of a domestic orthodoxy as it endorses, for example, "voluntary surrender to God! and the godly husband!" Her discussion of Defoe's *Family Instructor* argues that "what is at issue" in these books "is who has the power to be the instructor." While it clearly gives all authority to the male, Defoe's non-fiction account of sexual relations hovers between an earlier model that authorized the female's subjugation by physical force and a more recognizably modern one in which the female desires her own subordination, or "voluntary compliance." This, Flynn argues, is not the position Defoe takes in his own fiction which looks at life through the eyes of a female persona. In *Moll*

Introduction

Flanders and *Roxana* marriage is represented in terms that openly contest the idealized model of kinship identified with the ruling class. These heroines define themselves within a predacious economy where marriage offers their only means of survival. They prove that women cannot afford to distinguish money from love and are therefore forced to marry on terms that – according to the sentimental tradition – resemble prostitution. From this, we may draw a conclusion of no small importance in the history of desire. Defoe acknowledges that the virtuous domestic woman may indeed be the object of male desire, but when it comes to representing the woman as a desiring subject, Defoe offers a view from the bottom that is highly critical, not only of the reigning marriage practices, but also of the sentimental challenge to them. His women can desire a man for any number of reasons, but when she has to choose between money and love, money is better than sentiment alone.

That Defoe could express his political viewpoint through marriage manuals and fictional autobiographies of women testifies, among other things, to the unprecedented popularity that such literature was acquiring at the beginning of the eighteenth century. Defoe's use of these genres also suggests that its popularity had something to do with its capacity to express a dissenting viewpoint that was on the rise. Armstrong observes that around the turn of the century the proportion of conduct books written for women shifted abruptly in relation to the number of those devoted to men.[6] And as books for, about, and often by women came to dominate the field, it was also true that those books upholding the aristocratic ideal of behavior suddenly fell off in popularity. It is Armstrong's claim that the British Enlightenment gave rise to a new woman, a creature of feelings that naturally inclined to household management and caring for the sick, needy, and young. As the guardian and guarantor of private life, she was also the first example of modern psychology. She rose with remarkable speed to cultural prominence over her more-or-less noble counterparts and in the process transformed the whole idea of what it meant to be noble. Together with conduct books and other literature that claimed to be directed at women readers, novels helped to redefine what men were supposed to desire in women and what women, in turn, were supposed to desire to be. Most of the eighteenth-century novels that interest us today took part in this ideological struggle which, in less than a century, allowed an emergent social group to seize hold of the language of courtship and kinship and to make it articulate an alternative form of power. The new domestic ideal not only provided a basis on which numerous competing social groups could each identify their interests but also provided a form of power exercised through constant supervision and the regulation of desire, thus preparing the cultural ground in which capitalism could rapidly flourish. Indeed, the conduct books for women, though written by people of differing regions, sects, factions, and genders, rather singlemindedly represented the social world as one divided into public and private, economic and domestic, labor and leisure according to a principle of gender that placed the household and sexual relations under female authority. "By sexing the social world," according to Armstrong, "this body of writing produced a single idea of the household. And this ideal in turn helped to generate the belief that there was such a thing as the middle class well before one existed in any other form." By the end of the eighteenth century, people thought of society in terms of a class sexuality, for in contrast with both the landed aristocracy with its libertine appetites and the promiscuous mob was the sanctuary of middle-class love.

In "Wild nights: pleasure/sexuality/feminism," Cora Kaplan investigates the complicated configuration of gender and class that characterized English thinking in the wake of the French Revolution. Wollstonecraft's *Vindication of the Rights of Women* identifies the condition of women with the corruption of the *ancien régime*. Daughters were traded like objects in the marketplace among fathers and husbands without any concern for the desires of the individual woman involved or any need to educate her to make choices she was prepared to live with. To represent the aristocratic woman as degraded because she was the currency of an exchange among men, Wollstonecraft borrowed the rhetoric of earlier conduct books and fiction that challenged aristocratic sexuality. Unlike most authors who adopted such a rhetoric, however, Wollstonecraft did not criticize aristocratic sexuality in order to exalt the domestic woman. To the contrary, she attacked the dominant kinship practices in order to argue that the woman's condition had worsened with the division of labor into gendered spheres that characterized the emergent middle-class view. She saw women not as a revolutionary group but as one that must be completely re-educated. Wollstonecraft argues, in Kaplan's words, that "before the middle-class woman can join the middle-class man in advocating and advancing human progress she must be persuaded to become more masculine and respectable," by giving up her role both as "insignificant objects of desire" and as desiring subject. To position this viewpoint within the political debate of the time, Kaplan sees Wollstonecraft's feminist argument in opposition with the fundamental tenet of Rousseau's *Émile* that men and women should receive different educations because of innate differences of mind. Even as she accepted Rousseau's political agenda, Wollstonecraft opposed his notion of gender, arguing that female desire becomes more offensive when women are educated to become objects of male desire. To resist this form of self-definition, however, a woman must also forsake her role as desiring subject. Thus Wollstonecraft adopts the rhetoric of puritanical sexuality – a strategy the middle-classes used effectively to undermine the authority of the old aristocracy – to call upon women to reform themselves. They were to make themselves as knowledgeable and independent as men by renouncing their sexual pleasure, a price men did not have to pay.

Thomas M. Kavanagh is particularly concerned with how the "polarization of gender" affects both literature and our reading of it. The opposition structuring the new sexuality was the same in Laclos's France as it was in Wollstonecraft's England: if women wanted to have power as such, unlike men they had to renounce desire. Such is the distinction between the sexes in *Les Liaisons dangereuses*. But, cautions Kavanagh, Laclos's women cannot be understood as representations of our own notion of male and female. In order to locate the novel in history, Kavanagh looks to the conduct book in which Laclos discusses sexuality in relation to the politics of his times. Laclos uses this non-fictional mode to explain how both sexes are empowered even though each has very different powers; the male dominates the female in terms of physical strength, but the female excels in powers of imagination that enable her to manipulate male desire. On this basis, Kavanagh argues that the character of Merteuil is not meant to be unwomanly, but that of a woman who "consciously and consequently acts as the most womanly woman throughout this novel." Her defeat cannot represent the triumph of gender distinctions, then, but a far more complex and interesting historical process where a grander notion of gender was displaced by another, more limited kind. In admiring the female's imaginative powers and refusing to endorse her renunciation of desire, then, Laclos disputes a view such as Wollstonecraft's that identifies power with rational intelligence that men can acquire simply because they have been born men. Nevertheless, Laclos authorizes the very notion of sexuality he represents as constraining. For in contrast with Wollstonecraft, he assumes that female irrationality, for all its admirable powers, is rooted in her essential nature as the object of male desire rather than in a culture that teaches her to desire a subservient role.

Written with full awareness of the rhetoric of reform and how it worked through representations of gender, such endorsements of female sensuality invariably turned against themselves, as indeed Laclos's fiction did, to criticize the practices of a libertine culture. Sometime around the end of the eighteenth century, however, one may observe the novel losing interest in its critique of the dominant classes and taking up a rather different project. In the hands of Burney and Austen, fiction could still be said to oppose the domestic woman to women of title and wealth, but a woman's behavior was even more likely to be impugned if that behavior seemed motivated by desires which could also be attributed to the daughters of merchants and, later, to working-class girls. It is finally for their mercenary lust that the Bingley sisters strike us as less than desirable in Austen's *Pride and Prejudice*, and the same point is still more forcefully made in *Jane Eyre* by the acquisitive urge that attracts Blanche Ingram to Rochester and repels him from her. With the novels of Burney and Austen, furthermore, the conduct-book ideal of womanhood defined an ideal against which novelistic representations of women were held up as being more true to life. On the premise that no one really measured up to this ideal, Victorian fiction took up the task of retailoring the representation of women to indicate that each individual had slightly different desires; no two women could be right for the same man, nor any two men for the same woman. In Dickens, then, as in the Victorian love lyric, one finds the ideal marriage is not represented as being anything other than a fiction. With remarkable regularity, the best possible relationships to be achieved in this fiction turn out to be inferior substitutes for an original mother or father. As if to say that an idealized fiction of love had an unhealthy grip on human desire, furthermore, Thackeray treats Amelia Sedley harshly for conforming to the feminine ideal and punishes her husband Dobbin as well for confusing love with conformity. Not only novels by Dickens and Thackeray but all Victorian fiction testified in one way or another to the reality of a power that eighteenth-century conduct books could only imagine.

From the work of Rachel Bowlby, it appears that during the nineteenth century other forms of writing took over where the conduct book left off. If the eighteenth-century conduct book consistently promised to produce a woman who, in contrast with her aristocratic counterpart, possessed the virtues of frugality and self-restraint, the nineteenth century was all the more obsessed with regulating household consumption by regulating the female subject. A woman's taste was more important than ever before. According to Bowlby's study of the diaries for the *Bon Marché*, the authors of such guides to consumerism represented the store "not as a factory, but as a large, well-ordered domestic establishment. In this way, the diary brings the store closer to home." By the mid-nineteenth century, this suggests, middle-class power had become so well entrenched in England and France, and that power so clearly identified with the domestic woman and the private domain she was supposed to oversee, that books describing the character formation and household duties of this woman were no longer necessary. We might say that fiction had passed into social and economic fact. To be sure, some books directed the doctrine of domesticity toward the lower classes, promising social success as the reward for a feminine mode of behavior, and some books tried to revise the doctrine by urging women to acquire forms of knowledge that would make them economically independent. But these did not characterize the mainstream of books for women during the second half of the nineteenth century.

We should pause at this point and take note of the contrast between two important historical transformations in the conduct-book form. We can identify the beginning of the British Enlightenment with the moment when books that aimed at producing the domestic woman outstripped courtesy literature that presented forms of aristocratic behavior as the ideal to which both men and women should aspire. The triumph of the modern middle classes took place at least in part through the triumph of the female conduct book over courtesy literature. For this change in the representation of desire produced a culture divided into gendered spheres, the primary difference between "masculine" and "feminine" then creating the difference between public and private, work and leisure, economic and domestic, political and aesthetic. All the important themes subtending capitalism and enabling such economic practices to make sense in turn rested upon the assumption that such differences are as natural as gender itself. Indeed, we still understand ourselves and others within the same gendered universe of words and things. But this is not to deny there have been significant changes within the moment initiated and sustained by the production of a gendered universe. With the entrenchment of the new middle classes, the representation of gender and the regulation of desire became more important than ever before. In fact, it can be argued that the regulation of desire through representations of gender became the most efficacious form of social control, more so than the police, the military, the law courts, or even the schoolroom.[7] Beginning at birth and taking hold of the individual mind in the earliest years of childhood, psychoanalytic theory insists, each individual learns to think of himself or herself as first and foremost a boy or a girl and destined by natural desire to reproduce in some form the idealized social unit of mother, father, brother, and sister. At some point during the nineteenth century, literate people began to regard this kinship system as normal, natural, and good. Though a specifically modern form of family peculiar to capitalist nations, the family structured on gender differences appears to serve no particular interest groups and to have no particular political objectives. Thus it seemed only right to measure any and all other sexual practices against this model of kinship relations as if against a universal standard.

By the mid-nineteenth century authors of advice for women accordingly found it unnecessary to articulate the whole body of the woman, of the knowledge she must possess as a woman, or of the household that she was supposed to supervise. A fragment of these – her eyes, table manners, or china – could represent the whole. In Bowlby's analysis, furthermore, such fragmentation characterized female desire as well as her identity as the object of male desire. A woman's magazine *La Dernière Mode* illustrates how parts of the body, like objects that make up the household, were detached from the whole and then fetishized as they came to represent an idealized version of the whole. This mode of representation – or fashion system, as Barthes called it – not only objectifies the woman as a part object, but also "gives the woman her image in the mirror." The woman desires to be the exalted object, which she is not by birth or even by education, but which she knows the male desires her to be.

Thus we might say that the disjunction between surface and depth operated throughout the eighteenth and nineteenth centuries in a relation of signifier and signified. The woman's desirability, or value as an object of desire, had to be sought beneath the surface of her body that was the emblem of her family's wealth and station. Her value as a female was supposed to derive from certain qualities of mind, or nature as a desiring subject.

According to the MacCannells, what they call "the beauty system" continued the Enlightenment project by representing the female as an object that required improvement. Only we find that it is in terms of the body that this improvement is measured. We might mark this change in the history of desire with the appearance of hysteria in all its manifestations. A glance through the early case studies of Freud and Breuer or through Frued's *Dora* will reveal how hysteria inscribed a purely psychological conflict within the woman upon the surface of her body. In the early case histories, hysteria becomes nothing else but the woman's desire for self-regulation, paradoxically, gone out of control. When up against resistance on the part of desire, the desire for self-control could take the form of a speech impediment which prevented her from expressing desire, of a limp which confined her to the home, of genital disorders that limited sexual activity, or of eating problems which transferred the whole principle of household regulation onto the regulation of the woman's body in a way that might even prove life threatening. But the beauty system, unlike hysteria, inscribes a socially approved form of desire upon the female body: the desire to be what the male desires her to be. A girl, according to the MacCannells,

> is drawn into the beauty system by the force of her entire culture, by the design of the overall relationship between the sexes. When she looks into the mirror and sees ugliness reflected back upon herself, what she is actually experiencing is the value that her society has placed upon her category, that she has no value.

Glamour books, etiquette guides, and manuals for physical fitness divide the female body into zones and "through display or artifice bring it back to nature." No less so than hysteria, then, the beauty system displaces the depths onto the surface. Self-enhancing make-up, fashionable dress, social adeptness, and congeniality indicate not only a woman's capacity for self-regulation and her knowledge of

17

how to go about achieving self-regulation, but also her desire to oberve the procedures that ensure desirability. To the degree that she achieves one of the reigning stereotypes of beauty, the gap between self and stereotype – or, in other words, the difference between the female as subject and object – disappears, and the stereotype appears to be nature itself. The "natural woman" is of course the most difficult stereotype of all to achieve; it is as remote from the female as it is from the male and, like the aristocratic woman of an earlier time, the more desirable to both sexes for appearing so.

To demonstrate that the relationship between class and gender remains a problematic one to this day, Kaplan contrasts the class-bound feminism of Wollstonecraft with that of Adrienne Rich, who assumes the position of a radical feminist in contemporary letters. Kaplan writes,

> While Wollstonecraft acknowledged that a depraved sexual pleasure for both men and women was the effect of unequal power relations between them, radical feminism underlines the unpleasure of these relations for women. Where women have no choice over the aim and object of their sexuality, hetero-sexuality, in the words of Adrienne Rich, is "compulsory" – an institution more comprehensive and sinister than the different relations and practices it constructs. Worse, compulsory hetero-sexuality is part of a chain of gender specific tortures, both medical and conjugal: hysterectomy, cliterodectomy, battering, rape, and imprisonment are all elaborations of the sadistic act of penetration itself, penetration the socially valorised symbol of violence against women.

In constructing female sexuality as naturally different from that of the male, however, Rich "has," in Kaplan's opinion, "shifted the terms of the nature/culture debate without really shifting the paradigm around women and sexuality." The fantasy that one can create another, non-competitive social reality on the basis of gender was a contradiction in Wollstonecraft's day and remains so today. As Kaplan's comparative study clearly demonstrates, "the dream of an autonomous sexuality, not constructed through the desire of the other, male or female, is a transcendental fantasy of bourgeois individualism."

Introduction

However various with respect to literary period, language area, and critical procedures, the essays in this collection together raise certain issues for literary criticism. All of the authors believe there is a history of sexuality, and all use female conduct books to document that history. But where does that history lie? How is it to be discovered? What bearing does that history have upon literature and vice versa? The approaches to these questions are no less various, it appears, than the authors' understanding of culture itself. Several essays in this collection discover a relationship between representations of women in the literature of conduct and the use of such representations in literature. The essays by Flynn and Jones understand this relationship as one of difference, in which conduct books present the more conservative and literature, the more liberal attitude towards women. The literary viewpoint, whether authored by male or female, represents a minority viewpoint. Thus female poets of Renaissance France express dissatisfaction with a discourse that defines women as objects of desire, but which finds them undesirable when they display desires of their own. And Defoe's radical de-idealization of legitimate monogamy suggests that, with the possible exception of the wealthiest among them, women had to exchange their own bodies if they wanted to survive within the present economic situation. Despite the gap of a century or more between the courtly love poetry Jones discusses and the marriage manuals upon which Flynn bases her analysis of women in Defoe's fiction, the viewpoint of women in each case offers a means of expressing an alternative source of economic power from that underwriting the dominant view. But that the two essays agree in all these important respects raises a question, one that is brought to the forefront by the form of intertextuality that binds this collection of essays together. What difference does the gender of an author make? Must we identify the author with the desiring subject? If so, then why does Defoe find it advantageous to speak as a woman when launching his critique of economic conditions? Can we regard the female as a form of resistance when she is writing in the mode of the dominant class? These are some of the questions that arise from the essays by Jones and Flynn. To answer them requires one to historicize the very terms male and female.

This is the objective of Ashley and Kavanagh, both of whom use female conduct books to establish a set of norms for representing sexual behavior different from our own. Kavanagh finds Laclos's construction of such norms to be consistent with representations found in eighteenth-century French literature. Observing how Laclos represented women in an unfinished conduct book, Kavanagh takes issue with those who read Merteuil as if she were living in the twentieth century. Ashley demonstrates that late medieval conduct books revise an earlier model of female behavior for a merchant class ready to insist upon their own sexual norms. For these authors, as for Jones and Flynn, changes in the representation of women accompany more extensive historical changes and must be understood in relation to those changes. It is clear, for example, that with the period discussed by Flynn and Kavanagh, namely the Enlightenment in France and England, women have ceased to be defined primarily as iconic embodiments of wealth and title. Rather, the woman as object of desire has been linked in a meaningful way to the woman as desiring subject. And as Cora Kaplan demonstrates in her comparative study of Mary Wollstonecraft and Adrienne Rich, once this link has been forced, there can be no getting around it: any representation of sexual behavior invariably inscribes itself within the discourse of bourgeois individualism.

The relationship between class and gender raises a second order of problem for literary criticism. Once we become conscious of the historical dimension of sexuality, we may find ourselves able to document change in the distribution of features of gender and values attached to each. Yet there remains the question of causality. It becomes imperative to ask not only why do these particular changes occur, but also where and how. Ashley, Jones, Kaplan, Armstrong, and Bowlby all assume a materialist position in relation to their data, contending that the history of sexuality must be seen in relationship to economic struggles, that the struggle to represent ideal female behavior indeed accompanied the struggle of an emergent middle class to gain economic power.

In our opinion, however, the question of precisely how to configure sex and class remains a tricky one. It is possible, like Ashley, Jones, and Flynn – whose examples date from the Middle Ages to the early eighteenth century – to read sex allegorically in relation to political conflict, the female of course representing the subordinate social group. But when we encounter the materials serving as data for Kaplan, Armstrong, Bowlby, and the MacCannells, it is clear we are entering new historical territory where our designated materials will not submit to the same procedures that seem to provide a reasonable means of historicizing earlier literature. The knot can be untangled from two directions. First, we can abandon reflection theory, or the idea that literary history pursues a different but parallel course in relation to the other symbolic practices that compose history *per se*. Secondly, if we do consider literature – along with other kinds of writing – as one among many practices that appear to undergo change along with changes in political relationships, we may discover that writing does not necessarily reflect a change that has already occurred elsewhere in the culture. Indeed, following Foucault, we would argue that there have been times when writing created the semiotic conditions that allowed radical changes in economic and political relations to occur. The essays dealing with Enlightenment and post-Enlightenment culture indicate this is really what happened. They suggest that the redefinition of the female was a crucial feature of the hegemomy that brought the middle classes into power. These essays suggest further that with the emergence of the new middle classes, power itself changed; the dissemination of certain forms of literacy – or, in other words, hegemony itself – took precedence over the more commonly recognized institutions of state – the police, the courts, and the military, for example – in maintaining middle-class power. This recognition is probably the single most important consequence of reading literature in relation to the literature of conduct for women.

In 1928 Virginia Woolf suggested that an event of major historical proportions occurred when middle-class women began to write. Supporting this claim, as Woolf herself evidently knew, required nothing short of rewriting history. "Thus towards the end of the eighteenth century," in her words, "a change came about which, if I were rewriting history, I should describe more fully and think of greater importance than the Crusades or the War of the Roses. The middle-class woman began to write."[8] Despite recent interest in the history of representation *qua* representation, relatively few literary scholars and critics have explored the role of representation *in* history. While most of us pay lipservice to the power of literacy, we have not considered in a detailed and systematic way whether literature has played any part in political history. Indeed, it is the tendency of the disciplines in the United States and Britain to detach the writing we teach as literature from the other symbolic practices that compose history *per se*. Woolf's statement explains how this tendency has direct bearing on women. If writing is not figured into political history, then political power will continue to appear as if it (deceptively) resides exclusively in institutions that are largely governed by men, and the role played by women at various stages in the middle-class hegemony will remain unexamined for the political force that it was and still is.

Our decision, in editing this collection, to view women's writing as such a political force must in turn have obvious and direct bearing on our notions of what literature is and how we should approach it. It is unquestionably the tendency of the literary institution in this country to collaborate with history in relegating the writing known as literature to the status of a secondary modeling system, which is subordinate to one degree or another to the data properly composing history. It is worth noting that the moment when middle-class women began to write marked the moment when the writing of political economy took on unprecedented explanatory power. Writing itself appeared to lose political significance along with courtship procedures, marriage practices, and the organization of the household. And this occurred at the very time when these areas of culture assumed unprecedented power – or so the collective effort of this volume suggests.

While compiling this collection, we were reminded of the tendency of traditional histories to identify the important historical data as the products of men. We were attending a conference devoted to the Spanish Golden Age when a problem emerged very much like the problem that confronts many of us who deal with women's writing. A historian had been invited to respond to a paper concerned with the political viewpoint of artisan poets in sixteenth-century Mexico. He appeared perplexed, unsure of what he was supposed to do with this information, and skeptical of how the effects of this kind of literacy might be considered since it yielded little in terms of what this historian considered to be "evidence." He could only allow those truths to be declared truth which were based, in his words, "on counting cattle and bags of grain." It is difficult to believe this narrow notion of history could claim much respect. Yet on grounds that only a certain kind of information could be considered historical data, he sought to trivialize whatever such poetry had to say about the circumstances out of which it was produced. Not only did the historian understand human culture in terms of an unexamined emphasis on productive labor, but also he understood work only in terms of very specific products. Moreover, his representation did not acknowledge its basis in representation. The historian in question never counted a single head of cattle or bag of grain. He simply privileged account books over all other of modes of representation.

Indeed, so fixed is the idea that political meaning derives from a source outside of writing that all manner of printed material occupies no place within the academic disciplines. The argument for this collection relies in particular on women's conduct books, but there are more, many more, kinds of writing to be read and analyzed, all of which provide the material record of everyday life as it was supposed to be lived. And much of the excluded material was produced by, for, and about women. Like the conduct books for women, this material will flesh out the process which brought modern woman into being. It will explain how she rose with such incredible speed to cultural prominence. It will show that she was uniquely equipped to set in motion a process that would compel future generations to reproduce an idealized body and household compulsively, as if by natural desire. In this way, we may discover how the domestic woman – who may, for all we know, have existed in representation for as long as a century before she stepped forth from the pages of books to oversee middle-class parlors – became a function of each "normal" individual's psychic life. By occupying this place in the mind, this form of desire made it possible for masses of diverse individuals to coexist within modern culture.

To prove such an hypothesis to the satisfaction of those who believe history resides in an account of cattle and grain will take many years and many more researchers. Much of the material which will make up a more adequate account of the rise of the middle classes has as yet found no place within the disciplines. It has long been kept out of sight within the unclassified space of popular culture. Conduct books for women must be viewed as just one among many forgotten kinds of information which are similarly woven into the fabric of literature. In being the sort of data that conventional histories cannot account for, most of this material has the status of junk. But for the very reason it does resemble the stuff of an attic, such material can suddenly acquire enormous value as it finds a place for itself among the objects of knowledge. It is this kind of residual cultural information that can supplement the structures determining reality at a given moment in time, and do so in a way that requires some major revision of the conceptual framework within which those structures dominate.

The Ideology of Conduct

NOTES

1 This point has been discussed more fully by N. Armstrong in her (1987) *Desire and Domestic Fiction: A Political History of the Novel*, New York, Oxford University Press. See also M. Godelier (1982) "The ideal in the real," in R. Samuel and G. Steadman Jones (eds) *Culture, Ideology, and Politics*, London, Routledge & Kegan Paul, 12–38.

2 For a more complete discussion of the relationship between Jacobean literature and the debate between royalists and Puritans over the nature of the family, see L. Tennenhouse (1986) *Power on Display: The Politics of Shakespeare's Genres*, New York and London, Methuen.

3 J. Donzelot (1972) *The Policing of Families*, trans. R. Hurley, New York, Pantheon, 92.

4 K. M. Davis (1977) "The sacred condition of equality – how original were puritan doctrines of marriage?," *Social History*, 5, 570. Davis quotes the list of duties from J. Dod and R. Cleaver (1614) *A Godly Forme of Householde Gouernment*, London.

5 P. Crawford has documented the trend in such publications from the beginning to the end of the seventeenth century in her (1985) "Women's published writings 1600–1700," in M. Prior (ed.) *Women in Society*, London, Methuen, 211–81; see especially Appendix 2, 265–71.

6 See M. Curtin (1985) "A question of manners: status and gender in etiquette and courtesy," *Journal of Modern History*, 57, 407 and n. 26.

7 M. Foucault is responsible for this and many of our other insights. See especially his (1978) *The History of Sexuality*, vol. I, trans. R. Hurley, New York, Random House.

8 V. Woolf (1928) *A Room of One's Own*, New York, Harcourt, Brace, & World, 69.

Medieval courtesy literature and dramatic mirrors of female conduct*

---◆---

KATHLEEN M. ASHLEY

As many historians have pointed out, the late Middle Ages was an era obsessed with codified and externalized behaviors. For aristocrats, such codes promised to maintain social identities at a time of blurring boundaries between upper and "middle" classes. However, the wealthy bourgeoisie and other upwardly mobile groups subverted the boundaries as they increasingly adopted aristocratic codes to define their new sense of worth and place in medieval society. Although the flourishing of courtesy literature during the fourteenth and fifteenth centuries was connected to both these impulses, I will be concerned here primarily with conduct books addressed to non-aristocratic women and their influence on the French and English cycle plays.

Criticism on the cycle drama has been remarkably uniform in attributing to it the primary aim of religious instruction. Whether approached through typological patterns,[1] parody and symbolism,[2] the doctrine of repentance,[3] devotional rhetoric,[4] or communal rites and rituals,[5] criticism of the past 25 years has singlemindedly emphasized the drama's role in expounding and celebrating the history of man's salvation. I would like to suggest, however, that the cycle plays fulfilled many functions for late medieval society;

they were thus capable of presenting multiple, even at times contradictory, messages. The influence of conduct literature is particularly notable in several scenes where the religious drama slights its wider function as mirror of spiritual salvation for the whole community to mirror proper social behaviors for women in its audience.

This discussion will be organized around selected scenes from late medieval English and French drama, although the connection between conduct literature and cycle plays is a phenomenon with profound implications for our reading of late medieval culture. The ideology of the conduct book inscribed upon the cycle form transformed the religious drama and gave it new social functions in the late Middle Ages.

I will begin with the most ambiguous scene, the Annunciation. Its ambiguity lies, of course, in the eye of the scholar who wonders which interpretive code to apply to the episode which is only briefly described in Luke but which became one of the most symbolically rich within medieval exegesis, iconography, lyric, and narrative. The Towneley cycle Annunciation explicitly develops the theological doctrine of the Incarnation, with Deus giving a long speech (1–76) on its necessity within salvation history and on the symmetry of the recapitulation design, "A man, a madyn, and a tre: Man for man, tre for tre, / Madyn for madyn; thus shal it be" (32–4).[6] Gabriel, too, is fulsome on the details of the "prevate" or mystery of the Incarnation when he comes to Mary (77–106, 125–42). Despite the divine dogma and rhetoric, however, Mary does not immediately accept the news of her virgin conception but asks Gabriel first of all, "What is thi name?" (107) and then, "how shuld it be?" (112). Her hesitation, her questions, were interpreted within various medieval traditions of exegesis as evidence not of a lack of faith but of her "prudence" in the face of possible temptation. Thus the Annunciation had potentially *exemplary*, as opposed to purely *didactic*, functions. Mary as model for the proper behavior in such a situation becomes dramatically primary after the first 106 lines of theological exposition by God and Gabriel.

For the mystical tradition, the tempter was likely to be Satan, who roams about in the guise of an angel seeking vulnerable souls to delude with false visions and messages. The prudent believer must, according to this literature of spiritual caution, be wary of beautiful angels who may be the devil in disguise, and must first of all question the identity and motives of such an apparition. Mary, as I have argued elsewhere, appears to be exemplifying such spiritual caution when she confronts Gabriel in line 107.[7]

A second interpretive code, one drawn from conduct books for women, may also be applicable to the cycle Annunciation scenes. It calls for moral and behavioral prudence on the part of young women to resist the seductive words of young men who would lead them astray. Unlike Eve, who "dyd byleve to lyȝtely" and was deceived as are "many symple wymmen whiche lyghtely byleve the fooles / wherfore afterward they be broughte to doo folye," Geoffrey de la Tour Landry's fourteenth-century conduct book says that Mary prudently inquired of her messenger "the ende of the faytte or dede the whiche he dyd announce to her."[8] The *Book of the Knight of the Tower* concludes its chapter 107 with the moral that "Thus thenne ought the good wymmen to doo / as men speketh to them of yongthe / or of ony other thynge / whereof dyshonoure and blame may come to them." Unlike the prudence of the mystical tradition, this lesson is gender-directed to women and it concerns social rather than spiritual behavior, for the results of imprudence will be "blame" (not sin), whereas virtuous caution will bring "honor" (or society's praise).

The scenes of Joseph's "Doubts" which follow in all English cycles also play upon the possibility that Mary as a vulnerable young woman has been seduced by a handsome young man, not the "angel" she claims. Most critics have placed the drama of Joseph's discovery within the comic fabliau tradition of an old man married to a young and potentially wayward wife. I would also suggest the relevance of female conduct literature to Joseph's discourse.

In N-Town, *Joseph's Return*, Joseph rejects the claim that an angel had explained the child's divine paternity to Mary:

> Alas alas let be do way
> It was sum boy be-gan þis game
> þat clothyd was clene and gay
> and ȝe ȝeve hym now an Aungel name. (74–7)[9]

Joseph has read his conduct literature and knows the omnipresent danger of handsome youths and their fine words. In the York cycle, *Joseph's Trouble about Mary*, Mary's maid servants testify to her purity and isolation from men: "Hir kepars have we bene / And sho ay in oure sight, / Come here no man bytwene / To touche þat berde so bright" (118–21).[10] Only an angel has come to feed Mary, her chaperons insist. Joseph, however, rejects their testimony:

> þanne se I wele youre menyng is
> þe aungell has made hir with childe
> Nay, som man in aungellis liknesse
> With somkyn gawde has hir begiled,
> And þat trow I. (134–8)

The probability of angelic conception is obviously outweighed by the likelihood that some attractive man has tricked Mary.

Distinguishing the influence of the mystical prudence tradition from the influence of conduct literature within such a scene is very difficult; it should be noted, however, that there is never any suggestion that the angel might be the devil in disguise – Joseph thinks only that the "angel" is a human seducer. Even more important, in my opinion, is distinguishing Joseph's role in a *didactic* as opposed to an *exemplary* dramatic mode. If the cycle plays are perceived as dramatic expositions of salvation history whose primary message is theological, then Joseph does seem an old fool. Without understanding of the divine plan, he exists only as foil to Mary and thus as comic butt of the action. If, however, we acknowledge multiple messages within these plays, then their reception becomes considerably more complicated. Joseph may function as an exemplary character in his own right, not just at the end of the play – when the angel explains the Virgin Birth and Joseph accepts his role as human husband and father – but earlier in the midst of his "doubts." In his comic confusion, Joseph expresses propositions which were normative for late medieval culture: that marriage between partners of unequal age was socially disruptive and that young women unless carefully chaperoned and instructed were liable to the seductions of handsome, glib young men. The exception, Mary, does not disprove the validity of such rules. In addition to its fundamental task of dramatizing the doctrine of the Incarnation, the cycle drama was now charged with articulating rules of social conduct for its audience.

The presence of such multiple messages is even clearer in the Towneley *Salutation of Elizabeth*, a brief Visitation play dramatizing the episode from Luke (1:35–56) in which the annunciate Mary visits her aged but miraculously pregnant kinswoman Elizabeth. In Luke, the meeting of the two women is a vehicle for celebrating the

Incarnation as an example of divine power manifested within history. The centerpiece of our play is also Elizabeth's praise of Mary as blessed among women and Mary's song of response, the *Magnificat* – both closely paraphrased from Luke but more immediately available to the audience each day in the liturgy of vespers. But this crucial theological exchange occupies only about half (47) of the play's 90 lines. The other half (43) shows the friendly interaction of the two kinswomen, who engage in lengthy greetings at the beginning of the play and warm farewells at the end.

Such critical comment as there has been upon this play sees the human sentiment as an innocuous way of naturalizing abstract religious doctrine.[11] While such an approach probably reflects modern rather than medieval sensibilities, it does point to a more significant way to interpret the human relationships so carefully depicted in the medieval cycle drama: those relationships are intended to be exemplary in their own right. In the *Salutation of Elizabeth* the greetings, gossip, and leave-takings between Mary and Elizabeth model behavior for the medieval audience, especially its women members. Elizabeth greets Mary with joy as "blyssed blome" (4), "doghter and dere hart" (8), "dere kyns Woman" (15), and "frely foode" (85). Mary reciprocates by enquiring about Elizabeth's health, and the two exchange queries about friends and relatives back home (16–18, 22–7, 88).

That these are socially significant actions is clear from the *Young Babees Book*, a conduct book of the period which deals mainly with table manners but opens by pointing out that courtesy came from heaven when Gabriel greeted our Lady at the Annunciation and Elizabeth met with Mary at the Visitation.[12] The brief and general moral here is pointed toward children, but in conduct books addressed to women the idea is more fully developed. The *Book of the Knight of the Tower*, compiled in the late fourteenth century by Geoffrey de la Tour Landry for his daughters, devotes a whole chapter to the example of the blessed Virgin Mary's humility in the Annunciation and Visitation episodes. Mary is said to be "preysed of the holy scrypture for her good kynde and nature of her curtosye whanne she wente and vysyted her cosyn saynte Elysabeth. . . . And than bothe Cosyns humbled them self one toward the other / Wherfore good exemplary is here / how that parentes [relatives] and Frendes ought to see and vysyte eche other in theyr childbedde / and in theyr dysease and sekenesse / And humble them self one ageynst the other / as dyd these two holy and blessyd ladyes / as ye have herd."[13]

The Knight also contrasts the two holy kinswomen to those of proud and foolish heart who use their higher rank to take precedence over others. The virtue of humble courtesy exemplified by Mary and Elizabeth is here described in totally social terms, and the Knight points out that the greater the lineage and power of the woman the more she should bear herself courteously in order to receive the praise of "smalle folke" who are flattered when the great "make to them ony chere and speke fayre to them."[14]

The conduct book makes the Visitation a lesson in social behavior toward one's kinswomen and those lower in status, with the implication that such courtesy is profitable in worldly terms. We might compare the explanation of Mary's visit to Elizabeth given in the *Meditations on the Life of Christ*, a fourteenth-century devotional narrative written by a Franciscan for a nun on the premise that contemplation on the earthly life of Christ will help her avoid "trivial and transient things," fortify her "against trials and adversity," and lead to a "higher degree of contemplation." Though full of homely details of the life of Christ, the virtues it preaches are the Franciscan ones of humility and poverty, that is *abnegation* not *manipulation* of the world. Accordingly the humility it enjoins in its interpretation of Mary's journey to Elizabeth is not primarily social but spiritual, and directed toward inspiring grateful emotions in the contemplator. The *Meditations* counsels the nun:

> Consider her therefore, the queen of heaven and earth, going alone with her husband, not mounted but on foot and not attended by horsemen, knights, or barons, or by groups of servants and handmaidens. Instead she was accompanied by poverty, humility, and shame, and all the honest virtues. The Lord is with her: a large and honorable assembly she has, but no worldly vanity or pomp! . . . They began to converse, and our Lady asked about Elizabeth's conception, and Elizabeth about our Lady's, and they reasoned together about these things . . . praising God for both gifts, giving thanks and celebrating. The Lady stayed with Elizabeth for almost three months, aiding her and waiting on her in everything possible, with humility, reverence, and devotion, as though she had forgotten that she was the mother of God and queen of the whole world.[15]

The humility of the Visitation here teaches the paradox of the Incarnation, of the high deity made low flesh; it does not, as in conduct literature, teach the value of social graces for their own sakes.

But while the distinction between the conduct book's version of humility and the meditational narrative's humility may be clear, pinning down the virtue dramatized in the Towneley cycle's *Salutation of Elizabeth* is more difficult. In dramatizing the event, the play appears to combine both types of humility and its proportions reflect its harmonious conjunction of secular and sacred. Mary's socially instructive visit to her kinswoman Elizabeth modulates without strain into the spiritually edifying evocation of her state of grace, and the play concludes with an alternation of social and spiritual relationships as Mary says farewell to "myn awnt dere" (79), and Elizabeth tells Mary that "thou art full of grace; / Grete well all oure kyn of bloode" (87–8). Exemplary moral and behavioral lessons drawn from conduct books thus co-exist in Towneley with theological exegesis of Mary's role in the plan of salvation; their complementarity reflects Towneley's deep commitment to an Incarnational aesthetics, the wedding of divine and human in dramatic action and meaning. It is a wedding in which the distinction between secular and sacred essentially vanishes, for the two are perceived as part of the same continuum. As the *Young Babees Book*, earlier cited, puts it: courtesy came down from heaven when Elizabeth met with Mary. That Mary is now "full of grace" overflows in both the praise poem to God at the center of the play and in the socially exemplary courtesies between kinswomen at its beginning and end.

In other cycles, the incorporation of norms of female conduct from conduct literature may produce interesting distortions of earlier exegetical traditions which are still present. The late-fifteenth-century French *Passion* by Jean Michel, for example, includes a scene where Jesus comes to dinner at the Bethany home of Mary Magdalene and Martha. In the Biblical version of Luke 10:38–42, Martha rebukes Mary for sitting at the feet of Christ listening to him instead of helping her serve the dinner, but Christ tells the two that Mary has chosen "the better part." This very brief episode was interpreted for centuries by monastic theologians as a valorization of the contemplative life over the active life of service in the world. However, as Jacques Le Goff has suggested, as early as the twelfth century the new professions of merchants, craftsmen, and workers who were "concerned with finding religious justification for their activity and vocation," led to a growing respect for the active life represented by Martha, and certainly by the fifteenth century the lay, bourgeois impact upon religious culture was inescapable.[16]

Martha can therefore function as the heroine of the scene in Jean Michel's drama as she does not in Michel's predecessor, the playwright Greban, from whom Jean Michel adapted large portions of his *Mystère de la Passion*. Here, in the 170 lines, Martha dominates dramatically: Mary has only one speech of six lines and her brother Lazarus one of four lines, while Martha has five speeches and is addressed at least eight different times by Jesus and his disciples, who compliment her on her dinner, thank her for her hospitality, and recognize her service as a paradigm of almsgiving. Thus, although the climax and conclusion of the scene in the Bible is the point that Mary has chosen the "best part," and that is all that Greban dramatizes as well, here in Jean Michel's play Martha snaps back that Mary can live as she wishes, but she hopes that Christ will value her service as well (16,335–8).[17]

This astounding and totally unbiblical speech by Martha changes the entire sense of the scene. As I have argued elsewhere, there is a kind of schizophrenia here: ostensibly present to validate the claims of the contemplative Mary (as the rubrics to the scene suggest), the episode has been reformulated dramatically to sacramentalize the active life, for the meal that Martha serves Jesus and his disciples becomes a vivid image of the good deeds performed by the pious bourgeoisie in search of spiritual rewards.[18]

What I want to stress here is that the schizophrenia of the scene, the built-in tension between the claims of Mary Magdalene and Martha which is not totally resolved, comes from the drama's use of courtesy-book interpretations of the sisters. The *Book of the Knight of the Tower* again provides a commonplace source in chapter 101, where Martha is the chief example of how the housewife ought to take in the ministers of God. Martha

> was ever customed to lodge and herberowe the prophetes and the servaunts of god / whiche preched and taught the lawe / and ful charytable she was toward the folke / And by cause of the hooly lyf of her came the swete Jhesu Cryst to be herberowed in her hows.[19]

This was she, the account continues, who complained to Christ that her sister Mary would not help her to dress the meat, but our Lord answered humbly how Mary had chosen the best service. The conduct book, however, glides over the implied contradiction in messages without acknowledgment, picking up instead the "servyse" motif and applying it to Martha:

> This good and holy lady dyd servyse to Jhesu Cryste / whanne she herberowed hym self and his apostles with moche grete devocion & wyth a good herte / wherfor god dyd for her sake many myracles. . . . Every good woman ought to take here good ensample / how it is good to lodge and herberowe the servauntes of god / that is to say the predicatours / and them that prechen the feythe / and to discerne the good from evylle / Also the pylgryms and the poure peple of god.[20]

It is due to conduct-book interpretations of Martha's exemplary role that the focus of Jean Michel's episode has been shifted from the contemplative Mary to the active Martha, who throughout Michel's *Passion* becomes almost as important as her ever-fascinating sister, Mary Magdalene.

In the case of both the Towneley Annunciation and Visitation scenes and Jean Michel's Bethany scene, the source for the social rather than theological interpretation of exemplary women's behaviors is conduct literature. But we can be even more specific; behind the conduct book of the Knight of the Tower for his daughters is a collection of *exempla* of good and evil women's lives drawn mostly from the Bible. This collection, entitled the *Miroir des bonnes femmes* or *Miroir aux preudes femmes* (Mirror for noble/virtuous women) was composed *c.* 1300 and was a direct source for many of the Knight's examples, including those of the good hostess Martha and the prudent and courteous Virgin Mary.[21] It is unlikely that the *Miroir* has influenced the drama directly for, as John L. Grigsby has pointed out, "in contrast with the *Livre du Chevalier de la Tour Landry*, which enjoyed great popularity in France, England, and Germany, the *Miroir des bonnes femmes* has remained in obscurity."[22] Rather, its moral focus on proper behaviors for women has had an impact on conduct literature, which in turn influenced the cycle drama, one of whose aims became enactment of codes of female conduct for the audience's emulation. The cycles themselves, I would argue, often function like courtesy literature, modeling and mirroring civic and social identities appropriate to their urban and largely bourgeois parons, who claimed "gentle" status – a nobility based on virtuous deeds. Conduct literature, with its definitions of identity based on cultural behaviors rather than natural essences (nurture rather than nature), thus creates as much as it reflects the emerging power of the bourgeoisie.

Furthermore, as the drama focused more and more on human relationships and social roles, distinctions based on gender – conduct appropriate to the "gentlewoman" as opposed to the "gentleman" – were emphasized. Thus Mary models proper behaviors toward seductive men and pregnant kinswomen, while Martha is the perfect cook and hostess. Biblical events which had not been gender identified in previous exegesis may now be given such a reading. The *Book of the Knight of the Tower* takes from the *Miroir des bonnes femmes* the explanation that the holy women who wept for Christ when he was carrying the cross are examples that "every good woman ought to have pyte as she seeth that somme body dothe ony evylle to the poure people of god." The appropriate merciful female response is linked in this case with female essences: "woman of her nature oughte to be more swete and pyteous than the man / For the man oughte to be more hard and of more hyghe courage / And therefore they that have the herte nother meke nor pyteous maye be called mannysshe."[23]

At times in the drama the conduct becoming a gentlewoman clashes overtly with the religious context in which it is found. In a late scene from Jean Michel's *Passion*, for example, the Virgin Mary and the holy women are in Bethany awaiting word from Jesus, who appears to be in danger in Jerusalem. Suddenly John arrives to tell them that Jesus had been captured. Until this point, the scene has followed conventional expectations in developing the pathos in the predicaments of Christ, his followers, and his family. John, Christ's relative as well as his disciple, has a lengthy 115-line lament in which he expresses his fear of telling the Virgin Mary about the seizing of her son:

> quant bien parfondement je pense
> le grief, le tort, la viollence,
> la trahyson, le fier accés,
> les gens, la manière et l'excés,

le temps, la prinse et la lyeure,
les injures et la basteure
qu'on a fait et qu'on fait present
au benoist Jesus innocent,

. . .

je ne sçay quant je luy diray
duquel plus dolent je seray
ou de la mere ou de l'enfant.

(20,712–19, 726–8)

The *passio–compassio* topos is fully expressed throughout John's announcement of his news and Mary's initial response. Then "Nostre Dame" is given her own long lament (21,43–154) on her "cueur maternel doloreux," including impassioned exhortations to the holy women, Jesus, and the disciples, and condemnations of Judas.

Mary's first reaction is to rush to Jerusalem to succor her son but, incongruously, Jean Michel now turns the scene from a demonstration of the Virgin's maternal compassion into a lesson on how the well-bred lady behaves after curfew. When "Nostre Dame" announces her intention of going to Jerusalem to be with her son, John objects that no gentlewoman would go out after dark, for to do so would be to ruin her reputation:

> Mon ante et ma dame dolente,
> ne faictes pas ceste requeste;
> pas n'est licite ne honneste
> a preudes femmes de renon
> d'aller de nuyt.   (21,179–83)

The "preude femme" guards her good name and avoids compromising situations. The other holy women agree that John is right; Martha points out the danger of "scandal" if anything happens to them en route: "Ma dame, non, / la chose nous seroit trop male / et pourroit estre grant scandale / s'i nous venoit quelque fortune" (21,183–6). Mary Magdalene points out the danger of "la nuyt . . . fort obscure et brune" (21,187), telling Mary to stay overnight in Bethany until "le cler jour apparesse."

"Nostre Dame" does not protest these arguments, suggesting that

Mary's role as model for virtuous middle-class women takes precedence dramatically over her more traditional role as grieving mother of the about-to-be crucified Christ. The lamentation of the Virgin scene is here transformed – one might even say "deformed" – into a lesson on how to avoid a bad reputation drawn from conduct books for women. Injunctions against women's going out in public except on necessary errands were common in conduct books, as were exhortations to women to guard their "good name" (their "renommee.")[24] In the *Miroir des bonnes femmes*, the Virgin Mary is praised for remaining inside, leading to the moral that young women should stay home for "Li marcheans ne moustre mie la marcheaundise que il ne vuelt vendre."[25] The metaphor rather neatly conjoins those two groups whose visibility within late medieval urban life was crucial to the rise of the female conduct book: women and the bourgeoisie.

CONCLUSIONS

Within the fifteenth- and sixteenth-century religious drama the codes drawn from conduct books co-existed with earlier medieval codes from the literature of exegesis and spirituality. At times the conjunction was harmonious (as in Towneley cycle) and at times contradictory or tonally disruptive (as in Jean Michel's *Passion*.) The progression perceptible in the scenes discussed here is emblematic of the movement of late medieval culture. What began as an attempt to validate new lay life styles, to sacralize what had been defined as secular by monastic institutions, ended up replacing the older traditions totally and thus transforming the religious framework beyond recognition.

But what Huizinga considered a "waning" from the point of view of medieval symbolism might be construed as a creative cultural re-writing within a dramatic form of considerable flexibility. The popularity of the cycle drama for over two hundred years is, I would argue, a function of its success as a vehicle for effecting the symbolic transitions of power between church and state, between aristocracy and middle classes, and – perhaps most significantly – between male-based definitions of conduct which prevailed in the ecclesiastical and upper-class institutions of the high middle ages and the female-based definitions of conduct which seem to characterize the ideology of the newly powerful bourgeoisie in the late medieval and early renaissance period.

NOTES

* Research for this project was assisted by a National Endowment for the Humanities Travel to Collections Grant and funds from the University of Southern Maine Faculty Senate Research Committee.

1 V. A. Kolve (1966) *The Play called Corpus Christi*, Stanford, Calif., Stanford University Press; W. E. Meyers (1968) *A Figure Given: Typology in the Wakefield Plays*, Pittsburgh, Pa, Duquesne University Press.

2 J. Helterman (1981) *Symbolic Action in the Plays of the Wakefield Master*, Athens, Ga, University of Georgia Press.

3 E. Prosser (1961) *Drama and Religion in the English Mystery Plays*, Stanford, Calif., Stanford University Press.

4 R. Collier (1978) *Poetry and Drama in the York Corpus Christi Play*, Hamden, Conn., Archon Books.

5 P. Travis (1982) *Dramatic Design in the Chester Cycle*, Chicago,Ill., University of Chicago Press.

6 Citations from this cycle are taken from G. England (ed.) (1973) *The Towneley Plays* (1897), EETS e.s. 71, repr. Millwood, NY, Kraus.

7 K. M. Ashley (1979) "The specter of Bernard's noonday demon in medieval drama," *American Benedictine Review*, 30, 205–21.

8 Quoted in W. Caxton's translation in M. Y. Orford (ed.) (1971) *The Book of the Knight of the Tower*, EETS s.s. 2, 144.

9 K. S. Block (ed.) (1922) *Ludus Coventriae*, EETS e.s. 120.

10 R. Beadle (ed.) (1982) *The York Plays*, London, Edward Arnold.

11 J. Gardner comments on the "chatter of Mary and Elizabeth" as a "delightful early example of improvization," in his (1974) *The Construction of the Wakefield Cycle*, Carbondale, Ill., Southern Illinois University Press, 76. R. Woolf somewhat more subtly argues that the Towneley human endearments sustain the mood of Mary's reconciliation with Joseph after his doubts of the previous play; see her (1972) *The English Mystery Plays*, London, Routledge & Kegan Paul, 173–4. She contrasts the Towneley play with N-Town cycle's *Visit to Elizabeth* where "Elizabeth addresses Mary, not with human endearments, but with some of the most august of her late typological titles, such as 'trone and tabernakyl of þe hyʒ trinite' and by the significant adaption of the Biblical phrase *mater domini* to the supreme theological title of the Virgin, *modyr of god*, which is three times repeated." Woolf almost

always casts her aesthetic vote with scenes of "human" feeling rather than theological elevation.

12 F. J. Furnivall (ed.) (1969) *The Babees Book* (1868), EETS o.s. 32, repr. New York, Greenwood Press, 17.

13 Caxton translation (1971) 145–6.

14 ibid. 146.

15 I. Ragusa and R. B. Green (eds and trans.) (1961) *Meditations on the Life of Christ*, Princeton, NJ, Princeton University Press, 22–3, 24.

16 J. Le Goff (1980) *Time, Work, and Culture in the Middle Ages*, trans. A Goldhammer, Chicago, Ill., University of Chicago Press, 115.

17 O. Jodogne (ed.) (1959) *Le Mystère de la Passion* (Angers, 1486), Gembloux, Belgium, Éditions J. Duculot.

18 K. Ashley (1984) "The bourgeois piety of Martha in the *Passion* of Jean Michel," *Modern Language Quarterly*, 14, 227–40.

19 Caxton translation (1971) 134.

20 ibid.

21 Only two complete manuscript copies (MS 2156, Bibliothèque de l'Arsenal, in Paris, and MS Fr. 213, Bibliothèque municipale, in Dijon) and one partial copy (MS Fr. 32, University of Pennsylvania Library, Philadelphia) of the *Miroir des bonnes femmes* exist. The work has not been edited. Detailed descriptive articles on the *Miroir* were written by J. L. Grigsby (1961) *Romania*, 82, 458–81, and (1962) *Romania*, 83, 30–51, but to my knowledge no one else interested in conduct literature has investigated the *Miroir*'s contents or its impact. It is not mentioned in the major analysis of conduct books for women, A. A. Hentsch's *De la littérature didactique du Moyen Age s'adressant spécialement aux femmes*; nor does the recent book by D. Bornstein (1983) *The Lady in the Tower: Medieval Courtesy Literature for Women*, Hamden, Conn., Shoe String Press, cite the *Miroir*.

22 J. L. Grigsby (1963) "A new source of the *Livre du Chevalier de la Tour Landry*," *Romania* 84, 173. As Grigsby notes, the *Miroir* is found in only three Mss, while the *Livre du Chevalier* "can be found in thirteen Mss. and two early sixteenth-century printings, not counting the two English translations and the thirteen printings of the German translation" (173–4).

23 Caxton translation (1971) 135.

24 See for example Caxton translation (1971) 151–2.

25 *Miroir*, MS Fr. 213, Dijon, f. 134a.

2

Nets and bridles: early modern conduct books and sixteenth-century women's lyrics

ANN ROSALIND JONES

Recent analysis of early modern treatises on the nature of women suggests that debates over gender were articulated with basic issues of hierarchy and change in European society.[1] In the crossfire of gender polemics, however, women were consistently the objects of scrutiny and the targets of complex prescriptions for proper behavior. Even defenses of women were, in the great majority, written by men, and the practical conduct books that proliferated during the sixteenth century were directed by men toward fellow men on the rise, as in the etiquette manuals written for aspiring courtiers, or addressed to the fathers and husbands of potentially unruly daughters and wives, in the case of bourgeois and Protestant marriage manuals.

In the essay that follows, I offer a survey of sixteenth- and early-seventeenth-century courtesy books and marriage manuals in order to show how conduct books positioned women in the class transformations occurring throughout the male-dominated societies of Renaissance Europe. As the focus of these manuals shifted from the feudal king and his queen to the professional courtier and the lady-in-waiting, and from the landed aristocrat and his sumptuously attired consort to the bourgeois husband and his wife, women confronted new requirements for their morals and manners. Public self-display was the norm at court and in the urban coteries in which ambitious men (and, less frequently, women) met and competed for recognition and patronage. But the most widely disseminated feminine ideal was the confinement of the bourgeois daughter and wife to private domesticity in the households of city merchants, professional men and, in England, Protestant fathers and husbands. The court lady was required to speak; the bourgeois wife was enjoined to silence.

Male-authored literary texts reinforced these models. The witty yet virtuous court lady was sketched out in sonnet sequences and in élite comedy (Ronsard's Hélène in *Les Sonnets pour Hélène* and Beatrice in Shakespeare's *Much Ado about Nothing* are two exemplary heroines); the chaste, prudent wife became an admirable, if rare, character in city comedy; satires, in highly profitable popular forms, were aimed at women who transgressed gender decorum (Bertrand de la Borderie's *L'Amye de court*, the anonymous pamphlets *Hic Mulier* and *Haec Vir*). Yet the late 1500s was also a period in which women were beginning to enter the public sphere as writers, occasionally as poets. The ideologies of contemporary conduct books pervade their literary performances as well as those of men. By necessity, women writers acted out propitiatory obedience to expectations of women in order to defend themselves against attacks for making public their still unusual and suspect ambition to contribute to a culture still produced almost entirely by men. Two poets from different class and cultural situations, Catherine Des Roches and Isabella Whitney, illustrate the kinds of tactics adopted by women in order to negotiate the gender ideologies being used to consolidate emergent class identities in early modern Europe.

Conduct books as a genre in this period illustrate an uneasy confrontation between long-standing official discourses and new social practices. Medicine and philosophy had traditionally defined woman as the physical and intellectual inferior of man, given to hysterical and irrational outbursts; religion had defined her as subject to man since the Fall, owing him obedience to compensate for Eve's sins; law defined married women as covertes, subsumed under their husbands' economic and civic identity and incapable of making legal contracts on their own. These discourses represented female character and status as fixed – eternal givens founded on nature,

Scripture, and precedent. Conduct books appear to be based on a different assumption: men and women can be *produced*. They are malleable, capable of being trained for changing roles; proper instruction can fashion them into successful participants in new social settings and the etiquettes belonging to them.

But the question was not so simple. Historians of courtiership have shown that the availability of courtesy books actually intensified the social uncertainties arising from competition between the aristocracy and the new man.[2] Historians of women have argued that commitments to fixed social rank versus upward mobility underlay the increase in polemics on both sides of the woman issue throughout the sixteenth and seventeenth centuries.[3] The uproar over upstart women had some basis in an actual increase in women's opportunites. Like men, a few women were encountering new milieux outside the private domestic sphere – local and national courts, humanist coteries – where "merit," in the form of beauty, polished manners, and verbal skill, could improve the principal employment available to them: marriage into a higher rank. Anne Boleyn, the grand-daughter of a tenant farmer, rose to a position as spectacular as it was precarious at the English court in the 1520s; Stefano Guazzo in 1574 recorded seeing "about the French Queene, certayn meane Gentlewomen enter into such credit [through their music, painting, poetry, arts and sciences] that they are come to be maryed to the cheefe Gentlemen in Fraunce, without any peny given to them in dowry by their father;" when Annibal Guasco sent his daughter Lavinia to the court of the Duchess of Mantua in 1586, he foresaw the possibility of a secretary's career as well as marriage among the benefits she might expect.[4]

Yet the profession of lady-in-waiting, like membership in the urban salons in which women joined men in conversation and literary improvisation, included fewer women, for a shorter time, than did the career of courtiership and humanism for men. The reaction against feminine ambition seems vastly out of proportion to the number of women actually departing from traditional norms. Nonetheless, the fixity of those norms encouraged opponents of class mobility in general to ransack the classics and scholasticism for arguments in the new debates over women's nature. Anxiety about the artifices of the class-climbing man could be displaced into attacks upon unnatural women.[5] But conservative beliefs in the supposedly innate female virtues of obedience and humility, asserted in support of the "natural" hierarchy menaced by men on the rise, were also incorporated into the new feminine ideals being formulated by rising classes in the process of establishing group identities to rival or challenge the privileges of the aristocracy.

COURTESY BOOKS, THE COURT LADY, AND THE COSMOPOLITAN COTERIE

Courtesy manuals, written for members of a transitional occupation, are the most complex texts among conduct books. They argue for a kind of relativism that looks extremely progressive in the context of reactionary appeals to a stable gender system. Stefano Guazzo's *La civil conversatione* (1574, translated into English by George Pettie in 1581) is a case in point. Aiming at a wide range of sub-aristocratic classes, Guazzo posits variable custom rather than eternal principle as the basis for socially acceptable behavior. Whatever company Guazzo's courtier finds himself in, he is shown how to adapt gracefully and obligingly. So, too, Guazzo argues that daughters should be brought up according to a policy of flexible pragmatism. His liberal spokesman, Annibal Magnocavalli, recognizes that daughters will have diverse careers, marry men of differing ranks, and inhabit different geographical regions; therefore, they require diverse practical and moral training. Piety should be encouraged in a girl destined for the nunnery, but a more worldly education is necessary for a girl who is to go to court: she will need to "write, to discourse, to sing, to play on Instruments, to daunce, and to be able to perform all that which belongeth to a Courtier to doe" ("tutto ciò che adorna alle donne di palazzo," II, 78; 417). Wives, too, will need to conform to local customs rather than to a transcendent marital code: a Roman wife must submit to the seclusion imposed upon her by that city's conventions, but a Sienese wife should be ready for the open socializing accepted further north. Annibal sums up the consequences of class and regional variation as follows: "At this day, the manner of bringing up [daughters] is so different, I say not of one Countrey from another, yea but of one Countye, and of one Citie, that a manne can set downe no certaine determinate rule of it" (II, 74; 413).

But Guazzo's permissiveness has its limits: his commentary on the court lady reveals a fixation on chastity that interferes with his mapping of effective speech at court. His dilemma is that courtly etiquette coincides with other sixteenth-century ideologies of femininity in making a more or less explicit equation between women's sexuality and their speech. Outside the court, fathers and husbands were encouraged to silence their daughters and wives in order to preserve women's function as the repositories of family honor and the guarantors of domestic peace. But once a conduct-book writer like Castiglione or Guazzo admitted the presence of women at court and in other masculine gathering places, he faced the contradiction between longstanding discourses that condemned the public woman as a whore and the courtly code, which constructed women as decorative and inspiring adjuncts to men, necessary partners in the outward show of country house, palazzo, and literary salon. The sections of courtesy books addressed to the court lady imply that she was being given a share in the public sphere, in the "civil conversation" that led to useful connections and rewards for verbal expertise. But continuing anxiety about female sexual purity defined that sphere as a dangerous one for women. Etiquette books for the courtier offer him an array of positive models for imitation, but their instructions to women are couched in prohibitions and warnings. Threatened with the constant possibility of scandal, the court lady is advised to defend herself through a calculated rhetoric of words and gestures. What she must learn is how to assess the surveillance that operates at court and how to exploit a corresponding set of words and gestures for feminine self-display.

The rhetoric is intricate because the court lady's function was double. Officially she was to serve a princess or a queen, whose reputation depended not only on the beauty and splendor of her ladies-in-waiting but also on their chastity, which she was expected to oversee. Anne de France, in her instructions to her royal daughter (1504), warns her that any misbehavior on the part of her women will make people at court suspect her of secret vice;[6] Guazzo advises his Lavinia that chaste thoughts, apparent in her eyes and face, will endear her to her patroness more than anything else (C4v). But the lady was also at court to serve courtiers, to be a member of the chorus prompting men to bravery in tournaments and eloquence in conversation; she was expected to be a witty and informed participant in dialogues whose subject was most often love. Rather than prohibiting amorous repartee to women, the courtly code elicited it from them. To paraphrase Foucault, the court lady had to speak of sex;

43

she had to speak in public, and in a manner determined by the divisions between licit and illicit pleasure.[7] She performed a generalized erotic function directly opposed to the silent fidelity demanded of the private woman.

Castiglione's *Courtier* reveals the tension arising from this double assignment. His opening celebration of the mixed-sex conversations at the court of Urbino is followed by a hasty qualification:

> There was never agreement of will or hartie love greater between brethren than there was between us all. The like was betweene the women, with whom we had such free and honest conversation, that everye man might commune, sitte, dallye and laugh with whom he lusted. But such was the respect which we bore to the Dutchesse will, that the selfe same libertie was a very great bridle. Neither was there any that thought it not . . . the greatest griefe to offend her.[8]

Castiglione's effort in this passage is clearly to deny that verbal access to the ladies of Urbino implied sexual access as well. But Guazzo depicts a clumsier character, William, who exposes precisely the assumption that Castiglione denies. When Annibal announces that he will now discuss "la conversatione delle donne," William takes it for granted that he means bodytalk – that is, relations with the women "with whom men try their manhood withall in amorous encounters" ("con le quali si giuoca alle braccia," I, 324; 290). In William's view, "conversation," like "intercourse," has two meanings: with men it is civil; with women it is sexual. Men are refined through the artful practice of speech; women are corrupted by it. Annibal immediately disabuses William of this low-life notion, drawing together courtly commonplaces to assert that speaking with women sharpens men's wits, polishes their language, and elevates their thoughts. But the exchange is symptomatic: the courtly ideal of feminity cannot banish the conflict assumed to exist between women's conversation and their chastity. Thus speaking properly becomes a minefield for women, and its rules become bewilderingly complex.

Castiglione's comments on the *donna di palazzo* (significantly, she is not called a *cortigiana*/courtesan because the term already connoted a prostitute)[9] illustrate in their syntax a continual vacillation between the spontaneous natural modesty attributed to women and the necessity for artifice. The male courtier's *misura*, his graceful negotiation of a mean between extremes, is reduced for the court lady into elaborate directions for demonstrating sexual purity. Recommendations are followed by counter-recommendations and by acute analysis of how her behavior might be interpreted; "yes, but" and "neither/nor" are standard formulations. Beauty is posited as the court lady's first quality. Giuliano de' Medici says, "Beautie is more necessary in her than in the Courtier, for . . . there is a great lacke in the woman that wanteth beautie" (190; 342). But he immediately spells out the consequences of this desirability: "She ought also to be more circumspect, and to take better heede that she give no occasion to bee ill reported of, and so behave her selfe, that she be not onely not spotted with any fault, but not so much as with suspicion." Virtue is not enough; she must foresee the judgments observers will make of her. Giuliano explains why in a pragmatic acknowledgment of the power imbalance operating in courtly reputation: "a woman hath not so manie waies to defend her selfe from slanderous reportes, as hath a man." Here already is an ambivalent demand: the lady must be beautiful enough to attract men, but alert to the possibility that she will be criticized for doing it too well. She must look seductive, but she must be seen not to be seduced.

Giuliano's prescriptions for the court lady's speech call for a similar tightrope act. Her affability, which endears her to all men, must be accompanied by a modesty that keeps them at bay:

> there belongeth to her above all thinges, a certaine sweetness in language . . . whereby she may gently entertain all kinde of men with talke worthie the hearing and honest ("ragionamenti grati ed honesti") . . . accompanying with sober and quiet manners, and with the honestie that must alwaies be a stay to her deeds, a readie liveliness of wit.

The ideal becomes ever more demanding, as Giuliano seems to recognize:

> but with such a kinde of goodness, that she may be esteemed no less chaste, wise and courteous than pleasant, neate, conceited and sober ("arguta e discreta"), and therefore muste she keepe a certaine meane verie hard, and (in a manner) derived of contrary matters, and come just to certain limittes, but not to passe them. (191; 343)

His version of what the court lady is to talk about is based on a similar strategy of second-guessing observers who, he assumes, will scrutinize her mercilessly. Rather than deny that she takes pleasure in erotic chat, she must signify that she enjoys it within correct limits:

> This woman ought not . . . to be so squeimish . . . to abhorre both the company and the talke (though somewhat of the wantonest) . . . for a man may lightly guesse that she faigned to be so coye to hide that in herself which she doubted others might come to the knowledge of.

Another qualification follows:

> Neither ought she againe (to show her selfe free and pleasant) speake words of dishonestie, nor use a certaine familiarity without measure and bridle . . . but being present at suche kinde of talke, she ought to give [it] hearing with a little blushing and shamefacednesse.

To maneuver her way through the love chat central to her calling, then, the court lady needs a triple consciousness: she must know how to avoid appearing to be faking prudishness. A complex censorship of speech had also been recommended by Giovanni della Casa in one of his few remarks about women in *Il Galatheo* (1559): the court lady must replace frank sexual terms with euphemisms, and she must be especially careful to avoid unintended sexual puns.[10] Della Casa is obsessed with polite control of the body, but even he does not prescribe the blush required by Giuliano – a particularly tricky performance. The court lady is to accompany risqué conversation with an artfully produced version of what is naturally an involuntary symptom of embarrassment.

Six years after the publication of the *Courtier*, Agostino Nipho concretized Castiglione's ambivalent theory into specific models of feminine verbal strategy. Four chapters of his *De re aulica* (1534, translated into Italian in 1560) record reponses made by court ladies to their suitors. Nipho's affable ladies are almost incredibly adept at turning propositions delicately aside, and the preponderance of such maneuvers suggests that he expected them to occupy most of a woman's time. One lady places her lover neatly into the double bind built into Neoplatonic idealization of the mistress: "If I gave into your request," she says, "you would rule over a treasure much diminished from the one you enjoy now."[11] Another, whose lover praises her skill in turning aside his plea for an "indecent favor," exposes the difficulty of the technique required of her: "If I were as clever as you say," she tells him, "you would not even have noticed my counter-move" (120).

But the elaborate sprightliness of these *affabilità* jars with the natural sincerity Nipho also demands of the court lady. A woman's "sweetness of speech," he writes,

> should above all be simple, not feigned, ornamented or highly colored, but consonant with the purity of nature. For a woman who has nothing feigned or simulated about her seems worthy of every kind of praise, because she maintains the chastity and integrity that are proper to her. (115)

Spontaneity cannot be taught. What is it exactly, then, that Nipho is teaching? He forbids to women the self-serving flattery and acerbic wit he outlines for men, yet the speeches that he attributes to his lady, Phausina, as to others, suggest that the court lady is to practice artifices similar to men's: she is to provide an attentive ear for the verbal virtuosity of her superiors, and she is to use elaborate devices for praising herself indirectly. One of Phausina's remarks suggests that she is as expert at controlling group conversations as private ones. Three court ladies try to guess what Nipho's greatest pleasure in courting her is; one suggests bluntly that it lies in mutual hand-holding and embraces ("il piacevolissimo e scambievol maneggiar delle mani," 124). Phausina quickly suppresses this suspicion, assuring her listeners that the purity of Nipho's love, his freedom from the temptations that torment younger men, is the cause of his bliss – a point he has made himself throughout the book. Thus she compliments him for his self-control, herself for her chastity, and she administers a witty rebuke to the lady who presumed to trust the evidence of her senses rather than following the rules of the game. The ingenuity of Nipho's codes contradicts the unadorned speech he sets forth as a norm for women at court. He appeals to nature, but he teaches art.

Guazzo's representation of the feminine ideal brings further contradictions into view. His eulogy of an unnamed lady, probably a patroness at Casale, foregrounds the instability of the response the court lady is expected to arouse in men. Guazzo's phrasing makes clear the pleasure he feels in the alternation of desire and awe. The lady's speech, he writes, combines elegance, sweetness, and high-mindedness to such a degree that "the mindes of the hearers, intangled in these three nets, feele themselves at one instant to bee both moved by her amiability and bridled by her honesty" (I, 241; 300). This is a masculine image of Petrarchan desire, not a practical guide for women's behavior. The metaphors and paradoxes of love poetry, its nets of desire and silent eloquence, produce a model that few women readers could have put into practice. Guazzo's reverie reveals the tensions built into court life between the call for women's purity and the flirtatious volubility they were expected to provide for their male companions.

CATHERINE DES ROCHES: CHASTENING THE COURTIERS

One woman writer, however, put these intricate demands into highly successful practice in the poetry she wrote for an audience of humanist scholars and professionals much like Nipho, although they gathered in an urban household rather than the court of Urbino.[12] Catherine Des Roches, writing in Poitiers in the 1570s, adapted the precepts governing the conduct of the lady at court to her own role as the center of a literary salon. She constructs for herself a position of authority much like that of Castiglione's Cardinal Bembo, whose long Neoplatonic speech concluded the fourth book of *The Courtier* on a note of sublime masculine virtue and established a verbal code for generations of courtiers to come.[13] Through a series of gender reversals, she assembles a dialogue that assigns the woman speaker greater expertise in love theory and greater moral weight than her lover, at the same time that she invents a spotlessly chaste persona for herself in the midst of men's erotic celebration of her beauty.

Des Roches was one partner in a mother–daughter pair, Madeleine and Catherine, who published two collections of *Oeuvres* from Poitiers in 1578 and 1583. They turned to the public world for sustenance by necessity: Madeleine, twice a widow, held a salon to which Parisian experts in law made their way during Les Grands Jours, the special court sessions at which lawyers from the capital dispatched unfinished provincial cases.[14] Mother and daughter alike became famous among humanists and professional men for the learning and wit they exhibited on such occasions, and their fame spread beyond Poitiers in ways that profited them both. Catherine addressed odes on political subjects to the queen and king (Catherine de' Medici and Henri III), and Madeleine won a generous grant from the court as compensation for Protestant attacks on her property. Catherine apparently succeeded in making a living for them both. In their collection of letters, *Les Missives* (1586), Madeleine praises her daughter for her determination to support them both with her pen, "without any aid from others."[15]

Catherine works out a self-presentation in her poems that turns the directives of male-authored courtesy books into an enabling permission for less acceptable feminine ambitions. In the second of two songs she composed for a chorus of Amazons, for a masque in which they defeat Cupid and fend off the attacks of his earthly followers, the penultimate stanza typifies a central move throughout her writing: her appropriation of chastity as a condition and a justification for her activity as *dame de salon* and woman poet:

> Un coeur qui n'ouvre point aux voluptez la porte,
> Un penser généreux, une puissance forte
> Nous preserve tousiours de l'Amour et de Mars.
> Aussi en toutes parts la fame ne resonne
> Que du pouvoir hautain de la Royne Amazone
> Qui faict marcher les Dieux dessus ses etandars.
>
> (1, 120)[16]

A heart that never surrenders to love's pleasures,
A fruitful mind, an enduring strength
Guards us forever against Love and Mars:
And so, everywhere, the glory resounds
Of the lofty power of the Amazons' queen,
Who makes the gods march underneath her banners.

Catherine's insistence on her sexual integrity is particularly understandable in light of the coterie setting in which she performed. Her poems were initially recited directly to her audience, in a potentially unstable public space. The Poitiers salon resembled Castiglione's Urbino in the emphasis placed on quick wit and verbal elegance for men and women both: it was a gathering place for many men and few women, where face-to-face flirtation and erotic innuendo went hand in hand with poetic improvisation. The exposed situation of both

Des Roches, who would attract highly placed and influential men only as long as they avoided any breath of scandal, generated a set of defensive strategies clearly visible in Catherine's contribution to a collection of poems written by the Des Roches's visitors during the Grands Jours of 1579. The idea of assembling the volume came from Etienne Pasquier, a humanist lawyer and poet, who named it *La Puce* (*The Flea*). The occasion for the poems was his claim that he had seen a flea on the bosom of "la belle Catherine," a claim that led to an explosion of poems on the topic by some two dozen men, all entering with obvious glee into a competition over who could be most wittily lascivious in his paeans to the flea and its hostess. The men's poems play on "puce/pucelle" (flea/maiden/hymen), endlessly rework the *blason du tétin* (poem in praise of the breast), and identify the poet with the flea in verbs of action directed toward the woman's body: exploring, sucking, biting, penetrating.

Surrounded by an extravagant display of erotic entomology, what does the woman poet do? Acutely aware of her visibility in the coterie setting, Des Roches produces a self-portrait for a world that differentiated sharply between permissible sexual discourse for men and women. Only a courtesan poet could gain from sharing the salacious language used by the men writing in this contest. Catherine, instead, invents a witty yet irreproachably chaste persona for herself. She draws on Ovid's standard plot pattern in *The Metamorphoses* to transform the flea into a creature with whom she can identify: an ingeniously self-protective female, changed by Diana from a nymph fleeing Pan into a safer (if lower) form of life.

She explicitly takes on the role of a courtesy-book writer in a sequence of twenty-seven sonnets written to illustrate an exemplary exchange between two lovers, Sincero and Charite. (This may be one of the first versions of the letter-writing manuals so influential during the seventeenth and eighteenth centuries.) She introduces the poems as a guide to amorous etiquette, explaining in her preface:

> [Mes lecteurs] diront peut estre que je ne devois pas escrire d'amour, que si je suis amoureuse il ne fault pas le dire, et que si je ne suis telle il ne fault pas le feindre: je leur respondray à cela, que je ne le suis, ny ne feins de l'estre: car j'escry ce que j'ay pensé et non pas ce que j'ay veu en Syncero, lequel je ne connoys que

par imagination. Mais comme il est advenu à quelques grands
personnages de représenter un Roy parfaict, un parfaict orateur,
un parfaict courtisan, ainsi ai-je voulu former un parfaict
amoureux. (1, 52c)

Perhaps my readers will say that I should not write of love – that
if I am in love, I should not say so, and if I am not, I should not
pretend to be. To this I'd answer that I neither am in love nor
pretend to be. For in Sincero I write what I have thought, not
what I have actually seen, since I know him only through
imagination. But as it has happened to some great writers to
represent a perfect king, a perfect orator, a perfect courtier, so
have I wanted to fashion a perfect lover.

Thus Des Roches shifts love poetry into a didactic rather than a
confessional mode. Her construction of the exemplary couple draws
on a wide range of Neoplatonic treatises and lyric collections in
which the male writer demonstrates his philosophical and literary
polish through the speeches of characters capable of the élite refinement encoded in Neoplatonic dialogue. (Castiglione's Bembo was an
early example; contemporary examples in France included Scève's
Délie and Du Bellay's *L'Olive*.) In Catherine's text, however, a
woman directs the spiritual training of the man. In their first
dialogue, Sincero proclaims the intensity of his passion and asserts
his hope of ascending to heaven through her agency; Charite points
out the exaggerations and logical flaws in his declaration with the
gentle acerbity Nipho recommends. And while Sincero invokes
Petrarchan torment and desire, Charite repeats like an incantation
her definition of "l'amour saincte," the chaste mutual admiration she
insists will win them both emotional stability and worldly fame.
Moreover, Des Roches's appropriation of Neoplatonic precepts
allows her to praise herself/Charite with the subtle indirection
demonstrated by Nipho's Phausina. At the end of Charite's fourth
sonnet, she addresses a command to Sincero that is also a claim to
fame for her own sexual purity:

Faictes que la raison commande à vos desirs,
En esperant de moy les honnestes plaisirs
Que l'on doit esperer d'une chaste maitresse.
(1, 108)

Be certain that reason directs your desires,
And hope from me only the honorable joys
That may be expected from a chaste
   mistress.

Des Roches, then, inscribes the gender ideology of courtly conduct books at the center of her collected poems. She speaks of love from the middle of an erotically charged social and verbal arena, but she negotiates the minefield by asserting a rhetoric of feminine purity against the frankly sexual language of her male interlocutors. Her poetry needs to be understood as a set of subtly effective maneuvers within the contradictory definitions of womanly virtue, which, by the 1580s, had filtered down from royal and ducal palaces to the urban salons where ambitious professionals met and courted fame. These professionals, Des Roches demonstrates, could include women as well – as long as they obeyed and manipulated the rules of courtly discourse for their own ends.

BOURGEOIS MARRIAGE MANUALS: THE SHIFT TO DOMESTIC VIRTUES

Conduct books for fathers and husbands, including pedagogical treatises and marriage manuals addressed to male heads of households, make no attempt to balance the desirability and the dangers of women's entry into the public world: they forbid it. Their advice has a single focus, the chastity of the wife, which is assumed to need reinforcement through a range of physical and psychic controls. Throughout the sixteenth century women's dress, speech, and activity in the domestic realm were examined in more and more probing forms, motivated by two emerging social currents: hostility to aristocratic style and, in England, Puritan patriarchalism.

Domestic discourse linked physical enclosure and household tasks to the purity of women's bodies and the scarcity of their speech. The good wife was constructed as the woman who stays indoors, guarding her chastity as she guards the other property of her husband.[17] As her body is locked within the walls of the house, her tongue is locked in her mouth. Women are reminded that nature gave them teeth as a guard against careless speech. Giovanni Bruto, in his *La Institutione di una Fanciulla nata nobilmente* (1555), picked up the classical commonplace that nature hedged the tongue with rows of teeth to limit speech and made ears hollow to encourage listening, and Richard Brathwait repeated the warning in highly colored language in *The English Gentlewoman* (1631):

> What is spoken of Maids may be properly applied to all women: They should be seene and not heard. . . . What restraint is required in respect of the tongue may appear by that ivory guard or garrison by which it is impaled: See, how it is double warded, that it may with more reservancy and better security be restrained![18]

Simultaneously the Old Testament model of the good wife, much quoted from Proverbs, links her virtuous industry to her closed doors and few words. In contrast, the woman who lets herself be seen in the streets and at banquets is a harlot, described by Barnabe Rich in *My Ladies Looking Glasse* (1616) as "full of words, . . . loud and brabbling."[19]

The new directions of sixteenth-century marriage manuals can be clarified by a step backward in time and upward on the class scale. Earlier books written for the nobility had defined the aristocratic wife as a public figure, representing her husband's rank to the view of lesser citizens. In fifteenth- and sixteenth-century manuals written for queens and their attendants, high sumptuary requirements had been the rule. One example: in 1505 Queen Anne of France advised her daughter, should she ever be called upon to serve a queen, that ladies-in-waiting should dress fashionably and class-consciously:

> Be sure every day that you dress as well and carefully as you can, for in the eyes of the world, believe me, it is inappropriate, even shocking, to see a nobly born girl or woman ignorantly or inelegantly dressed. Neither men or women can be too elegantly or neatly dressed, in my view – as long as they are not over-finicky, or so obsessed over it that they cease to serve God. (25)

She adds that queens and the wives of the upper aristocracy, who are expected to be on constant public view, should dress more lavishly than other women, a view almost exactly similar to that in a text written a century earlier, Christine de Pisan's *Livre des Trois Vertus* (1405). Elaborate costume is a required sign of rank, a class duty along with generous hospitality and the knowledge of correct forms of speech toward all lesser-ranking groups. Throughout her *Enseignements*, Anne repeats that exemplary behavior in public is the noblewoman's main duty: "Noblewomen are necessarily more observed than others, so they must be more careful. For in all things they are and must be the mirror, pattern and example for others" (65).

In total contrast to the feudal ideal, advice books for merchants and the lesser gentry define the wife as a domestic worker, conspicuous not for beauty or splendor but for practical virtues, which are celebrated in opposition to aristocratic leisure and display. This attitude was recorded early on by Leon Battista Alberti, writing for the Florentine merchant patriciate in his *Libri della Famiglia*, finished in 1421 and, although unpublished, a typical statement of the new class attitude.[20] A later Italian text, Torquato Tasso's *Discorso della virtù feminile, e donnesca* (1582), shows how persistent the distinction between royal grandeur and bourgeois modesty had come to be. Tasso dedicated his book to the Duchess of Mantua, to whom he announced that he was writing not for "the citizen's wife, or to a private lady, even less to an industrious mother of a family."[21] For these categories of women, he says, thriftiness and usefulness must be the main concerns. For a queen, they are "lightness, delicacy and decorum," which he links to "fine linen robes, embroidered with silk and gold." Chivalrous nostalgia and a transparent desire for ducal patronage motivate a good deal of Tasso's praise of feminine elegance, but he typifies the early modern split in his focus between regal display and domestic simplicity.

English writers make equally precise distinctions when they discuss proper dress for women. Rich, who dedicated his *Looking Glasse* to the wife of a knight, Sir Oliver James, concedes that if a woman can afford the finery (silk, silver, gold) suited to her high rank, "she useth them to the glory of God, that hath created them to that end and purpose, to decke and ornifie such worthy persons" (42). But once the issue of wifely conduct is raised, Rich quotes Proverbs on domestic industriousness in a practical vein that suggests he is no longer defending the sumptuary rights of the aristocracy: "She seeketh out wool and flax, and laboureth cheerfully with her hands; / She overseeth the waies of her household, and eateth not the bread of idlenesse." And he ends with a dismissal of courtly refinements as vices, out of reach and dangerous to the good woman, who "is not shee that can lift up her heeles highest in the galliard, [or] that is lavish of her lips or loose of her tongue" (44). Moral virtue is defined as the property of lower ranks here, while verbal looseness is implicitly paralleled to big spending.

Brathwait takes a similar position in *The English Gentlewoman*, addressed to women of the lesser nobility, whom he obviously wants to protect against corruption and betrayal by "courtezans" and foppish gallants (a widespread reaction against Jacobean court and city life). In the opening emblems, the gentlewoman is pictured holding a coat of arms and dressed richly in ruff, farthingale, and brocade – but not, Brathwait emphasizes in his chapter on "Apparrell," in excessive splendor. She is also shown in an illustration of "Decency," preferring natural flowers to artificial, prideful plumes; and in his chapter explicating "Decency," Brathwait advises unmarried women and men of this class to take the safest – that is, the lowest – path as far as dress and demeanor are concerned:

> Do you think that a j[u]tting Gait, a leering Looke, a glibbery Tongue, or gaudy Attire can move affection in anyone worthy of your love? Sure, no. . . . To be an admirer of one of these were to prefer a Maymarrian [Maid Marian] before a Modest Matron. (95)

Such precise discriminations play no part in marriage manuals written for city fathers and the petty gentry, in which the attack on fancy dress and elaborate manners as a sign of vanity and dereliction of feminine duty supports a new sense of class values constructed against the old and the new aristocracy. A case in point is Robert Greene's dedication to *A Quip for an Upstart Courtier, or a quaint dispute between velvet breeches and cloth breeches* (1592), in which the symbolism of clothing underlies the writer's praise of Thomas Barnabie as a fellow "maintayner of Cloth breeches (I meane of the olde and worthie customes of the Gentilitie and yeomanrie of England").[22] When Greene turns to women, however, his defense of simplicity brings him into contradiction with the romance genre he uses for the exemplary tales of his *Penelope's Web* (1601). The royal heroines of this narrative marriage manual perform in fantastic plots, which, against all class verisimilitude, still represent them as exhibiting the practical skills and the modest virtue of the bourgeois wife. Barmenissa, rejected by her sultan husband, supports herself in her exile by working with "the Needle and the Wheele;" Cratina attracts a king through her humility and chastity, which Greene presents as the qualities of a "country wife."[23] More abstractly, marriage as an institution began to be associated with an unadorned and therefore genuinely noble state, as in the formula delivered by a courtier in George Whetstone's *Heptameron of Civill Discourses* (1582):

> Gorgeous and rich Apparayle delighteth the Gazers eye: and (perhaps) offendeth the wearers heart: where Maryage, in homely Attyre, is everywhere honored.[24]

The pressure on non-aristocratic wives to prefer bodily and moral plainness to worldly glitter and to practice profitable private industry instead was directed toward a variety of readers from the mid-sixteenth century onward. Ambitious parents and upstart or un-thrifty husbands seem to be the main targets for domestic ideology, but its promoters also promise happier marriage to single women. Thomas Becon, defending marriage against Catholic celibacy and aristocratic adultery in his preface to *The Christian State of Matrimony* (1543), advises men against marrying wives richer than they are. Higher-ranking wives will be "froward and scolding," "so ladylyke and high in the insteppe . . . that they think that theyre husbands ought of very duty to give them place."[25] Humble and domestically trained women are a better prospect:

> Get unto thee such a wyfe, as fereth God, loveth hys word, is gentle, quiet, honest, silent, of few wordes, servisable, obsequious, modest, loving, faithfull, obedient and redy to do whatsoever becometh an honest marryed woman.   (B5r)

The lady-like refinements Becon warns husbands against were also forbidden to a housewife-to-be by Giovanni Bruto in his sharply anti-courtly treatise on the education of a nobly born maiden. *La Insitutione di una Fanciulla nata nobilmente* was dedicated not to a noblewoman, in fact, but to the daughter of a Genoese merchant living in Anvers, Marietta Cattaneo. Throughout, Bruto sets the humanist education and the dancing and music lessons given daughters of the aristocracy against an ideal of feminine virtue that calls the reigning class hierarchy into question. He tells Marietta that her nobility consists in the "generosità" she has been given by nature, and he encourages her to model her piety and domestic skills "not only upon ladies nobler than herself, richer and more powerful, but, far more important, on those who are virtuous and wise . . . knowing that the world contains many noble and elevated women inferior to her" (iiiir). He also insists that weaving, spinning, and sewing are suitable tasks for a girl of her rank. His English translator, Thomas Salter (*A Mirrhor mete for all Mothers, Matrones and Maids*, 1579), expanded Bruto's preface to include an attack on mothers and schoolmistresses, whose longing for luxury in dress he interprets as a symptom of parental and pedagogical irresponsibility:

> likewise such garments as be gallant, garnisht with gold, which (notwithstandyng how gorgeous so ever they be to the eye, are but durt and drosse), we see bothe Mothers and Mistresses to be so curious as so nere as they can, they will not permit so muche as a mote to remaine upon them, and yet God . . . knowes them to be so negligent and careless over their Daughters, and Maidens, as thei never regarde nor respect their behaviours.[26]

Aristocratic vanity is banished, to be replaced with practical education and genuine Protestant values.

"Servisability" in girls and wives is also called for in a sermon by Edward Hake, published as *A Touchstone for this Time Present* (1574), in which thunderous satire reinforces a concern for masculine advancement. Hake opposes honest labor to conspicuous consumption in a series of exhortations that foregrounds the economic needs of penurious young men and condemns the expensive self-adornment of women of various classes:

> I would to God that maydes at the least wise might be brought up, of not in learning, yet in honest trades and occupations.
> . . . the Substaunce which is consumed in two Yeares space upon the apparail of one meane Gentlemans Daughter, or uppon the Daughter or Wife of one meane Citizen, would be sufficient to finde a poore Student in the Universitye by the space of fowre or five Yeeres at the least. (D2r-v)[27]

Such urging toward utilitarian rather than aesthetic considerations in marriage runs throughout Guazzo's third book of *Civil*

Conversation, "Domestic Conversation," in which he warns husbands that although beauty in a wife may promise handsome and therefore successful children, public opinion, which opposes beauty and virtue, must shape marital choice: "And even if a woman who combines beauty and chastity can be found, such rare beauty will nonetheless be suspect, and critical judgments will be made against the reputation of husband and wife both" (326). He also warns wives that free speaking and elegant dress will be read as sure signs of unchastity, an irremediable catastrophe. He recommends instead "a grave expression, lowered eyes and calm features" and ends the discussion by mocking a hyper-elaborate court coiffure (355–7). Pettie intensifies Guazzo's warning by referring to a law of the street which added official force to the dress code: "I will tell you moreover, that it is ordained by the civile law, that if a man offer abuse to an honest matrone, [she] being attyred like a harlot, there is no remedy against him by law" (II, 36).

Guazzo's last word on wifely decorum involves a subtler argument: true beauty is the beauty of exertion, of physical fitness:

> Nothing can increase a husband's love more than his wife's good government of the household, for he not only rejoices in her usefulness and energy, but forms a good opinion of her chastity . . . seeing that through her efforts in useful and honest occupations, she takes on a healthy glow. [Pettie writes, "A lively naturall colour and that vertuous vermillion that neither sweat nor teares can wash away."]   (366; II, 4)

Housework, that is, is set up as the source of an alternative, earned beauty, while the cosmetic contrivances of the upper classes are cast out of the household.

The link between wifely plainness and chastity is bluntly spelled out in William Vaughan's *The Golden Grove* (1608; book 2, "The Family"). The wife "must not be too sumptuous and superfluous in her attire, as, decked with frizled hair, embroidery, precious stones, and gold put about, for they are the forerunners of adultery."[28] Like English writers who followed him, Vaughan spelled out the economic function of the middle-class family: he deals with the "acquisitive facultie" as the last among "the chiefest parts of a family," linking domestic profit to the repression of wasteful display and of sexual temptation.

One apparently liberal exception to the redefinition of wifely beauty reinforces the power of the husband according to a deceptive logic of equality. Sir Thomas Smith, in *The Commonwealth of England and the Maner of Government thereof* (1583), posits a divinely ordained balance between the husband's natural authority and the wife's physical charm as the basis for a harmonious union, incorporating the wife's beauty into a safely enclosed circuit of exchange, which he likens to Aristotelian oligarchy:

> So then the house and family is the first and most naturall (but private) appearance of one of the best kinds of a commonwealth, that is called *Aristocratia*, where a fewe, and the best do governe: and where not one alwaies, but somtime and in some thing another doth beare the rule. Which to maintaine for his part, God hath given to the man greater wit, bigger strength, and more courage, to compell the woman to obey by reason, or force: and to the woman beauty, faire countenance, and sweet words, to make the man obey her againe, for love.[29]

Wifely beauty is conceived of here as a private virtue, relevant only to the couple and apparently invisible to the larger world. Moreover, beauty is set up as women's only source of power in an asymmetrical division of gender characteristics that firmly assigns all real power to the husband.

As Smith's *Commonwealth* shows, the Protestant defense of marriage gave new importance to family relations, but it shaped those relations according to a newly elaborated theory of patriarchalism.[30] As the king ruled over his kingdom, the father ruled over his family flock; as Christ was head of the church, the husband was head of the wife. One consequence for women was that wifely speech came under intimate scrutiny. English marriage manuals monitor women's speech indoors and out, on the assumption that natural female garrulity must be carefully controlled in the interests of the domestic unit. Vaughan warns husbands that an excess of severity may cause embarrassing verbal outbreaks: "There is nothing in the world as spiteful as a woman, if she be hardly dealt withall." For purely pragmatic reasons, the wife must be allowed a cautious degree of freedom: "otherwise (a woman's nature is such) she will by stealth find out some secret place or other to tattle in, or to disport herself" (o5r). Vaughan attempts to convince wives as well that it is to their disadvantage to make domestic secrets public: "she must not discover her husbands imperfections and faults to any, for by disclosing them, eyther she makes herself a iesting stock, or els she ministreth occasion for knaves to tempt her to villainy" (o6v).

The same fear of women's speech as a threat to the private sanctum of marriage permeates Richard Snawsel's *A Looking Glasse for Married Folkes* (1631), an expansion of a dialogue by Erasmus. In this dramatic sketch against shrewish wives, Snawsel has Eulalie, an exemplary wife, reproach a shrew for describing her husband's drunken fits. "O Xantip," says Eulalie, "you make my heart ake to hear you. Therefore, marke this, that when you doe thus disgrace your husband, you shame your selfe."[31] Eulalie also tells a story about a wife who softened her husband's heart by keeping her tears at being beaten a secret, and she quotes Scripture in support of wifely reticence: "we women are apt to speake . . . but the Apostle James willeth us to be swift to heare, and slow to speake" (42–3). The second heroine of the dialogue was added by Snawsel: Abigail, a Puritan wife who acts as a marriage counsellor, brings about a reconciliation between Xantip and Ben-Ezer by advising the wife on how to speak humbly and obediently and by exemplifying womanly meekness in her own speeches to the husband. She says to Ben-Ezer, "Wee are but women, and therefore somewhat bashfull, as it beseemes us, to speak unto you, being a man . . . yet, under leave and correction, we will do our good will to declare those things which we have learned" (94). The dialogue is a Protestant courtesy book: it offers women instances of proper speech, within the narrow confines of the speech defined as proper to wives. Snawsel teaches the grammar of Puritan obedience.

But women's speech, even in the service of Christian piety, eventually met stiffer resistance than Snawsel's little book suggests. Conduct books of the early seventeenth century suggest that a backlash against women's religious testifying was beginning to gain force. Gervase Markham, in *The English Huswife* (1615), writes that it is the wife's responsibility to urge her family to "an upright and sincere religion" through her own example, but he forbids her

> to utter forth that violence of spirit which many of our (vainely accounted pure) women do, drawing a contempt upon the ordinary Ministrie, and thinking nothing lawefull but the fantazies of their owne inventions, usurping to themselves a power

of preaching and interpreting the holy word, to which onely they ought to be but hearers and beleevers.[32]

Brathwait is equally severe, dismissing women's comments on the Scriptures as "the strange opinions of Shee-clarkes, which, as they understand them not themselves, so they labour to intangle others of equall understanding to themselves." He concludes, "Women, as they are to be no speakers in the Church, so neither are they to be disputers of controversies of the Church" (90).

Handbooks aimed at English housewives suggest that their tasks were more broadly defined, more varied, and more physically practical than those assigned to the court lady. They were to supervise servants, cure the sick, administer charity as well as manage household, bakery, and dairy. But at the same time their speech was increasingly subordinated to their husbands' will. Rites of humility are clearly spelled out in William Gouge's much reprinted collection of sermons, *Of Domesticall Duties* (1622, 1627, 1634). The minister chastens body and speech alike. He defines "wifely courtesy" as "that vertue whereby a wife taketh occasion to testifie her acknowledgment of her husband's superiority by some outward obeisance."[33] He means that she is to bow down to her husband when he leaves or returns from a journey, in gratitude for favors he has bestowed upon her, and daily, "when she sitteth down or riseth up from table." Nor is she to undercut his authority by calling him pet names (such as "Ducke, Chicke, Sweethearte, Pigsnies"); she must address him as "husband," registering his superiority at every utterance. Moreover, wives are to carry out these gestures of submission not in self-interest but as a truthful sign of the state of their conscience:

> Here lyeth a maine difference betwixt true, Christian, religious wives and mere naturall women; these may be subject on by-respects, as namely that their husbands may the more love them, or live the more quietly and peacably with them. . . . But the other have respect to Christ's ordinance, whereby they are commanded subjection. (319)

There is no room for calculated effect in Gouge's Christian marriage.

The consolidation of Protestant and rising-class ideology in England appears throughout Gervase Markham's *The English*

Huswife, published in 1615 along with *Country Contentments*, a treatise on the "Princely exercise of Hunting." Markham advertises this volume as suited to men "whose more serious imployments will not afford them so much leisure as to follow this pasttime which almost consumeth the whole day; but must draw their pleasure into a more streighter circle, proportioning an hower or two in the morning for the full scope of their delights" (34–5). He offers speed and efficiency in attaining high gentry style to his male readers, but he has a different purpose in his household handbook, in which he promises he will lay out both "the inward and outward vertues which ought to be in a compleat woman." Technical advice for the "English husband-man" expands into moral commands for the housewife, who is instructed in religious and supervisory duties as well as medicine, brewing, baking, and preserving. Markham's recommendations draw together requirements for wifely obedience, bourgeois thrift, and patriotic simplicity. He links one obligation to the next according to a logic of foresightful and sober acquisition, which ends in adducing the housewife's dress and diet as proofs of class and national solidarity:

> Next unto this sanctity and holiness of life, it is meete that our English Hous-wife be a woman of great modesty and temperance as well inwardly as outwardly; inwardly as in her behavior and carriage toward her Husband, wherein she shall shunne all violence of rage, passion and humour, coveting lesse to direct then to bee directed, appearing ever unto him pleasant, amiable and delightfull . . . outwardly as in her apparrell and dyet, both which she shall proportion according to the competency of her husband's estate and calling, making her circle rather straight than large, for it is a rule if we extend to the uttermost we take awaie increase . . . but if we preserve any part, we build strong forts against the adversities of fortune.

Markham's style for the virtuous bourgeois wife is actually an anti-style, a class-reinforcing rejection of higher ranks' exotic fashions that reverses the inner/outer split by now presumed to underlie aristocratic immorality and surface show:[34]

> Let therefore the Hus-wifes garments be comely, cleanly and strong, made as well to preserve the health, as adorne the

person, altogether without toiish garnishes, or the glosse of light colours, and as farre from the vanity of new and fantastique fashions, as neare to the comely imitations of modest Matrons. ... Let her dyet ... be apter to kill hunger then revive new appetites, let it proceede more from the provision of her own yarde, then the furniture of the markets; and let it rather be esteemed for the familiar acquaintance she hath with it, than for the strangeness and raritie it bringeth from other Countries. (3–4)

Markham's housewife, then, inherited a set of instructions that opposed and rewrote earlier class images that had included different ideals of womanliness in Europe. He transforms the symbolic splendor and public visibility through which the noblewoman shored up and extended her husband's influence into the practical activity of a frugal and energetic preserver of newly earned goods and homespun virtues, and he recommends an analogous kind of speech: not the cultivated elegance through which the court lady complemented and stimulated the courtier, but the plainspoken, pragmatic dealings of country wife with her neighbors. Markham's prescription for the compleat woman, like the contrasting prescriptions for womanly conduct that preceded it, illustrates that femininity is a constantly changing construction, open to debate and revision (although women rarely took an active part in such debates in the sixteenth century) as class interests shift and enter into conflict with one another.

ISABELLA WHITNEY: MARKETING MANNERS

Marriage manuals' prohibitions and controls of public appearances and public speech by women were certainly one reason that so little writing by women of the petty gentry or urban bourgeoisie was published in sixteenth-century England – and perhaps also a reason that when they wrote, they wrote protest in pamphlet form, most often under pseudonyms.[35] One exception to the rule of modest silence, however, was Isabella Whitney, a London serving-woman whose poems were printed in two inexpensive collections in the 1570s. Whitney made a virtue of necessity; more precisely, she turned necessity into virtue. Rather than flouting emergent ideologies of the private woman, she appropriated bourgeois gender discourse for her own profit.

Whitney is best known through Betty Tavitsky's research, especially her edition of Whitney's "Last Wyll and Testament," a high-spirited farewell to the streets and merchants of London that reveals Whitney's interest in reaching a broad urban readership.[36] Whitney published two pamphlets with Richard Jones, a printer who specialized in popular pamphlets and miscellanies, and who may also have published other poems by Whitney anonymously in his anthologies.[37]

Whitney appears to accept the exclusion of women from the public sphere. She justifies her own writing as a stop-gap measure through which, as "maid" (unmarried woman), she must support herself. In a verse letter in the pamphlet, *A Sweet Nosgay of Pleasant Posye*, "To her Sister Misteris A.B.," she piously acknowledges the duties of a married woman; indeed, her emphasis on useful activity sounds much like Markham's. She does not challenge contemporary expectations of women; she simply asserts a temporary difference in situation between her sister and herself:

> Good sister so I you commend,
>   to him that made us all:
> I know you huswifery intend,
>   though I to writing fall:
> Wherefore no l[o]nger shall you stay,
>   from businesse, that profit may.
>
> Had I a Husband, or a House,
>   and all that longes therto
> My selfe could frame about to rouse
>   as other women do:
> But til some houshold cares me tye,
>   My bookes and Pen I wyll apply.   (D2r)[38]

In an undated text, *The Copy of a Letter lately written in meeter by a yonge Gentilwoman: to her unconstant lover*, Whitney continues to work within the confines of correct womanly behavior. Ingeniously, however, she adopts the role of a marriage counsellor in order to write an eminently public and publishable letter to a man who has broken his promise to marry her. In Whitney's hands, the lament of the abandoned mistress, enjoying a vogue in England after George Turberville's translation of Ovid's *Heroides* in 1567, is turned into a set of recommendations for marital success that has more in common with Hake's sermons than with the anguished reproaches of Ovid's Ariadne or Medea. Like Des Roches, Whitney deploys contemporary gender ideology in order to establish a profitably respectable speaking and writing position for herself. She echoes conduct-book commonplaces on the good wife in order to write her way out of the discursive double bind that positioned loquacious women as whores, on the one hand, or, in the case of Ovidian lament, as exemplary tragic victims.

From the opening of the *Letter*, Whitney shifts from accusation to an advisory role toward the man who has failed to keep his marriage to another woman secret. She speaks to him in a tone of familiar yet detached camaraderie:

> You know I always wisht you well
> so will I during lyfe:
> But sith you shall a Husband be
> God send you a good wife.   (A4r)[39]

After listing classical villains (Jason, Theseus, Aeneas) to add weight to her criticism of the man who has betrayed her, she turns to classical heroines to construct a didactic counter-portrait of wifely virtue. Preaching to the would-be husband from the elevated position of marriage counsellor, she takes on a role that had belonged only to men writers in the middle decades of the sixteenth century:

> For she that shal so happy be
> of thee to be elect:
> I wish her virtues to be such
> she nede not be suspect.   (A4r)

And she goes on to moralize Ovid in a historically specific crosscutting of literary and ethical discourses, using his heroines in *The Metamorphoses* to exemplify virtues central to the ideal of feminine behavior being promulgated in Puritan sermons and in the middle-class conduct books to which Greene's *Penelope's Web* would later belong:

> I rather wish her HELENS face,
>   then one of HELENS trade:
> With chastnes of PENELOPE,
>   the which did never fade.
>
> A LUCRES for her contancy,
>   and THISBE for her trueth.   (A4v)

Whitney's performance throughout the Letter appears to demonstrate her acceptance of dicta regarding wifely modesty and restrained speech, yet her citation of such requirements actually allows her to turn the power relations between herself and the man who has broken off their engagement upside down. Rather than bewailing her abandonment, she rewrites her fiancé's freedom to leave her and choose another woman as the move of a foolish man, a "noddye" who requires the counsel that a jilted woman turned marital advisor is eminently capable of giving.

In the second half of the pamphlet, in quatrains on the subject of undependable suitors, Whitney echoes the mistrust of foppish gallants evident in anti-courtly treatises such as Brathwait's *English Gentlewoman*. But in a striking reversal of assumptions about gender, she displaces the seductive artifice traditionally attributed to women onto deceptive men courting women:[40]

> Trust not a man at the fyrst sight!
>   but trye him well before:
> I wish al Maids within their breasts
>   to kepe this thing in store.
>
> Beware of fayre and painted talke,
>   beware of flattering tonges:
> The Mermaids do pretend no good,
>   for all their plesant Songs!   (A6r)

In the last two lines, her return to female figures as examples of vice demonstrates the extent to which notions of woman as temptress dominated the gender ideology of her time (and the literary sources upon which sixteenth-century writers of either sex drew). Even when her aim is to criticize the opposite sex, the ammunition that comes to hand is determined by a history of suspicious and condemnatory discourses about women.

Nonetheless, Whitney's *Admonition* establishes her as a survivor rather than a victim, and as an expert on feminine self-protection:

> And sith the fish that reason lacks
> once warned will beware:
> Why should we not take hede to that
> that turneth us to care.
>
> And I who was deceived late
> by ones unfaithfull teares:
> Trust now for to beware, if that
> I live this hundred yeares.   (A8v)

Both halves of the pamphlet weave marriage manual formulas together with classical allusions to produce a popularly aimed poem in which Whitney simultaneously masters abandonment and interpellates a respectful readership. By grafting two vocabularies she finds in place – the lexicon of Ovidian victimizers and victims and the pieties of bourgeois marriage theory – and using them as permission for her work as a woman writer, she constructs an alliance with a public potentially more loyal and certainly more profitable than the "unconstant lover" to whom the Letter is ostensibly addressed.

These poets' negotiations of cultural prohibitions and permissions demonstrate that conduct books and women's lyrics occupied the same ideological terrain in the second half of the sixteenth century. The nets and bridles that restrained women's participation in literary culture also provided them with entries into it in ways that mentors of élite manners and Protestant preachers could hardly have foreseen. Des Roches made a name and a career for herself within the confines of court-oriented etiquette, which assigned women a role of public visibility and verbal flirtation yet instructed them in the uses of chastity as a defense against censure for seeming too accessible; Whitney claimed a sturdy bourgeois credibility by purifying the passionate regrets of the Ovidian heroine into the judiciously practical moral authority claimed by male class-spokesmen writing and translating bourgeois marriage manuals in the mid-1500s. Together, Des Roches and Whitney represent a miniscule, almost invisible sample of European women, but they reveal the ingenuity that was required to divert early modern controls upon women into channels for their survival through literary self-representation.

Des Roches's feminized Neoplatonism and Whitney's prudent

advice to lovers shattered no ideological enclosures in 1571 or 1582. But when their poetry is recognized as a productive use of the diversifying discourses of ideal femininity that surrounded them, it breaks down a conceptual enclosure that is still too much with us: the notion that social life and aesthetic invention occupy separate spheres. I have been arguing instead that ascendant class ideals, mobilized in polemical dialogue with feudal values, defined sixteenth-century behavior and channeled literary production in intricately interconnected ways. By writing at all, women departed from governing codes of conduct in spirit, but they did so by the letter, by appropriating positive prescriptions rather than immobilizing prohibitions. Des Roches read Castiglione as saying, "Speak chastely, in this dangerous new coterie world, but speak;" Whitney read her Puritan brothers as saying, "If you must speak, speak as a true godly woman for the greater good of your sex." These poets' compromises with new conceptions of proper feminity in a historical period now generally conceded to have had largely negative consequences for women may be to our present theoretical benefit.[41] Sixteenth-century women writers offer evidence that literary-historical survival depends not upon isolated genius or immunity from social conflict but from creative manipulation of the gender ideologies that clash around poets, and in them, as they compose their stanzas. Hypothetical and coercive both, the social relations of daughter to father, wife to husband, and beloved to suitor intermesh with the poet's relations to past tradition, to contemporary languages of class, and to readers in her present and in her future.

NOTES

1 For this argument in relation to scholarly treatises on the nature and duties of women, see C. Jordan (1985) "Rethinking gender: Renaissance defenses of women," MLA paper.

2 F. Whigham analyzes the effects of courtesy books in his (1983) "Interpretation at court: courtesy and the performer–audience dialectic," *NLH*, 14, Spring, and in his (1984) *Ambition and Privilege: The Social Tropes of Elizabethan Courtesy Theory*, Berkeley, Calif., University of California Press.

3 R. Kelso, in her survey of European conduct books, suggests that the new emphasis on secular activity for men led to a re-emphasis on

Nets and Bridles

Christian humility and withdrawal from the world for women: (1956, 1978) *Doctrine for the Lady of the Renaissance*, Urbana, Ill., University of Illinois Press, 23–6. For England, see the doctoral dissertation of S. Cahn (1981) "Changing conceptions of women in sixteenth- and seventeenth-century England", University of Michigan, and L. Jardine's argument that unofficial changes in inheritance patterns, to the benefit of women, were a cause of new attacks, in her (1983) *Still Harping on Daughters: Women and Drama in the Age of Shakespeare*, Totowa, NJ, Barnes & Noble, ch. 3. An excellent study of French class loyalties and women's roles in salons, arguing that the birth versus merit debate was a central issue, is C. Lougee (1980) *Le Paradis des femmes: Women, Salons and Social Stratification in Seventeenth-Century France*, Princeton, NJ, Princeton University Press.

4 For details about Anne Boleyn's training as a lady-in-waiting, see A. Plowden (1979) *Tudor Women: Queens and Commoners*, London, Weidenfeld & Nicolson, 40–3. Guazzo's remark is quoted from E. Sullivan (ed.) (1925) *La Civil Conversatione del Signor Stefano Guazzo* (Venice, 1575), trans. G. Pettie (1581) London, Constable, II, 78; 418. In my citations, page numbers refer first to Pettie's translation, then to the Italian text. Annibal Guasco's very interesting epistle to his daughter is entitled *Ragionamento à D. Lavinia sua figliuola della maniera del governarsi in corte, andando per Dama* (1586), Turin.

5 See F. Whigham on "cosmesis" (ch. 4) and sumptuary laws (ch. 5) in *Ambition and Privilege*; and P. Stallybrass (1986) "The body enclosed," in M. Ferguson, M. Quilligan, and N. Vickers (eds) *Rewriting the Renaissance: The Discourses of Sexual Difference in Early Modern Europe*, Chicago, Ill., University of Chicago Press. A discussion of radical uses of images of unruly women is N. Z. Davis (1975) "Women on top: symbolic sexual inversion and political disorder in early modern Europe," in *Society and Culture in Early Modern France*, Stanford Calif., Stanford University Press. For the often contradictory amalgamation of classical and patristic writing with contemporary ideas about women, see I. Maclean (1980) *The Renaissance Notion of Woman*, Cambridge, Cambridge University Press.

6 *Les Enseignements d'Anne de France à sa fille Susanne de Bourbon* (1505), repr. (1878) Moulins, Des Rosiers, intro. A. M. Chazaud, 81.

7 I am drawing on Michel Foucault's comment on the situation of doctors involved in sex research at the beginning of the eighteenth century: "One had to speak of sex; one had to speak publicly, and in a manner that was not determined by the division between licit and illicit, even if the speaker maintained the distinction for himself," in his (1978) *The History of Sexuality*, trans. R. Hurley, New York, Pantheon, 24. When a woman spoke in the sixteenth century, however, she had to observe

licit/illicit distinctions very carefully, determined as they were by the tensions between courtly and domestic discourse on women.

8 J. H. Whitfield (ed.) (1974) *Il Libro del Cortigiano* (Venice, 1528), trans. Sir Thomas Hoby (1561) London, H. M. Dent. Page numbers after my citations refer first to Hoby's translation, then to the Italian text: B. Maier (ed.) (1964) Turin UTET, second edn.

9 Arturo Graf records the use of "cortigiana onesta," the highest category to which courtesans were assigned, in a Roman census and a diary entry of the early sixteenth century, "Una Cortigiana fra mille: Veronica Franco," in A. Graf (1926) *Attraverso il Cinquecento*, Turin, Chiantore, 226.

10 G. della Casa (1560) *Il Galatheo*, Florence, first published in Milan (1559), 38a–39a. Like Giuliano, della Casa warns that more may be imputed to the court lady's words than she intends: "Those ladies who are or wish to be well mannered should be careful to avoid not only improper actions but also improper words, and not only those that are improper or shocking, but even those which could be or could seem so" (32b).

11 A. Nipho (1560) *Il Cortigiano del Sessa*, trans. from the Latin by F. Baldelli, Genoa, 120.

12 Lougee's study of seventeenth-century coteries (*Le Paradis des femmes*) is informative about their social functions, as is the biography of the Des Roches by G. Diller (1936) *Les Dames Des Roches: Etude sur la vie littéraire à Poitiers dans la deuxième moitié du XVIe siècle*, Paris, Droz.

13 For an incisive analysis of the vocabulary of Neoplatonism as the code of an endangered, self-protective courtly élite, see J. Guidi (1980) "De l'amour courtois à l'amour sacré: la condition de la femme dans l'oeuvre de B. Castiglione," in A. Rochon (ed.) *Images de la femme dans la littérature italienne de la Renaissance*, Paris, Centre de Récherche sur la Renaissance Italienne, Université de la Sorbonne nouvelle. For a similar argument relating to an earlier period, see F. Goldin's discussion of French and German courtly love poetry as "the ideal image" through which the "best educated and most powerful secular class in the Middle Ages regarded itself and justified its existence," in his (1967) *The Mirror of Narcissus in the Courtly Love Lyric*, Ithaca, NY, Cornell University Press.

14 Diller discusses the financial history of the Des Roches, including their winning of a royal grant, in *Les Dames Des Roches*, pt 1, ch. 1.

15 Paraphrased from the Houghton Library edition of *Les Oeuvres des Mesdames Des Roches de Poitiers mère et fille* (1586) Paris, Abel l'Angelier, "Epistre à ma fille," 2a.

16 I have used the British Museum Library edition of *Les Oeuvres de*

Mesdames des Roches de Poitiers, mère et fille (1578) Paris, Abel Angelier.

17 A good study of bourgeois Protestant marriage and household handbooks is S. Hull (1982) *Chaste, Silent and Obedient: English Books for Women, 1475–1640*, San Marino, Calif., Huntington Library.

18 R. Brathwait (1631) *The English Gentlewoman*, London, 64, 88.

19 B. Rich (1616) *My Ladies Looking Class*, London, 44.

20 Leon Battista Alberti's handbook for the Florentine patriciate has been edited, with a useful introduction, by G. Guarini (1971) *Della Famiglia*, Lewisburg, Pa., Bucknell University Press.

21 T. Tasso (1582) *Discorso della virtù feminile, e donnesca*, Venice, 5.

22 R. Greene, *A Quip for an Upstart Courtier*, in A. Grosart (ed.) (1881–6) *The Life and Complete Works of Robert Greene*, repr. (1964) New York, Russell & Russell, XI, 20.

23 R. Greene (1601) *Penelope's Web*, London, E4r.

24 G. Whetstone (1582) *An Heptameron of Civill Discourses*, London, X2r–v.

25 T. Becon (1543), preface to *The Christian State of Matrimony*, trans. from the Dutch by M. Coverdale, London, B3v.

26 T. Salter (1579) *A Mirrhor mete for all Mothers, Matrones and Maidens*, London, A7r–v. For a useful critique of the now discredited assumption that Renaissance humanism supported women's access to education and the public sphere, see J. B. Holm's (1984) analysis of the Bruto/Salter book, "The myth of a feminist humanism," *Soundings*, 68, Winter.

27 E. Hake (1574) *A Touchstone for this Time Present*, London, D2r–v.

28 W. Vaughan (1608) *The Golden Grove*, London, o6r.

29 Sir Thomas Smith (1583) *De Republica Anglorum: A Discourse on the Commonwealth of England and the Maner of Government thereof*, ed. L. Alston (1906), Cambridge, Cambridge University Press, 23.

30 Arguments that Protestantism worked in favor of women are summed up and debated in several recent studies, including K. Davies (1977) "The sacred condition of equality – how original were Puritan doctrines of marriage?", *Social History*, 5, May, 563–81; L. Stone (1977) *The Family, Sex and Marriage in England, 1500–1800*, New York, Harper & Row, 195–206, 216–18; and L. Jardine's chapter 2, " 'She openeth her mouth with wisdom': the double bind of renaissance education and reformed religion," in her (1983) *Still Harping on Daughters*.

31 R. Snawsel (1631) *A Looking Glasse for Married Folkes*, London, repr. (1975) Norwood, NJ, Walter Johnson, 34–5.

32 G. Markham (1615, 1631) *The English Huswife*, London, 2. For an argument that women's prophesying and preaching had been justified on the basis of traditional views of women's passivity and excitability and that they were firmly suppressed by the end of the seventeenth

century, see P. Mack (1982) "Women as prophets during the English Civil War," *Feminist Studies*, 8, Spring, 19–45.

33 W. Gouge (1634) *Of Domesticall Duties: Eight Treatises*, London, 281.

34 Compare a similarly anti-aristocratic stance from T. Powell's later (1635) *The Art of Thriving, or the plaine pathway to preferment*, London. Speaking of the daughters of a London merchant, he writes, "Instead of Song and Musick, let them learn Cookery and Laundry, and in steade of Reading Sir Philip Sidney's Arcadia, let them read the grounds of good huswifery. I like not a female Poëtesse at any hand: let great personages glory [in] their skill in Musicke, the posture of their bodies, their knowledge in languages, the greatnesse and freedome of their Spirits and their arts in arraigning of men's affections, at their flattering Faces: this is not the way to breede a private Gentleman's daughter" (114–15).

35 B. Travitsky (1984) "The lady doth protest: protest in the popular writings of Renaissance Englishwomen," *ELR*, 14, Autumn, 255–83.

36 B. Travitsky (1980) "'The Wyll and Testament' of Isabella Whitney," *ELR*, 10, Winter.

37 R. J. Fehrenbach (1981) studies the anthologies of Whitney's publisher in "Isabella Whitney and the popular miscellanies of Richard Jones," *Cahiers élisabéthains*, 19.

38 I have used the British Museum Library edition of *A Sweet Nosgay of Pleasant Posye: contayning a hundred and ten Phylosophicall Flowers* (1573), but a useful facsimile has been edited by R. Panofsky and included in his edition (1982) of *Sir Hugh Platt: The Floures of Philosophie (1572)*, Delmar, NJ, Scholars' Facsimiles and Reprints, vol. 374.

39 I have used the Bodleian edition of *The Copy of a letter, lately written in meeter, by a yonge Gentilwoman: to her unconstant lover, with an Admonition to all yong Gentilwomen, and to all other Maydes in general to beware of mennes flattery*, London, n. d. Excerpts from this apparently unique copy are printed by B. Travitsky in her (1981) *The Paradise of Women: Writings by Englishwomen of the Renaissance*, Westport, Conn., Greenwood Press, 118–20.

40 Travitsky, too, was struck by this reversal of traditional blame of women as deceivers ("The lady doth protest," 262).

41 For the now classic statement of this view, see J. Kelly-Gadol (1977) "Did women have a Renaissance?" in R. Bridenthal and C. Koonz (eds) *Becoming Visible: Women in European History*, Boston, Mass., Houghton Mifflin. See also the editors' introduction to *Rewriting the Renaissance*.

3

Defoe's idea of conduct: ideological fictions and fictional reality

CAROL HOULIHAN FLYNN

Conduct manuals document nostalgic belief in a "natural" self that "ought" to be in harmony with its needs and desires. The Utopian scheme of conduct manuals is essentially ahistoric in its quest for a lost unity of body and soul, sense and reason that could exist only in an Edenic imagination, but contextually these elegiac documents record an historical struggle for control that can be located in real time and in a real place. In his conduct manuals and his novels, Daniel Defoe, ostensibly the poet laureate of English, Whiggish, individualistic capitalism, locates one of the central confusions of his century, the contradictory desire for freedom and limitation, for equality and subordination.[1] Insisting upon "Justice" between men and women in marriage, he also reveals the strains that the fiction of justice exacts when domestic harmony and "affective individualism" depend upon a subordination of the woman in the house.

While espousing his domestic ideals, Defoe wrote almost endlessly about domestic difficulties. In his conduct manuals and in his fiction he measures the cost of "mutual subordination," the domestic internalization of rules that should ensure familial harmony. His careful attention to the "civilizing process"[2] reveals the double bind of domesticity and sexuality, exposing in the process the perils of "affective individualism."[3]

An early champion of feminist ideals, Defoe insists upon "justice" between husband and wife (*CL*, 77). But he speaks for a system at war with its own imperatives. At the time that women were being granted certain freedoms, they were nonetheless being contained by categories of domestic use that assumed spheres of influence circumscribed by domestic necessity. This containment appears "necessary," the logical response to the dangers the unaccommodated woman represented. Yet the containment also needed to be considered "natural,"a voluntary submission to the good.

Defoe's conduct manuals establish a framework of social control contradicted by the numerous "examples" that emphasize the struggle for dominance between men and women "learning" to behave. The contradictions result from the dual message the conduct manuals deliver: proper behavior must be learned, restraint that goes against fallen nature must be developed, but that behavior must also appear voluntary and "natural." Liberty must be measured by "Christian Limitation," an elastic talent for suppression that elicits "Moderation where we have no positive Restraints imposed" (*CL*, 46). Although outlawing physical coercion, Defoe demands an "affectionate" compliance. As a champion of the "companionate marriage," he seems to attack any form of physical coercion in his domestic vignettes pleading for voluntary self-regulation. Restraint? I will have nothing to do with it, announces a pious, lenient husband laboring to bring his wife to God's – and his – ways. He relies instead upon God's heavy, "just" hand to bring a wayward wife to her senses (*FI* I, 386–7).

The ideal situation in Defoe's domestic economy, voluntary surrender to God's and the godly husband's will, is best expressed by simple spokespeople: the poor peasant giving thanks for his little bounty, the tender child of six asking to be instructed in God's ways.[4] The real circumstance of the manuals, however, cancel unwitting gestures of faith, revealing instead the code's discrepancy. Conduct discourse becomes a site of struggle for power, for an individuation that depends upon a suppression of free will and sexuality. While speaking out firmly against physical measures, to reproduce eager, affectionate implements of God's will, Defoe invokes God the father to instill within his subjects obedience. Lacking the simple faith of the old and feeble, or the young and idiotic, his less willing subjects are brought to the patriarchal good through "accidents" providentially plotted, that result in maiming, illness, fever, and madness. Once chastened, they usually become necessarily abject, ready to assume their duties with all the ardor appropriate to affective domestic structures.

The message underlying these domestic success stories strains against its ideological imperative. Wives, Defoe maintains endlessly, must not be "upper servants," yet his most recalcitrant women, poised to be stricken into submission, complain loudly (and convincingly) of just that state of servitude. Notorious equivocation marks the work of the writer who could wish that all men could be masters, even if they had to buy slaves to become so.[5]

The domestic vision not only contradicts its demands for both equality and subservience, but also exists hermetically sealed off from the larger world of economic concerns that subjects nuclear domesticity (of the middling sort) to constant risk. In the conduct books, the passions, rather than the economy, threaten to disrupt the companionate marriage, a state curiously immune to economic stress. In its privileged state, middle-class marriage takes on an aristocratic patina of permanence. "Matrimony," Defoe declares in *Conjugal Lewdness*, "is a chast and modest Scheme of Living; 'tis a State, not a Circumstance of Life; . . . it is durable as Life and bounded only by the Duration of Life" (343). But matrimony in Defoe's novels is a "circumstance" of life bounded by material considerations, reflecting the insubstantiality of comfort and the inevitability of physical needs and desires. Good wives moor uneasily in their "safe Harbours," subject always to the random violations of their domestic peace while husbands mysteriously wander off, to lose their fortunes, or die.

In the novels, the ideal of correct behavior gives way to strategies of survival as both Moll and Roxana "murther" their children and sell their bodies to save themselves. Negotiating through a world in which a woman alone "is just like a Bag of Money or a Jewel drop't on the Highway, which is a Prey to the next Comer" (*MF*, 128), Moll and Roxana use their sexuality aggressively to exert control over a reality always in flux. Conduct becomes not that which "ought" to be done, but that which must be done. Their solutions vary dramatically. Moll Flanders escapes the double bind of mutual subordination by existing in a dream-like state that incorporates domestic and economic contradictions paratactically. By refusing to subordinate style as well as experience, Moll comically triumphs through fantastic acts of renewal over the censors Defoe employs in his conduct books. Roxana, however, tragically collides with the moral and economic system in a disaster that clarifies the irony of Moll's triumph and invalidates the code of behavior Defoe sets out in his tracts.

Defoe's fictional representations of "reality" expose the "imaginary" relation his code of conduct bears to his society. Louis Althusser argues that

> all ideology represents in its necessarily imaginary distortion not the existing relations of production (and the other relations that derive from them), but above all the (imaginary) relationship of individuals to the relations of production and the relations that derive from them. What is represented in ideology is therefore not the system of the real relations which govern the existence of individuals, but the imaginary relation of those individuals to the real relations in which they live.[6]

While Defoe's conduct manuals represent the "necessarily imaginary distortions" that characterize the "companionate marriage," his novels move closer to "the real relations" in which Moll Flanders and Roxana live in their attention to the contradictions inherent in the demand for individualism and subjection, justice and hierarchy. This essay will examine the equivocal nature of Defoe's ideological fictions, his conduct manuals, and then discuss the ways his fictional "realities" reveal the instabilities of the conduct code in the "real" world. "If this unhappy Story were a Romance, a Fiction, contrived to illustrate the Subject," Defoe complained in *Conjugal Lewdness*, "I should give it you with all its abhorred Particulars, as far as decency of Language would permit" (34–5). In his fictions Defoe addressed the "abhorred Particulars," the material circumstances he set out to order in his conduct codes. Attention to both fictional and nonfictional forms demonstrate the strains of sustaining an "affective individualism" in a "system at war with itself."

IDEOLOGICAL FICTIONS: THE CONDUCT OF LIFE

The Family Instructor, *Religious Courtship* and *Conjugal Lewdness* establish a code of conduct that depends upon domestic stability. From the start, however, the imperative to "reform" the household unsettles relationships, setting husband against wife, parent against child. While Defoe does not attempt to conceal the discord that accompanies reformation (in fact he seems to revel in it), neither does he contradict his edicts. The family must conform to God's will, God's will interpreted by a patriarchal spokesman. Even if that spokesman is overbearing, unsympathetic, rash, what he speaks invests him with an authority that cannot be denied.

The struggle for authority becomes immediately apparent in the *Family Instructor* (1715). The innocent questions of a young child inspire a lax father to reform himself and his family. The boy complains that he has not been instructed "properly." Mother and Nurse taught him prayers "every Night and Morning," but he "only said them by rote." He has been taught "to play, and sing the Songs my nurse teaches me, and read in my Sister's Song Book," but now he spurns such feminine discourse and hungers to be taught by the Father to serve God, taught in "hard Words" like Attribute and Infinite (*FI* I, 13, 16, 17).

In this first instruction, the Father and Mother unify to reform their more rebellious older children. Demonstrating her allegiance to her husband, Mother burns offending playbooks and novels and boxes her oldest daughter's rebellious ears, while Father outlaws Sabbatarian walks through the park eventually to drive both daughter and son out of his house. The daugher, initially the most defiant, flees to a sympathetic aunt who treats her with kindness, and marries her eventually to her lenient, yet religious son.

In this fortuitous union, we can see the way the companionate marriage actually works. While the husband, a paragon of sobriety and tact might disavow the use of force and restraint, he continues nonetheless to campaign for religious reform. In this gentler household, proper instruction remains masculine instruction. Catechizing his children, the softer father still demands that they confess their mother's inadequacy as teacher:

father: Did no Body ever tell you [who made you.]
child: No *Pappa*.
mother: Sirrah, did not I tell you so?
child: No, *Mamma*
mo: Nor Nurse either?
child: No *Mamma*
mo: You tell a Lie Sirrah

child: No indeed *Mamma*

hus: Nay, *my dear*, Children and Fools, *you know*, &c.

(FI I, 371)

It never becomes clear here who "lies." If the irreligious mother did instruct, her feeble lessons scarcely registered in ears better tuned to hear the law of the father. As in the previous dialogue, lessons made by the mother and nurse are fit only for sisters reading their song books, part of a marginal discourse scorned by more knowledgable "Children and Fools."

After resisting her husband's sweet doctrine for a number of years, the rebellious daughter turns rather dramatically to her domestic duties when in his not so mysterious way, God strikes her ill. She falls into a fever upon learning that her rebellious brother, who disregarded a prophetic dream to join a military regiment, has lost his arm in battle. Believing herself to be on her deathbed, she resolves to reform and to beg her father his forgiveness. Her brother is not so lucky. Returning home after wasting his fortune, he still refuses to repent. Melancholy and disturbed, he attempts suicide three times only to die

> in a miserable Condition Atheisticall and impenitent, having never seen his Father, nor so much as desiring it, till on his death Bed, being delerious, he cried out for his *Father*! his *Father*! That he had abused his Father! and begged to see his Father! That he might ask him Forgiveness! but he died before his Father who happened to be in the Country, could be sent for. (*FI*. I, 443–44)

The first *Family Instructor* closes abruptly in this patriarchal sentence that insists absolutely upon the law of the father. The father's own rash, violent attempt to reform his household becomes privileged material that cannot be dislodged by the ironic implications of unheard deathbed cries while Defoe remains outside the struggle for compliance by relying on God's intervention into the affair of the rebellious wife. Asserting through her maimed brother that "God is Just," he can scourge the rebel sister-wife with the brother's plight to bring her "leniently" into submission. Her mild husband need never raise a hand against his unruly companion when God proves to be so conveniently "just" and compelling. External, supernatural force brings to heel an insubordinate wife eager to submit to the rigors of the companionate marriage.

Defoe's Idea of Conduct

Defoe's second *Family Instructor* (1718) emphasizes even more baldly the struggles for domestic authority in its depiction of the trials of two religious husbands saddled with two rebellious wives. The men, a "citizen" and a "friend" from the country, compare notes on their attempts to "instruct" their households. The friend struggles to bring his wealthy, aristocratic bride to acknowledge his and God's authority. Several hundred pages of insubordination and mockery culminate in her flight from the household. The young wife proves so determined to escape her husband's authority that she finds herself rashly imagining that she would rather poison her spouse than relinquish her power. Obsessively defying her family, she dreams of an act of rebellion that destroys not only her husband and household, but also her children. This vision sends her into fever, incipient madness, and eventually into a state of grateful repentance.

The citizen's tale is more complicated, for his wife is no flighty young thing in need of religious instruction, but a partner of many years who is not irreligious, not blasphemous, but bored and irritated by her husband's "performance" of his public function as family instructor. Her criticism – it is to her "a Piece of cold insignificant stuff . . . an Abomination" (*FI* II, 52) – so maddens her husband that rather than cast pearls to swine, he stops family prayers altogether. The disruption of family instruction creates chaos: "all Appearance of Order and Duty is lost." Eventually the family divides, three children joining the wife upstairs, where "she pretends to pray and read with them by her self as if her Husband was a heathen, her other children out-casts, and her Family Reprobates" (42). In retaliation, the father holds services downstairs, locking the mother out of the family circle. She tries the door two or three times before retiring to her room where she cries vehemently for hours.

What is at issue here is not the imperative to "instruct" so much as the power to be the instructor. The citizen's wife objects to his "lordly" posture towards her, his demand for authority while he preaches mutual subjection. When she reports that her children also object to their father's preaching, the citizen interrogates them not only on their behavior, but also on their "Thoughts" of his performance. "Had you never any dislike of it in your thoughts?" he quizzes his daughter. "No, never Sir, I can't imagine why you ask, Sir," (*FI* II, 45) she answers. "Liars," mutters the mother when she learns of her children's defection. "The Decay of Family-worship, like a Gangreen in the religious Body, spread itself from one Limb to another, till it affected the Vitals, and proved mortal," Defoe warns (*FI* II, 8), but his examples demand that "family worship" be led in the name of the Father. As he argues in *Religious Courtship*, man and wife need to unite, to worship God as one (143), and that one becomes patriarchal in its union.

Defoe gives a double message in his story of the rebellious wives, a plea for mutual subjection and an insistence upon feminine subordination. "I know I am your upper Servant, but sure I am not such a Servant but I may have liberty to laugh a little at my Master, – when I think proper" (*FI* II, 48), taunts the friend from the country's pert wife. Her jibe tells much, revealing in its perverse insubordination precisely the position she holds and does not hold. Her husband objects to the term "upper Servant," but not to her necessity to come gently to her duty. The citizen in his stubborn rage for authority demands such "companionate" submission that even after his wife has gone mad, spent a year in an asylum, and returned with loss of memory but "in a very good Disposition as to the religious Part," he still remains dissatisfied. Since she cannot remember offending her husband, she is not truly capable of repentance. He looks upon her "as one dead" (*FI* II, 72, 75).

The wife not only must submit to family instruction, but also must submit consciously, even joyously. Justifying his use of such violently rebellious wives to make his moral, Defoe explains that in the real world wives are usually not so provoking, but then his exemplary husbands "are brought in talking more mildly and patiently than most Husbands do, in like Cases of Provocation" (*FI* II, 174). In driving his rebellious wives mad to make a dramatic point, Defoe also manages to warn his female reader that her conscious adoption of a "separate but equal" posture of subservience is essential to her mental and physical health. By resorting to such extreme solutions to domestic problems, mad wives and prodigal sons calling out *Father!* on their deathbeds, Defoe is establishing the need for "voluntary" compliance that becomes what Althusser would call "imaginary." His domestic harmony covers over the powerful impulses of rebellion that are really suppressed by force rather than affection. While on another occasion, he can argue eloquently against clapping wives in madhouses to control them,[7] Defoe seems to find lunatic asylums quite useful in enforcing his own ideological fictions of mutual subjection. His dependence upon force therapeutically applied reveals the iron hand of harmonious, "affective individualism."

Conjugal Lewdness: or Matrimonial Whoredom. A Treatise Concerning the Use and Abuse of the Marriage Bed (1727), reveals even more clearly the split between matrimonial equality and subordination. It is Defoe's most liberal and most conservative word on marriage in its demand for domestic "Use" of the Marriage Bed and the feminine body. While calling for "Justice" between man and wife, for "there is no Decency can be preserved where Justice is not done"(77), it also calls for constant "Procreation of the Species, and the Generation of Mankind," the "just" and only "End of Matrimony" (303). As a feminist speaking to "the ladies," Defoe claims to be:

> So little a Friend to that which they call Government and Obedience between the Man and his Wife . . . that the Ladies will take no Offence at me, I dare say. I don't take the State of Matrimony to be designed as that of Apprentices who are bound to the Family, and that the Wife is to be us'd only as the upper Servant in the House. (26)

The companionate marriage is most eloquently defended here as reciprocal obligation "founded in Love . . . performed in the heighth of Affection; its most perfect Accomplishment consists not in the Union of the Sexes, but in the Union of the Souls; uniting their Desires, their Ends, and consequently their Endeavours, for compleating their mutual Felicity" (27). But such mutual Felicity can only be an "imaginary distortion," for in the marriage bed, "Abuses" abound.

In presenting four hundred pages of "Abuses," Defoe betrays a fear of what he calls "the frail part." "Where the spiritual part is over-ruled by the fleshly, where the sensual directs the rational," and the "Order of Things is inverted; Nature is set with her Bottom upward; Heaven is out of the Mind, and Hell seems to have taken possession" (271). Mutual felicity requires suppression of the flesh. Defoe admires St Francis for

> fall[ing] upon his Body, with the Scourge and the Discipline. Ha! Brother Ass, says he, *that was the best Title he could give his Carkass*, do you want Correction? Is your Blood so hot still? Then he would fast forty Hours, and all the while whip and tear himself with a Wire Scourge, till he made the Blood come. (314)

Disavowing papist disciplines, Defoe demands nonetheless strenuous dieting, for

> we not only dig our Graves with our Teeth, by mingling our Diseases with our Food, nourishing Distemper and Life together, but we even eat our way into Eternity, and Damn our Souls with our Teeth, gnawing our Way through the Doors of the Devil's Castle. (323)

While Defoe requires mutual suppression of the appetite, the material he most fears is feminine, "Nature . . . set with her Bottom upward." It was common knowledge that women were "more amorous than Men," more apt to consume themselves with their passion. Dr Venette spoke for his age when he warned that as "Sparrows do not live long, because they are too hot, and too susceptible of Love, so Women last less time; because they have a devouring heat, that consumes them by degrees," while the "Female Physician," Dr Maubray warned against the "*attractive Faculty*" of the womb which ingests the sperm "after the same manner as a *famishing stomach* snatches at the victuals from the *Mouth* of the Eater."[8]

The perpetually hungry womb needed to be filled up. To defend his demand for procreation, Defoe cites Solomon's attack upon the barren woman who is "*never satisfied*," and worse still, will "never say, it is enough" (157). A woman who refuses the encumbrances of children but demands sexual satisfaction is guilty of having "the Use of the Man" without acting "the Part of the Woman; she would have him be the Husband, but she would not be a Wife, and, if you bear the blunt Stile that some people put it into, she would only keep a St——n" (133–4). The fear of being used like a stallion, only to fail and to be *said* to fail to satisfy voracious feminine appetites generates much of the hysteria circulating throughout the tract and invokes hard matrimonial measures. In his tale of the "barren doe," Defoe makes his clearest attack on the problem.

A member of "the merry Club, called, *The Assembly of Barren Does*," a bride "ready to die with the Thoughts" of childbirth, asks her cousin for contraceptive advice. Her cousin argues that contraception is no better than murder, for "the Difference is only here, that by this Medicine you destroy a younger Conception than you would do in the other Case" (141). When this argument fails, the cousin resorts to "art" and prescribes not a contraceptive but a placebo that sends the guilty bride into a fever. Fearful that she has murdered an unborn child (that appears to exist only in her imagination), the doe in her delerium confesses her crime to an attendant nurse who in turn betrays her indiscretion to a mother-in-law most eager to report to her son who is predictably outraged.

"Mutual subjection" and affective individualism exacts correct behavior, but perhaps even more significantly, it demands correct thinking. "Had you never any dislike of it in your thoughts?" the citizen asked his defecting daughter. "No, never, sir; I can't imagine why you ask, sir." The barren doe must not only do her duty, but also *want* – earnestly – to do it. Although she did not actually act out her crime, she *thought* it in her desire to maintain physical autonomy while feeding her sexual appetite. Force, in this case the threat of parliamentary dissolution of the marriage, "terrified her to the last Degree; she behaved her self to him with great submission, and indeed, more than he desired" (145). She is made to "wear out" two years, "tho with many hard Struggles and frequent Reproaches from her Husband, who was extremely soured in his Temper by it, and did not stick to use her hardly enough about it upon all Occasions," until "to her particular satisfaction" she proves at last with child, "for she earnestly desired to be with Child, to put an End to all these Dissatisfactions" (150). Such *earnestly* affectionate submission becomes in the doe's tale the product of authoritarian force accompanied by reflection. Ironically, however rigorous the reflection, however abject the submission, in the companionate marriage mutual subjection can never be absolutely sincere. Within this domestic discourse is a fear not only of the voracious womb, but also the voracious imagination always "venting" itself, a subversive truth that will "ooze out" in spite of the moral censor.[9] In *Religious Courtship* the youngest, wisest sister inspires her irreligious suitor to repent, but being wise, she distrusts his conversion. The elder sister objects to her niceness: "I think my Sister is mad: what kind of Confession of Principles do you insist on pray? I hope you don't set up to examine the Heart" (*RC*, 172). But of course she does, and so does Defoe when he acts as the moral enforcer of a mutual subordination that can only be "imaginary," and therefore always suspect.

FICTIONAL REALITY: THE NOVELS

> I took Possession at once of a House well Furnish'd, and a
> Husband in very good Circumstances, so that I had a prospect of
> a very happy Life if I knew how to manage it; and I had leisure to
> consider of the real Value of the Life I was likely to live; how
> different it was to be from the loose ungovern'd part I had acted
> before, and how much happier a Life of Virtue and Sobriety is,
> than that which we call a Life of Pleasure.   (*MF*, 188)

Landed in a "safe Harbour," Moll Flanders sounds like conduct
book exemplar. "In very good circumstances," the "managed" life of
virtue and sobriety promises happiness. But circumstances change,
and after five years of "Ease and Content . . . a sudden Blow from an
almost invisible Hand blasted all my happiness, and turn'd me out
into the World in a Condition the reverse of all that had been before
it." When Defoe, the author of conduct manuals, demands self-
control and moral management, he presupposes a domestic life of
stability and substance safe from arbitrary intrusions from invisible
hands. His citizens and their wives worry over mutual subordination
and family worship, but they are always certain that they possess a
parlor to pray in. His novelistic domestic economies, however, reveal
a terrible instability. Husbands wander off as if "the Ground had
open'd and swallow'd them all up, and no-body had known it,"
(*R*, 12), lovers turn religious and decamp, domestic spaces open onto
a hostile world, their goods "torn" out, their shells "gutted," children
can become treacherous sources of betrayal. With money in your
pocket you are home anywhere, Moll notoriously boasts, at home
everywhere and nowhere. "I had stay'd here five weeks, and live'd
very comfortably indeed (the secret anxiety of my mind excepted),"
Moll reports, on the road (*MF*, 191). Her anxious comfort charac-
terizes a society expanding so dramatically that it depends upon
spectacular reverses as a matter of course.

"I had a prospect of a very happy Life," Moll mused, "if I knew
how to manage it." Preaching domestic economy, Defoe presents
unmanageable circumstances, comically in Moll's case, tragically in
Roxana's. Both women, veritable posture mistresses in their flexibility, shift and turn to maintain an impossible balance. The moral
imperatives of the conduct manuals become what Moll calls "by the
way," irrelevant incidentals in a world of tragic-comic accidents

where your husband turns out to be your brother and your serving-maid is actually your daughter. Such domestic revelations, a staple of romance, would be used comically by novelists like Fielding and Smollett. In his novels, however, Defoe creates recognition scenes darkly providential, scenes that establish uneasy familial dystopias. Family structures turn perverse, while the "natural" self apparently regulated in the conduct manuals strains against material circumstances that make nuclear domesticity not only "imaginary," but unimaginable.

MOLL FLANDERS

In *Moll Flanders* and *Roxana* Defoe tells his domestic tale twice, once comically, once tragically. Moll's version, like Roxana's, is studded with contradictions, but unlike Roxana, Moll makes no attempt either to reconcile or to untangle mutually impossible conditions. Her narration approaches the dream state in its generous inclusions of all the domestic parts that cannot yet ought to fit. Defoe the dreamer-laureate of capitalism, the bankrupt who disastrously invested in brick yards and civet cats and spent hard time on the road eluding irate creditors and dissatisfied family members, recuperates in this story the financial success and domestic bliss that is in reality impossible to achieve. The English Tradesman, he boasted, "is a kind of Phoenix, who often rises out of his own ashes, and makes the ruin of his fortunes to be a firm foundation to build his recovery."[10] In his (1905) "Fragment of an analysis of a case of hysteria," Freud argued that there could be no "no" in the unconscious: P. Rieff (ed.) (1963) *Dora: An Analysis of a Case of Hysteria*, New York, Collier-Macmillan, 75. In her spectacular triumphs over necessity, the ever-renewed Moll exists on just such an unconscious level, disavowing the no, the ought, the very grounds of conduct that the Family Instructor requires.

The moral consciousness Defoe demands in his manuals requires a stability and leisure Moll only seldom enjoys. What she needs to "rise out of her own ashes" is a radically reconstructed innocence, a talent for constant forgetting, and the energy to keep moving. The law of the father, a law essentially static and immutable, so necessary to the family instructor, signifies nothing in a world of flux where fathers generally take to the road, leaving their domestic mistakes behind.

Patriarchy collapses parodically, uncertainly verging into a matriarchy both critically unstable, but at the same time, fantastically effective. Two instances particularly undermine the notion of patriarchically "companionate" conduct: the time when Moll learns the incestuous secret of her identity, and Moll's sojourn at the Sign of the Cradle.

The story of Moll's origins begins cozily enough, in a fireside tale celebrating the fantastic opportunities that the new world, that "Newgate," offers the Phoenix-like practitioners of Defoe's darling economy. "Many a *Newgate*-Bird becomes a great Man," Moll's mother confides "with a great deal of good humour'd Confidence . . . and we have . . . several Justices of the Peace, Officers of the Train Bands, and Magistrates of the Towns they live in, that have been burnt in the Hand" (86). The tale turns from a public celebration of "the great man" to a personal revelation of the impossibility of reconciling the "secret" of her origins to her consequentially incestuous circumstances. Outwardly, all appears successful. While branded with the mark of her past, the good-humored mother testifies to the wonders of the economic system that rewards resourceful phoenix-like Newgate birds. But at the core of that system, Moll knows "that the whole Relation was Unnatural in the highest degree" (91). Moll exists uneasily as the product of the mother's Newgate experience and the consumer of the New World dream. Her blasted domesticity indicts both economic systems as forcefully as Gay's *Beggar's Opera*, dismantling in the process the myth of the regenerated colonial experience that her own eventual success as another "Newgate" Phoenix will depend upon. Defoe and Gay both demonstrate the instability of an economy that depends upon illicit recycling and always deferred reckoning. Like Macheath redeemed from his necessary gallows, Moll escapes her incestuous marriage which "a very good cargo" (that spoils in the crossing) to sail into various irregular, "unnatural" relationships that succeed to fail to succeed at last in a colonial economy that depends upon the "unnatural" relation Moll profits from. Within such a context, Moll's eventual redemption, profitable gentility trickling down from her incestuous new world estate, becomes radically compromised.

While the American experience both criticizes and depends upon the resilience of Newgate birds, Moll's stay at the Sign of the Cradle even more systematically exposes the contradictions of an economic and sexual economy at war with its imperatives. Her unwanted pregnancy reveals the "real" cost of Defoe's "imaginary" edict to breed. Maternity for Moll – and for mortals outside of conduct books – is too expensive when domesticity is so unstable. To keep moving, and to stop is to die, Moll sheds children with an abandon that is both necessary and lethal. Jemmy's baby becomes particularly problematic, because it threatens to blow up what she anticipates to be her "safe Harbour" with her (potentially bankrupted) clerk. At the Sign of the Cradle, Moll leaves behind the pretense of domesticity to enter a commercial haven that both "nauseates" and pleases her appetite while meeting her economic needs.

The strains of this compromised domestic system become most apparent and most "concealed" under Mother Midnight's management. Both "Beldame" and Mother, Moll's governess manages to nurture her charges, but she is also found guilty of "stealing away" a victimized daughter into prostitution. Her establishment harbors whores, yet conceals "indecencies," behind clean linen, tidy bills of fare, and appetizing dishes of chicken and sweetbreads. The "Mother's" centrality to a system that both uses and protects women might hint at a triumphant matriarchal structure that transcends circumstances of sexual and financial transaction.[11] But its precarious and unnatural nature emphasizes the costs of a domestic economy that in Moll's case depends upon a dislocation that can resolve itself only in a well-run, neutral management of childbearing and rearing that exists only in fantasy. "Let none be encouraged in their loose practices from this dexterous management, for she is gone to her place," Moll warns, "and I dare say has left nothing behind her that can or will come up to it" (171).

The dislocations implicit in Defoe's breeding imperative become most evident when Moll debates sending out her child to nurse. She scrupulously makes a well-founded argument against the deadly practice of wet nursing, insisting that "'tis only a contriv'd Method for Murther; that is to say, a killing their Children with safety" (173).[12] But all the while she makes a passionate case against wet nursing, she is arguing with a woman who has nursed her as "Careful, and Tender" through her own pregnancy "as if I had been her own Child," better (we know) than Moll's "true" mother, author of her confusion. Even more ironically, after mulling over the dangers of the nursing system, after underlining the cost of domestic existence, Moll delivers the child to a nurse that is not only "wholesome look'd" and "likely" (177), but one who proves "easie" about payment and loving in her care. Moll's success in shedding her children locates Defoe's domestic ideology within a larger economic context which depends upon the "lewdness" and abuses that are outlawed from the companionate marriage of "affectively bonded individuals." Whether or not in the "real" world Moll's wet-nurse would be so easy, she is for Moll's purposes indispensable. Without the ever elusive security necessary for breeding, superfluous children must be shed in a system that depends more on cash than compassion. Even the loyal Mother Midnight proves "equally impenetrable in that Part which related to Affection . . . when you are gone, what are you to me?" she asks (174). Her particular fidelity to Moll does not discount its economic matrix, but only suggests its rarity.

Like a Phoenix, Moll regularly rises out of problems that remain contextually insoluble. In her process of exposing the circumstantial inequities of her domestic and economic systems, she manages to retain a conditional innocence hardy enough to allow her to reward her rich Virginian son, incestuous fruit of a bigamous marriage, with a stolen watch, guilty material she can redeem with her generosity. In fact, when she encounters her tender son, "my one, and only Child" (332–3), she finds herself so pleased with his prudence and management that she feels "as if I had been in a new World, and began secretly now to wish that I had not brought my *Lancashire* Husband from *England* at all." Such uncensored desire underscores the fantastic freedom Moll enjoys. If there is no negation in the unconscious, in Moll's dream, all sexual and economic contradictions exist not resolved so much as expressed, fragmentary pieces of a real world where resolution can only be imaginary. In Roxana's world, the contradictions overwhelm such imaginary solutions.

ROXANA

The idea of "home" drives Defoe's most consistently tragic character, Roxana, through her paces. Like Moll, Roxana plays with the materials of her body in an attempt to exert control over a reality always in flux. But while Moll succeeds in retaining an innocence that frees her to operate with energetic impunity, Roxana becomes fixed in the guilt that accompanies her gain. Through her, Defoe explores most relentlessly the contradictions of a sexual economy

that demands subordination and self-determination while he emphasizes the impossibility of attaining enough domestic security to
make possible the ideological fictions of correct conduct. Roxana's
failure makes even clearer the irony of Moll's fantastic triumph
as well as the strains of discord that affective individualism
exacts.

Of all Defoe's characters, Roxana remains the most persistently
hungry, even when she is "wallowing" in wealth. In her primal scene,
deserted by her foolish husband, Roxana sits "in Rags and Dirt, who
was but a little before riding in my Coach; thin, and looking almost
like One Starv'd, who was before fat and beautiful," while her house,
once handsome, "was now stripp'd, and naked." Like Moll, she has
been and will continue to be a good breeder, and pays now for her
fertility with five hungry children that drive her to thoughts of
"murther." Rather than "eat up my very Children themselves"
(17–18), she drops them onto the parish or into unfriendly familial hands. She does not enjoy Moll's impunity, however, for one
"burthen in the belly," a daughter and namesake, returns to bear
witness to the cost of her strategies. Unlike Moll's bigamous son, that
paragon of prudence, easily fobbed off with a reconstructed story
and a pickpocketed watch, Roxana's daughter Susan rashly hounds
her mother for her birthright.

Roxana's strategies always anticipate future "dreadful Scenes"
(162) of devastation that must be resisted. To attain "freedom," she
measures, almost parodically, her liberty through a self-imposed
"limitation." Roxana exploits the "slavery" of unaccommodated
woman dramatically and publicly, turning herself into "a Roxana,"
mistress to the court, contained in a seraglio of her own making.
"Home," that structure that can be "gutted" by furious landlords,
deserted by wayward husbands, becomes a public "house" of pleasure as notorious as the Sign of the Cradle. Domestic space literally
sprawls into the street "full of Coaches with Coronets, and fine
Glass-Chairs," while a mob of suppliants require "a strong Party of
the Guards . . . to keep the Door, for without that, there had been
such a promiscuous Crowd, and some of them scandalous too, that
we shou'd have been all Disorder and Confusion" (178). Stocking
her house with materials that will later prove tainted, her infamous
"Turkish Dress," her massive pieces of plate too large for "ordinary"
use, Roxana transforms her rooms and her person to achieve what
she calls "Sweet Liberty" at the cost of her self. To attain indepen-

dence, she feigns compliance and submission, perversely imitating the subordination Defoe both demands and disavows in his conduct manuals. By playing the slave, by presenting her body as eroticized material and fetish of her sexuality, Roxana establishes a freedom so precarious that eventually she is forced to "eat up" her own child to escape exposure, that dreaded condition of "Disorder and Confusion."

However compromised her code of conduct might appear, Roxana prefers it to marriage, in which the women is reduced to "a meer Woman ever after, that is to say, A Slave . . . at best but *an Upper-Servant*" (148). Her Dutch merchant defends the passive dependency wives must assume, arguing that since the man bears "the Anxiety of Living," it is fit for the woman to do nothing but "eat the Fat and drink the Sweet . . . sit still, and look round her; be waited on and made much of; be serv'd, and lov'd, and made easie." His defense of "mutual subordination" partially satisfies Defoe's own ideological fictions, but only irritates Roxana's memory of her "dreadful Scene." In trusting the exertions of a "mere man" a "mere wife" might find herself "stripp'd to the Cloaths on her Back . . . until she sees her Children starve; herself miserable, breaks her Heart; and cries herself to Death" (150). To protect herself from such perilous dependency, Roxana, speaking "*Amazonian* Language," judging that "Liberty seem'd to be the Men's Property," chooses to be a *Man-Woman*, for as I was born free, I wou'd die so" (171).[13]

The context of her declaration exposes the fragile nature of Roxana's freedom, for she has just delivered her Dutch Merchant's bastard, a circumstance that impedes her materially and psychologically. "I wou'd willingly have given ten Thousand Pounds of my Money to have been rid of the Burthen I had in my Belly," she confides, "but it cou'd not be so" (163). Roxana arranges for the merchant's bastard with icy reluctance, confessing that "I did not love the child nor love to see it." Resolving that "it should not be able to call me mother" (228), she admits "often" wishing "it wou'd go quietly out of the world" (263). But as her legitimate daughter Susan demonstrates, children do not go quietly.

Unlike Moll, who was able to achieve respectability and financial stability in spite of the dubious nature of her origins, her maternity, and her fortune, Roxana becomes trapped in the double bind of security and respectability. After turning herself into an instrument of her own sexuality, a fetish designed to stave off her primal "dreadful Scene," she also strives for a decorum always in danger of being stripped away. In her zeal for disguised sobriety she imitates perversely the conduct manuals' call to reform. Like the rash "Family Instructor" so eager to reform his family even if he has to kill them to attain compliance, almost "overnight" Roxana vows to "shift [her] Being," and "put off all [her] Equipages, and Servants, Coaches, and Horses; change [her] Liveries, nay, [her] own Cloaths, and if it was possible, [her] very Face" (208). Just as her sexuality can become fetishized into an exotic Turkish dress, her piety becomes reified by the grave weight of her modest Quaker garb. "Compleatly concealed," Roxana boasts that "there was not a QUAKER in the Town look'd less like a Counterfeit than I did" (213). Her misplaced assurance undercuts the domestic ideology of conduct that depends upon concealment of rebellious passions so thorough that their suppression seems natural – not "Counterfeit."

All such decorum requires is the sacrificial murder of one child hungry for knowledge. The daughter, Susan, a nagging, fanatical witness to Roxana's early tableau of ragged, hungry need, through a quirk of providence, served as housemaid in the public arena of "Roxana's" splendid debaucheries. In search of her own origins, she sees past Roxana's respectable Quaker dress to a more fundamental truth. The eroticized costume that transformed the Man-Woman into compliant slave proved so compelling that Susan cannot forget its seductive power. While Roxana has been rationalizing her "debaucheries" by returning obsessively to her original hunger, her daughter, the unknowing servant in "Roxana's" household, has been dwelling on the glory of her mother's apotheosis in her fabulous Turkish costume. To protect herself from her daughter's "broken Account" of her Turkish dress and courtesan past, Roxana gives Susan over to the diligent Amy to be dispatched. In her passivity, her compliance to a system of respectability that numbs feeling, Roxana chooses outwardly proper conduct that depends upon the infanticide that underlies the sexual economy she attempted to master. This is not to say that Defoe's *Family Instructor* taught patriarchs to kill their children to make them better. Rather, the society that Defoe repeatedly tries to measure, depends upon subjection to contradictory demands for security and freedom, substance and desire, survival and morality.

With the death of Susan, the narrative collapses. Roxana makes one last attempt to reclaim her early maternity in visiting her other daughter, "the very Counterpart of myself" (329). But after one short paragraph packed with calamities, Roxana is blasted off the page for her crime. In her isolated unregenerate state, she mirrors not the confidence of the "Family Instructor" in his state of grace, but demonstrates instead a hopelessness as thorough as the melancholy of the prodigal son missing one arm and one father, calling out for forgiveness on his deathbed. But while the son appeals to a father who pervades his domestic landscape, a father out of town, but present in the narrative, Roxana appears stripped of authority structures. "I was brought so low again, that my Repentance seem'd to be only the Consequence of my Misery, as my Misery was of my Crime" (330). The weariness accompanying this "seeming" repentance locates the problem Defoe comes up against in this most realistic of his fictions. The ideological fiction of mutual subjection and affective individualism depended, in the conduct manuals, upon subordination to patriarchal authority that Defoe, defender of women, defender of capitalism, both abhorred and demanded. Moll Flanders escapes problems of domestic authority through the adventures Defoe dreams for her, managing to exist by denying with energetic enthusiasm the contradictions of her equivocal state. But Roxana pays for Moll's holiday as she incorporates within herself the price of the contradictions of her physical economy. While Defoe argues in *Conjugal Lewdness* that matrimony is "a state" rather than a Circumstance, in his fictional narratives, the circumstantial aspects of domesticity rule as arbitrarily as "the invisible hand" that "blasts" Moll's happiness and turns her out into the world. Falling into "a dreadful Course of Calamities," Roxana discloses ultimately a seeming repentance circumstantial, consequential, and utterly without application. Subject always to the fall not into knowledge, not into experience, but into calamity that can be repeated endlessly, Defoe stops dreaming comic solutions to tragic problems of necessity and desire. Far from instructing the family, *Roxana* blows it up, destroying in the process the simple faith in domesticity that only a "Phoenix-like" reader or one of Defoe's favorite "children and fools" could maintain. Roxana, tainted, tarnished, polluted with the murder of her burden in the belly, bears witness to the strains of feminine conduct in a system "at war with itself." Her failure exposes the cost of an "affective individualism" that subordinates sexuality and maternity to a system that "murthers" its children to feed its desires.

Defoe's Idea of Conduct

NOTES

1 Defoe wrote *The Family Instructor* in two parts in 1715 and 1718. I have used the first edition of the *FI* (1715) when possible, but for the second part (1718) I have used a text published in 1809.

The Family Instructor: In Three Parts With a Recommendatory Letter by the Reverend Mr. S. Wright (1715) London, will be referred to in the text as *FI* I.

The second part of *FI*, *The Family Instructor; in Two Parts relating 1. To Family Breaches, and their Obstructing Religious Duties. 2. To the Great Mistake of Mixing the Passions in the Managing and Correcting of Children* (1718) London, will be referred to in the text as *FI* II.

Religious Courtship: Being Historical Discourses, on the Necessity of Marrying Religious Husbands and Wives Only (1722) London, referred to in the text as *RC*.

Conjugal Lewdness; or, Matrimonial Whoredom (1727), ed. M. Novak (1967), Gainesville, Scholars' Facsimiles and Reprints, referred to as *CL*.

Moll Flanders, ed. G. A. Starr (1981), Oxford, Oxford University Press, referred to as *MF*.

Roxana. The Fortunate Mistress, ed. J. Jack (1981), Oxford, Oxford University Press, referred to as *R*.

2 See N. Elias (1978) *The History of Manners: The Civilizing Process*, New York, Pantheon, originally published in Switzerland, 1939, on the pains of becoming "civilized."

3 J. Hagstrum (1980) *Sex and Sensibility: Ideal and Erotic Love from Milton to Mozart*, Chicago, Ill., University of Chicago Press, and L. Stone (1977) *The Family, Sex and Marriage In England, 1500–1800*, London, Harper & Row, both admire the eighteenth century for its emotional possibilities, arguing that sexuality and sensibility could be unified gracefully to serve a household dedicated to an affectionate mutuality. Defoe's compulsive attention to the costs of such accommodation undermines their enthusiasm at best.

4 As G. Starr observes, "the slave, the child, the youngest sibling, the apprentice, the unlettered peasant, and the savage are Defoe's favorite spokesmen" for his conduct codes, in his (1971) *Defoe and Casuistry*, Princeton, NJ, Princeton University Press, 37–8. The marginalized, often retarded, state of such advocates for subservience and accommodation is worth considering.

5 The desire comes from *Applebee's Journal*, cited by P. Earle (1977) *The World of Defoe*, New York, Atheneum, 170. Defoe wished "for my country's good that it might please God that all our people were masters and able to keep servants, tho' they were obliged to buy their servants, as

other nations do, and as we do in His Majesty's dominions." M. Douglas (1969) *Purity and Danger*, London, Routledge & Kegan Paul, develops at length the equivocations implicit in sexual and economic systems that both encourage and yet, by necessity, deny, individuation, systems "at war with themselves."

6 L. Althusser (1971) "Ideology and idealized state apparatuses," in *Lenin and Philosophy and Other Essays*, New York, Monthly Review Press, 165.

7 In his (1728) "Augusta Triumphans: or the Way to Make London the Most Flourishing City in the Universe," London, Defoe attacks the practice of clapping wives into private madhouses where they were "stripp'd, whipp'd, ill fed and worse us'd" for the convenience of wastrel husbands bent upon using up their fortunes, 31.

8 Both Venette and Maubray are considered in P. G. Bouce (ed.) (1982) *Sexuality in Eighteenth-Century Britain*, Manchester, Manchester University Press, 48, 84. See also F. Nussbaum (1984) *The Brink of All We Hate: English Satires on Women*, Lexington, University of Kentucky Press; and R. Thompson (1979) *Unfit for Modest Ears*, Totowa, Rowman & Littlefield, for documentation of the misogynist fears of voracious women.

9 Defoe discusses at length the necessity for "giving vent" and "undbend-[ing] the Mind" which works "with such a vehemence in the Minds of those who are guilty of any atrocious Villany," in *MF*, 325–6, a passage remarkable for a pressure its inappropriate location brings to bear on a wayward text. He also discusses the desire to confess in *Applebee's Journal*, 2 March 1723, and the *Review*, November 1704. (See Starr's note, *MF*, 396.)

10 As cited in J. R. Moore (1958) *Daniel Defoe: Citizen of the Modern World*, Chicago, Ill., University of Chicago Press, 103.

11 In her (1982) "Matriarchal mirror: women and capital in MF," *PMLA*, 97, 212–26, L. A. Chaber argues that triumphing over "semantic double dealing and social tabooes," Moll receives a "legacy of power and humanity" that renders her "human, if not fully humane," and is able to recuperate her fortunes in a colonial America that "combines the best of the threatened conservative idyll of England's agrarian past with the capitalist dream of unlimited mobility and growth" (222–3). Chaber's article is particularly sensitive to the ideological complexities of Defoe's fictions, but emphasizes, perhaps at the expense of the work, a triumph for Moll that can only be, ultimately, ironic.

12 G. Rosen (1976) "A slaughter of innocents: aspects of child health in the eighteenth-century city," *Studies in Eighteenth-Century Culture*, 5, 293–316, and R. Trumbach (1978) *The Rise of the Egalitarian Family: Aristocratic Kinship and Domestic Relations in Eighteenth-Century*

England, New York, Academic Press, both discuss the practice of wet nursing in the eighteenth century.

13 An early sympathetic opponent of Roxana's arguments is S. Peterson (1955) "The matrimonial theme of Defoe's *Roxana*," *PMLA*, 70, 166–91.

4

The rise of the domestic woman*

NANCY ARMSTRONG

It is only by seeing women in their own homes, among their own set, just as they always are, that you can form any just judgement. Short of that, it is all guess and luck – and will generally be ill-luck. How many a man has committed himself on a short acquaintance, and rued it all the rest of his life!

(Jane Austen, *Emma*)

Although aimed simply at making young women desirable to men of a good social position, countless conduct books and works of instruction for women represented a specific configuration of sexual features as the only appropriate object for men at all levels of society to want for a wife. At the same time, such writing provided people from diverse social groups with a basis for imagining economic interests in common.[1] Thus it was the new domestic woman rather than her counterpart, the new economic man, who first encroached upon aristocratic culture and seized authority from it. This writing assumed that an education ideally made a woman desire to be what a prosperous man desires, which is above all else a female. She therefore had to lack the competitive desires and worldly ambitions

96

that consequently belonged – as if by some natural principle – to the male. For such a man, her desirability hinged upon an education in frugal domestic practices. She was supposed to complement his role as an earner and producer with hers as a wise spender and tasteful consumer. Such an ideal relationship presupposed a woman whose desires were not of necessity attracted to material things. But because a woman's desire could in fact be manipulated by signs of wealth and position, she required an education.

In assuming this, eighteenth-century conduct books and educational treatises for women forced open a contradiction within the existing cultural territory that had been marked out for representing the female. These authors portrayed aristocratic women along with those who harbored aristocratic pretensions as the very embodiments of corrupted desire, namely desire that sought its gratification in economic and political terms. The books all took care to explain how this form of desire destroyed the very virtues essential to a wife and mother. Narratives of her ideal development would come later. The educational handbooks for women simply mapped out a new field of knowledge as specifically female. In doing so, they declared their intention to recover and preserve a woman's true (sexual) identity in a world run according to other (political and economic) measures of men. With this as its justification, the writing devoted to defining the female wrought an important change in the understanding of power. It severed the language of kinship from that of political relations, producing a culture divided into the respective domains of domestic woman and economic man.

After reading several dozen or more conduct books, one is struck with a sense of their emptiness – a lack of what we today consider "real" information about the female subject and the object world that she is supposed to occupy. Under the sheer force of repetition, however, one does see a figure emerge from the categories that organize these manuals. A figure of female subjectivity, a grammar really, awaited the substance that the novel and its readers, as well as the countless individuals educated according to the model of the new woman, would eventually provide. In such books one can see a culture in the process of rethinking at the most basic level the dominant (aristocratic) rules for sexual exchange. Because they appeared to have no political bias, these rules took on the power of natural law, and as a result, they presented – in actuality, still present – readers with ideology in its most powerful form.

The Ideology of Conduct

THE BOOK OF CLASS SEXUALITY

Until sometime around the end of the seventeenth century, the great majority of conduct books were devoted mainly to representing the male of the dominant class.[2] For the purposes of my argument, it does not really matter whether or not aristocrats were actually the ones to take such instruction seriously. What does matter is what the literate public considered to be the dominant social ideal. Ruth Kelso and Suzanne Hull have shown that during the sixteenth and seventeenth centuries there were relatively few books for instructing women as compared to those available to men. Their research also shows that books addressing a readership with humbler aspirations increased in popularity during the seventeenth century.[3] Although by mid-century they outnumbered conduct books that exalted the attributes of aristocratic women, the distinctively Puritan flavor of some marriage manuals and books on household governance made it quite clear that they were not endorsing the preferred cultural norms.[4] But neither was their advice for women supposed to challenge the aristocratic ideal. Whatever their political attitude toward the aristocracy, no one presumed to represent a more desirable woman but simply one that was more practical for people of less means and prestige. An exclusive concern for the practical matters of running a household classified certain handbooks for women as domestic economies, which meant they belonged to an entirely different genre than conduct books that aspired to be courtesy literature. Although some books argued that domestic economy should be part of an ideal gentlewoman's education, they did not come into their own until the last decade of the seventeenth century.[5] Until then, different levels of society held recognizably different ideas of what made a woman marriageable. During the first decades of the eighteenth century, however, categories which had apparently remained fairly constant for centuries underwent rapid transformation.

The distinction between conduct books and domestic economies changed so that each reached out to the other's reader. So popular did these books become that by the second half of the eighteenth century virtually everyone knew the ideal of womanhood they proposed. Joyce Hemlow considers this writing the purest expression of the same interest in manners that one finds in Burney: "the problem of the conduct of the young lady was investigated so thoroughly that the lifetime of Fanny Burney, or more accurately the years 1760–1820, which saw also the rise of the novel of manners, might be called the age of courtesy books for women."[6] To this I would add an important qualification. While the lifetime of Burney – and, one might note, of Austen as well – should indeed be seen as the high point of a tradition of conduct books for women, it would be misleading to suggest that the two kinds of writing – women's courtesy books and novels of manners – sprang into being and passed out of currency together. The production of conduct books long preceded novels of manners and in fact virtually exploded during the period following the failure to renew the licensing act in 1695, thus preceding the novel of manners by several decades.[7] Although today we no longer find authors designing curricula to educate young women at home, the conduct book is still alive and well. Besides all the books and advice columns telling women how to catch and keep a man, as well as magazines imaging the beautiful home, the modern woman will probably have taken at least one home economics course before graduating from high school. Perhaps because its most basic tenets became social facts with the formation of the national curriculum that included female pupils as well as males, conduct books have grown more specialized during our own century – concentrating now on thin thighs, then on the manners of a business woman, and with equal frequency on such specific domestic skills as French cuisine or English gardening that men are supposed to learn as well as women.

It is safe to say that by the mid-eighteenth century the number of books specifying the qualities of a new kind of woman had well outstripped the number of those devoted to describing the aristocratic male.[8] The growth of this body of writing thus coincided with the rise of the popular press, itself a part of the larger process that Raymond Williams has aptly named "the long revolution."[9] Lord Halifax's *Advice to a Daughter* first appeared in 1688 and ran through two dozen editions, winning great popularity for nearly a century until Dr Gregory's *Father's Legacy to His Daughters* and Hester Chapone's *Letters on the Improvement of the Mind* supplanted it. John Mason's study of courtesy literature shows that the number and variety of ladies' conduct books began to increase with the publication of such books as *The Ladies Dictionary* (1694) and *The Whole Duty of Women* (1695).[10] Where men are concerned, his study shows that by mid-century the form gradually mutated into other forms – satire, for example – once the production of the ideal social leader who dominated Renaissance treatises was no longer imagined as its primary goal. Meanwhile, the conduct book for women enjoyed a different fate. Educational literature that addressed a female readership quickly became very popular once it broke free from the aristocratic model, and despite a falling off after the 1820s, many books remained in print well into the nineteenth century.

Throughout this period, countless female conduct books, ladies' magazines, and books of instruction for children all posited a similar feminine ideal and tended toward the same objective of ensuring a happy household. Indeed, the end of the eighteenth century saw not only the publication of proposals for institutions devoted to educating women, but also the development of programs designed to instruct women at home. Erasmus Darwin's *A Plan for the Conduct of Female Education in Boarding Schools* (1798) and the Edgeworth's *Practical Education* (1801) are only two of the more famous efforts at institutionalizing the curriculum proposed by conduct-book literature. In representing the household as a world with its own form of social relations, a distinctively feminine discourse, this body of literature revised the semiotic of culture at its most basic level and enabled a coherent idea of the middle class to take shape. That the relative number of conduct books appeared to decrease as the eighteenth century came to an end was not because the female ideal they represented passed out of vogue. To the contrary, there is every reason to think that by this time the ideal had passed into the domain of common sense where it provided the frame of reference for other kinds of writing, among them the novel. With the history of conduct books for women in mind, for example, one can understand how Richardson's tediously protracted description of the household in *Pamela* could be supplanted by Austen's minimalist representation precisely because the rules governing sexual relations laid out in the conduct books could be taken for granted. Austen could simply allude where Richardson, in defiance of an earlier notion of sexual relations, had to elaborate for hundreds of pages. More than that, Austen knew perfectly well her readers had identified those rules not only with common sense, if not always with nature, but also with the form of the novel itself.

Conduct books addressed a readership comprising various levels and sources of income and included virtually all people who distinguished themselves from the aristocracy, on the one hand, and from the laboring poor on the other. Although written in various regional, professional, and political voices, each with the specific concerns of a local readership foremost in mind, the conduct books written during the first decades of the eighteenth century nevertheless proposed an ideal that was reappearing with wonderful regularity. Their evident popularity therefore suggests we might detect the presence of a "middle class," as we mean it today, much earlier than other writing from that time in history indicates. Even if we use Hemlow's later dates of 1760–1820 to mark the high point of the writing of manners, we must still confront an historical paradox. Conduct books imply the presence of a unified middle class at a time when other representations of the social world suggest that no such class yet existed. Most other writing in fact suggests that the eighteenth-century Englishman saw himself within a static and hierarchical society, radically different from the dynamic struggle of landlords, capitalists, and laboring poor that would accompany the rise of the middle class during the early decades of the nineteenth century. Harold Perkin provides this encapsulated view of how social relationships were understood in eighteenth-century England: "The old society then was a finely graded hierarchy of great subtlety and discrimination, in which men were acutely aware of their exact relation to those immediately above and below them, but only vaguely conscious except at the very top of their connection with those on their own level."[11] These men apparently felt allegiance only to those immediately above and below them in economic chains, and they probably harbored antagonism toward those who occupied similar positions in other chains of dependency. According to Perkin, the absence of anything resembling a modern middle class is particularly apparent in England, where there was no word for *bourgeoisie* "until the nineteenth century," because "the thing itself did not exist, in the sense of a permanent, self-conscious urban class in opposition to the landed aristocracy" (61). The English view of society proved to be incorrigibly vertical, he continues, for no sooner did one generation of townsmen succeed in business or trade than they sought to raise their social status by becoming country gentlemen.

If conduct books addressed a fairly wide readership with fairly consistent social objectives, then they present us with an historical contradiction of major proportions – a middle class that was not actually there. It was no mystery who occupied the top of the social

The Ideology of Conduct

ladder as well as the bottom, but there are only the most irregular and diverse data concerning those in the middle. Reviewing his information concerning the period from 1688 to 1803, Perkin describes what he calls "the middle ranks" of the "old society:"

> The middle ranks were distinguished at the top from the gentry and nobility not so much by lower incomes as by the necessity of earning their living, and at the bottom from the labouring poor not so much by higher incomes as by the property, however small, represented by stock in trade, livestock, tools, or the educational investment of skill or expertise. (23)

We should note that Perkin organizes this field of information negatively in that his description accounts for those people who were neither aristocracy nor laboring poor. Everywhere within this field there were hierarchies – professional and economic – marked by "an infinity of graduated statuses." By the same token, he claims, every occupation was marked "by internal differences of status greater than any which separated it from those outside" (24). This is not to say that Perkin's map of eighteenth-century society is any less a representation than that which can be extrapolated from the conduct books of an earlier time. I am simply suggesting that during the early eighteenth century most authors regarded differences of status as the only accurate way of identifying individuals within the middle ranks of their society. They did not, in other words, perceive what common interests might have united all those at the same social level. That the female conduct book presupposed horizontal affiliations among the literate public where no such affiliations would exist as a matter of practice for another sixty to a hundred years has obvious bearing on social and literary history alike. It marks a basic change in the public understanding of social relations as well as a change in what constituted good taste in reading. But I should hasten to add that the question raised by this body of discourse is not the same one addressed by Ian Watt or Richard Altick in their studies of the novel-reading public. We cannot ask the conduct book to explain what new social elements had been introduced into the readership that so altered its taste.[12] The available data do not allow us to do so. If changes in socioeconomic categories came after similar changes in the categories governing female education, we must ask instead what the new domestic ideal said to a heterogenous economic group that ensured this ideal would keep on making sense well into the nineteenth century – after political relationships assumed a modern configuration.

During the eighteenth century the conduct book for women became such a common phenomenon that many different kinds of writers felt compelled to add their wrinkles to the female character. Besides men like Halifax, Rochester, Swift, and Defoe – all of whom tried their hands at writing conduct books for women – there were also pedagogues such as Timothy Rogers, Thomas Gisborne, and T. S. Arthur, clergymen like Revd Thomas Broadhurst, Dr Fordyce, and the darling of Austen's generation, Dr Gregory, as well as a number of women authors such as Sarah Tyler, Miss Catherine E. Beecher, and the Countess Dowager of Carlisle, all of whom have long since faded from cultural memory. Like Hester Chapone, Hannah More, and Maria Edgeworth, some authors made their reputations by writing conduct books, while other conduct-book authors like Mary Wollstonecraft and Erasmus Darwin were known primarily for writing in more prestigious modes. Even when the author's name is obscure, as most of these names indeed are, one can usually infer a social identity from the female virtues to which the writer grants highest priority, for these virtues are inevitably linked to functions which that writer feels are essential to good household management.

Taken together, these local voices comprise a text displaying obvious distinctions between town and country, between old money and new, among income levels and various occupations, and particularly among the different amounts of leisure time people had to occupy. By dividing the social world on the basis of sex, this body of writing produced a single ideal of the household. But the domestic ideal did not so much speak to middle-class interests as we now understand them. In fact, it is accurate to say that such writing as the conduct books helped to generate the belief that there was such a thing as a middle class with clearly established affiliations before it actually existed. If there is any truth in this, then it is also reasonable to claim that the modern individual was first and foremost a female.

The handbook that gained such immense popularity in England at the end of the seventeenth century was a hybrid form that combined materials from earlier devotional books and books of manners ostensibly written for aristocratic women, with information from books of maternal advice to daughters, as well as with descriptions of the housewife's practical duties as depicted in humbler handbooks of domestic economy, almanacs, and recipe books. Written by Timothy Rogers, an otherwise unremarkable educator with dissenter's sympathies, *The Character of a Good Woman, both in a Single and Married State* provides a particularly useful example of the genre as it appeared at the beginning of the eighteenth century. The book holds true to its subtitle and represents the ideal female as a bipartite character. Among the qualities of the unmarried woman that the author extols are modesty, humility, and honesty. In earlier writing, these conspicuously passive virtues were considered the antidote to natural deficiencies that had been the female's heritage ever since the Fall of Man. In keeping with Enlightenment strategies, however, the new mode of instruction declares it will cultivate the inherently female qualities that are most likely to ward off the vanity which contemporary social life instills. Published in 1697, *The Character of a Good Woman* does not represent women as more prone to corruption and thus more in need of redemption than men; it exalts female nature because, as the author claims, women are "generally more serious than men . . . as far beyond in the lessons of Devotion as in the tuneableness and sweetness of your voice."[13] Here passive virtue is both in keeping with female nature and essential to preserving that nature.

The passive virtue of the unmarried woman constitutes only half of the paradigm that rapidly gained currency during the eighteenth century. To the qualities of the innocent maiden, conduct books appended those of the efficient housewife. As if straight from Renaissance handbooks on domestic economy, these books developed categories that defined the ideal woman in her married state. Her representation was as practical and detailed as the maiden's was abstract and homiletic in style. Except for unqualified obedience to her husband, the virtues of the ideal wife appeared to be active. A list of her duties could have included household management, regulation of servants, supervision of children, planning of entertainment, and concern for the sick. It quickly becomes apparent, however, that the main duty of the new housewife was to supervise the servants who were the ones to take care of these matters. The table of contents for *The Young Ladies Companion or, Beauty's Looking-Glass*, which was written in 1740, demonstrates a typical mix of topics drawn from courtesy literature as well as from the practical handbooks: (1) Religion, (2) Husband, (3) House, Family, and Children, (4) Behavior and Conversation, (5) Friendships, (6) Censure, (7) Vanity and Affectation, (8) Pride, (9) Diversions.[14] At this point in history, the social differences implicit in the different materials that went into conduct books have faded. The features of the devout maiden have been bonded to those of the industrious housewife, forming a new but utterly familiar system of signs.

Contained within the framework of gender rather than status, the earlier meaning of traditionally female features – practical duties and abstract virtues alike – changed even while they seemed to pass into the eighteenth century untouched by the individual imagination. Different categories of female identity, which were drawn from quite diverse traditions of writing and aimed at various social groups, formed a single representation. In their combination, contrary notions of taste transformed one another to form a standard capable of reaching across a broad spectrum of social groups. Once the practical duties of the common housewife had been included within the framework of courtesy literature, they became more and more tightly restricted to those tasks that were performed within and for the household alone. In contrast with earlier domestic economies, the eighteenth-century conduct books ceased to provide advice for the care of livestock or the concoction of medicinal cures. Producing goods to be consumed by the household was apparently no longer their readers' concern. In this respect, even the eighteenth-century instructional literature modeled upon the earlier domestic economies was influenced by courtesy literature. The more practically oriented books still emphasized frugality, for example. But in their instructions for the preparation of food, frugality became a matter of good taste and a way of displaying domestic virtue, not of stretching the resources to meet the needs of the household. In proposing a menu "proper for a frugal as well as a sumptuous table," for example, *The Compleat Housewife or, Accomplished Gentlewoman's Companion* (1734) converts the notion of propriety from an economic norm to a new national standard. A meal commensurate with one's means, in other words, became a meal "suitable to English constitutions and English Palates, wholesome, toothsome, all practical and easy to be performed."[15]

If the female's abstract virtues endowed the duties of the housewife with value, the spiritual virtues honored in earlier courtesy literature became limited in how they might help her perform her practical duties. Once female virtue became so linked to work, conduct books banished from the ideal woman the features that had once seemed desirable because they enhanced the aristocratic woman. In a conduct book of the early nineteenth century, T. S. Arthur goes so far as to assault the ideal of cloistered virtue that for centuries had been considered desirable in unmarried aristocratic women. Arthur also reveals what had – by the end of the eighteenth century – replaced this form of virtue as the basis for female virtue. In his view, "What is called the religion of the cloister is no religion at all, but mere selfishness – a retiring from *actual duty in the world*, into an imaginary state of sanctimoniousness" (italics mine).[16] Thomas Broadhurst's *Advice to Young Ladies on the Improvement of the Mind and Conduct of Life* (1810) shows an equally prevalent tendency toward anti-intellectualism directed at women who sought an élite education – once the privilege of well-born women – and the pleasures of intellectual life:

> She who is faithfully employed in discharging the various duties of a wife and daughter, a mother and a friend, is far more usefully occupied than one who, to the culpable neglect of the most important obligations, is daily absorbed by philosophic and literary speculations, or soaring aloft amidst the enchanted regions of fiction and romance.[17]

Such attacks on both religious and intellectual women condemn female virtues associated with the dominant social ideal of earlier culture. In this manner, the conduct books sought to define the practice of secular morality as the woman's natural duty. If certain agrarian and artisan forms of labor were considered unfeminine by virtue of their inclusion in the conduct book, then certain manifestations of aristocratic taste and learning were declared corrupt and opposed to the mental accomplishments of the good wife and mother. In the process, her duties were pared down to those that seem remarkably frivolous but that were – and to some extent still are – considered nonetheless essential to domestic happiness.

I would like to suggest that the peculiar features and extraordinary durability of the domestic ideal had everything to do with its capability to suppress the very conflicts so evident in the bewildering field of dialects comprising this body of writing until the second half of the eighteenth century. The authors of conduct books were acutely sensitive to the subtlest differences in status, and each represented his or her readers' interests in terms of a differential system that opposed country and town, rich and poor, labor and leisure, and no doubt more refined or local socioeconomic interests. Within such a semantic field, the representation of any male role automatically defined a partisan position. In deciding what role a male should ideally fulfill, then, the authors of both fiction and conduct books had to stand on one side or another in a number of these thematic oppositions. And to do so would limit a readership accordingly. The female, in contrast, provided a topic that could bind together precisely those groups who were necessarily divided by other kinds of writing. Virtually no other topic appeared to be so free of bias toward an occupation, political faction, or religious affiliation. In bringing into being a concept of the household where socially hostile groups felt they could all agree, the domestic ideal helped create the fiction of horizontal affiliations that only a century later could be said to have materialized as an economic reality. As part of an effort to explain how domestic fiction happened to survive and acquire prestige while other forms of writing rose and fell in popularity, the following description demonstrates how formulation of the domestic woman overcame the conflicts and contradictions inherent in most other Enlightenment efforts at rewriting the conditions of history.

A COUNTRY HOUSE THAT IS NOT
A COUNTRY HOUSE

It is relatively easy to distinguish those conduct books meant for rural readers from those addressing people in town. Despite these and all the other signs of competing economic interests that presupposed a politically diverse readership, the eighteenth-century books for women nevertheless agreed that the country house should be the site of the ideal household. By this they meant the country house should cease to provide a model of aristocratic culture and to offer instead a model that would be realized in any and all respectable households. This way of representing life in the country house made it possible for competing interest groups to ignore their economic origins and coalesce around a single domestic ideal. The opposition between city and country, which marked a major division between economic and political interests at the time, only enhanced the advantages of the domestic ideal. Urban tradesmen and merchants, for example, ordinarily would have thought they had little in common with independent farmers and grain dealers, and traditional representations of the country house only reinforced this political opposition. The country house of seventeenth-century England had encouraged popular belief that those at the very top of the social hierarchy were the ultimate end of production. In such a hierarchical system of relationships, people who were entitled to a privileged position were expected to display their wealth in certain highly prescribed ways.[18] In its most idealized form, the old society appeared to be governed by a patron who distributed wealth and power down a series of hierarchically organized relationships until virtually every client benefited from this generosity. Such, for example, is the form that social authority assumes in the country-house poems of the seventeenth century.[19]

So important were forms of sumptuary display to maintaining the social order during the sixteenth and seventeenth centuries that a series of royal proclamations detailed the permissible forms of aristocratic display. Using wealth to display the signs of high social status was forbidden to those whose birth and title had not qualified them to do so. In her proclamation of 6 July 1597, Queen Elizabeth voiced concern about the "confusion in all places being great where the meanest are as richly appareled as their betters."[20] By "meanest" she was obviously referring to non-aristocrats whose money could disguise a lack of noble origins. To remedy this situation, she reiterated a national dress code which specified, among other things, that "none shall wear in his apparel cloth of gold or silver tissued, silk of color purple under the degree of an earl, except Knights of the Garter in their purple mantles" (176). Besides listing clothing and materials that must be used according to rank, degree, and proximity to the Queen, the proclamation also limited the total amount one could spend each year on clothing. These restrictions extended to women whose body, like that of the male, was an ornamental body representing the family's place in an intricately precise set of kinship relations determined by the metaphysics of blood. The order extended from viscountesses to baron's daughters and wives of barons' eldest sons, from gentlemen of the privy chamber to those who attended duchesses, countesses, and so forth. The list concluded with an order that "no person under the degrees specified shall wear any guard or welt of silk upon any petticoat, cloak or safeguard" (179).

These attempts to regulate aristocratic display were intended to prevent wealth from obscuring kinship rules that maintained the social hierarchy. This political imperative might well have motivated

James I to issue proclamations ordering the nobility out of the city and into the countryside where they were supposed to win popular support by displays of hospitality. Leah S. Marcus has argued that James meant these measures to counter political resistance that was gathering in the city but that also appeared to extend into the countryside in the riots of 1616 when attempts by landlords to fence in common land met with violent resistance.[21] In a speech to the Star Chamber in that same year, James, like Elizabeth before him, represents the city as a place attracting so many people that "all the countrey is gotten into *London*; so as with time, England will onely be *London*, and the whole countrey be left waste."[22] He claimed that wives and daughters, attracted by foreign fashions, forced their husbands and fathers to abandon the country for London where a woman's virtue would inevitably be tarnished. To correct all these abuses, he issued an injunction to "keepe the old fashion of *England*: For it was wont to be the honour and reputation of the English Nobilitie and Gentry, to liue in the countrey, and keepe hospitalitie" (343–4). James, in other words, saw the good country life as a means of maintaining popular support for the crown. With this in mind, he saw to it that the aristocratic practices centered in the country house would represent all that was truly British.

Eighteenth-century conduct books for women therefore contended with two particularly powerful traditions, one having to do with the rules for displaying the aristocratic body and the other having to do with the practice of hospitality in the countryside. These symbolic practices authorized aristocratic power – power based on birth and title alone – whose site was the country manor house. It is reasonable to assume that, in opposing these traditions, female conduct books changed the ideal of what English life ought to be when they replaced the lavish displays of aristocratic life with the frugal and private practices of the modern gentleman. This was no doubt the primary political aim of such writing and the main reason why it suddenly attracted so many authors and readers. But the new representation of English country life itself depended on another rhetorical strategy that denigrated the ornamental body of the aristocrat to exalt the retiring and yet ever vigilant domestic woman. Such a representation would eventually hollow out the material body of the female who challenged the metaphysics of blood so that the body might be filled with a gender-based self, or psychology, but it is my purpose in this essay to show how the conduct books' definition of the desirable woman first enabled a substantial number of competing interest groups to identify their economic interests with the same ideal.

This strategy for deflecting the political opposition between country and city can be isolated in any number of handbooks. *The Compleat Housewife, or Accomplished Gentlewoman's Companion* (1734) promises to give its reader a set of "Directions generally for dressing in the best, most natural, and wholesome Manner, such Provisions as are the Product of our Country, and in such a Manner as is most agreeable to English Palates" (2). How the ideal of a table that was fitting and proper for any size purse in the realm actually served agrarian interests becomes apparent when we consider what kind of food the handbook forbids. In claiming it is "to our Disgrace" that Englishmen have "so fondly admired the French Tongue, French *modes*, and French Messes" (2), the author speaks on behalf of agricultural interests. But it is important that he attack the urban taste for things imported by assaulting the "unwholesome" diet which supposedly caters to aristocratic taste. Restricted to domestic matters, his political commentary avoids raising the opposition between agricultural interests and those of an increasing number who were importing goods for urban markets. A few years later, in 1740, *The Young Ladies Companion or, Beauty's Looking-Glass* similarly lashes out against immoderate household expenditures. Using terms that would have been especially meaningful to ambitious townspeople, this author elaborates the economic disaster that ensues from aping aristocratic standards:

> when usual Presents are made, and an expensive Marriage is solemniz'd, gaudy cloaths and Equipage are bought, and perhaps, a London house furnished, a considerable Part of this Portion will be disburs'd and the forlorn Hero of this shewy, noisy farce, will discover too late how much more eligible it had been to have marry'd a LADY well born, of a discreet, modest, and frugal Education, and an agreeable Person with less Money, than a haughty Dame with all her Quality Airs about her. (113)

Despite regional differences, the author who writes for readers in town and the one who addresses a rural readership agree with each other on the components of the ideal domestic life. Both situate the model household in opposition to the excesses of aristocratic behavior, and both contest the prevailing system of status distinctions in order to insist on a discrete and frugal household with a woman educated in the practices of inconspicuous consumption. They maintain that such behavior is a more accurate indication of good breeding than the traditional distinctions of title or wealth. *The Young Ladies Companion or, Beauty's Looking-Glass* also lays out the economic basis for desiring the woman of "discreet, modest, and frugal Education" over and against one of great fortune who was likely to be a "haughty Dame with all her Quality Airs about her" (115). The woman who brings more wealth to the marriage turns out to be a bad investment in this account. She is described as "the dearest purchase now in England, . . . not excepting the *South-Sea Stock*," the notorious financial corporation whose stock rose in several months time from £100 to £1000 in 1720 and then plummeted several months after that. By way of contrast to the woman who brings a large dowry but requires an ostentatious style of living, this gentleman considers the frugal wife a solid investment. "For every thousand Pound" the wealthier woman brings, he calculates, her needs will multiply accordingly: "she spends more than the interest of it; for besides her private expence, the gay furniture, the rich Beds, China-Ware, Tea-Table, visiting rooms, rich coach, etc. must be chiefly placed to her Account" (115). To this way of thinking, the woman who feels so obliged to display signs of status – in the manner of aristocratic women – will soon prove too expensive to keep.

It is important to note that the qualities of the desirable woman – her discretion, modesty, and frugality – described the objectives of an educational program in terms that spelled out a coherent set of economic policies for the management of the household. The authors of these educational books for women turned the virtues of the new woman into a language resonating with political meaning. These virtues were simultaneously the categories of a pedagogical theory, the form of subjectivity it engendered, the taste that resulted, and the economy that such taste ensured. In arguing for a new set of qualities to desire in a woman, these books therefore made her capable of authorizing a whole new set of economic practices that directly opposed what were therefore supposed to be seen as the excesses of a decadent aristocracy. Under the dominion of such a woman, the country house could no longer authorize a political system that made sumptuary display the ultimate aim of production. Instead, it proposed a world where production was an end in itself rather than a means to such an end.

The frugal domestic economy that these conduct books idealize in their educational program for women was one fueled by interest from investments rather than by labor. It differed in this significant respect from the household represented in the sixteenth- and seventeenth-century Puritan handbooks, as well as from the country ideal preferred by James I. This modern household did not identify the source of one's income with a certain craft, trade, region, or family; its economy depended on money earned on investments. Such money made the household into a self-enclosed world whose means of support were elsewhere, invisible, removed from the scene. The few statements quoted above, like those in the discussion to follow, strongly suggest that the good country life so depicted no longer revealed one's origins or political allegiances. The negation of traditional differences between those at the very top and those at the bottom of the social scale cleared the cultural ground for a class sexuality that valued people according to intrinsic personal qualities. A group of people consequently came to understand themselves as part of an educated élite who, in Harry Payne's words, prided themselves on "gentility, science, innovation . . . and economic realism."[23] Such an ideal representation of the ruling class had the advantage – in theory at least – of making available to many in the middle ranks the good country life that had formerly seemed available only to those of title.

Not only did the pleasures of country life actually crown the success of several generations of English businessmen during the course of the nineteenth century, but also the lesser gentry and prosperous farmers apparently took pains to educate their daughters according to the principles of this conduct-book ideal. By 1825, then, one finds a conduct book modeling the exemplary household on that "of a respectable Country Gentleman, with a young family whose Net Income is from £16 000 to £18 000 a year, and whose expences do not exceed £7000."[24] The author nevertheless described this household in the conventional manner to contrast it sharply with the corrupt and extravagant habits attributed to the old aristocracy. At the same time, one can notice that such criticism of the aristocracy had lost most of its political edge. Sexual differences appear to have become much more important than economic differences in defining an individual's place in the world, and conduct books from the early decades of the nineteenth century had already come to see the country house, not as the center of aristocratic (male) power, but as the perfect realization of the domestic woman's (non-aristocratic) character. During the high Victorian age, this model of middle-class domesticity began to determine the way the aristocracy represented themselves as well. Mark Girouard cites a number of instances that testify to this curious loop in British cultural history:

> In the 1870s Lord and Lady Folkstone chose to be painted singing "Home, Sweet Home" with their eldest son. A portrait of Lord Armstrong, the millionaire arms dealer, shows him reading the newspaper in his dining room inglenook at Cragside, over the fireplace of which is inscribed "East or West, Home is Best." An essential part of the new image cultivated by both new and old families was their domesticity; they were anxious to show that their houses, however grand, were also homes and sheltered a happy family life.[25]

In comparing the domestic ideal as represented in conduct books to its appearance on the English countryside, one discovers a gap of more than a century between these written accounts and their social realization.

I call attention to this discontinuity in order to claim importance for representation itself. I want to suggest that by developing a language strictly for relations within the home, conduct books for women inadvertently provided the terms for rethinking relationships in the political world, for this language enabled authors to articulate both worlds while they appeared to represent only one. To this capability we can probably attribute the persistent sense that the conduct book spoke to male readers even while it addressed itself specifically to women. In so doing, the new domestic ideal succeeded where Defoe's island kingdom had failed. It established a private economy apart from the forms of rivalry and dependency that organized the world of men. The new domestic economy derived power from interest-bearing investments, a form of income that effectively destroyed the old agrarian ideal by effacing the whole system of status signs which lent that ideal its value. At the same time, the new country house harked back to an earlier agrarian world where the household was a largely self-contained social unit. In appearing to be logically prior to ideology in this respect, the new language of the household acquired power akin to that of natural law.

LABOR THAT IS NOT LABOR

Conduct books appear to be as sensitive to the difference between labor and leisure as they are to the tension between town and country or to the line separating the rich from the poor. This distinction was always implicit in the number of idle hours it was assumed a woman had to fill. In figuring out a way to convert this time into an ideal program of education, however, the books took labor and leisure off their separate conceptual planes and placed them in a moral continuum. Here a woman was ranked according to the specifically female virtues she possessed rather than to the value of her family name and social connections. But in order to create such a female system of values in the first place, the conduct books represented the domestic woman in opposition to certain practices attributed to women at both extremes of the social scale. A woman was deficient in female qualities if she, like the aristocratic woman, spent her time in idle amusements. As the conduct books represent them, such activities always aimed at putting the body on display, a carry-over from the Renaissance display of aristocratic power. For a woman to display herself in such a manner was the same as saying that she was supposed to be valued for her body and its adornments, not for the virtues she might possess as a woman and wife. By the same token, the conduct books found the laboring woman unfit for domestic duties because she, too, located value in the material body. Conduct books attacked these two traditional notions of the female body in order to suggest that the female had depths far more valuable than her surface. By implying that the essence of the woman lay inside or underneath her surface, the invention of depths in the self entailed making the material body of the woman appear superficial. The invention of depth also provided the rationale for an educational program designed specifically for women, for these programs strove to subordinate the body to a set of mental processes that guaranteed domesticity.

It is important to observe how the conduct books differentiated the new woman from the woman who served as the means of displaying aristocratic power. As if of one mind, they agreed that any woman's value necessarily depreciated as she took up the practice of self-display. "It is true," remarks one book, "that the mere splendour of wealth and title will at all times attract a circle of admirers, as frivolous and uninformed as many of their possessors." Those who aspire to the fashionable world become "low minded satellites of fashion and greatness." They can never equal those whom they endeavor to mirror, the author continues, but "merely flatter themselves that they deserve a brilliancy and consequence from the more dignified body around which they move."[26] Although it appears to speak from an utterly conservative position, one quite in keeping with the ideology that prompted the royal proclamations of Elizabeth and James, this statement is shaped by a revealing contradiction that allows it to serve a set of interests absolutely opposed to those represented by the aristocratic body of Renaissance culture.

According to the logic of this statement, the genuine person of leisure is worth "more" than women who "merely" flatter themselves by virtue of their proximity to aristocratic power, but this is not the distinction that matters most in the author's system of values. While affording a precise way of differentiating members of the fashionable world, "splendour" and "brilliancy" nevertheless fail to provide a reliable way of assessing women. For the author of this conduct book, women who devote themselves to practical matters are less likely to be "frivolous and uninformed" than women who possess "wealth and title." But even though the practical kind "are infinitely to be preferred to that large class of superficial females whose sole ambition it is to be seen and noticed in the circle of gaiety," any outward and visible signs of value, even those of a practical nature, imply some emotional lack in the woman that significantly lowers her value on the marriage market. There is no doubt in the author's mind that "If a woman were only expert in the use of her needle, and properly skilled in domestic economy," she still would not be prepared to meet her domestic obligations.[27]

Before abandoning this example, we should take note of the fact that its attack on aristocratic conduct is more than an argument for a certain kind of woman or even for a certain kind of household; it is also an argument against the traditional notion of amusement. What happens to amusement reveals the most characteristic – and indeed powerful – rhetorical strategy of the conduct books. First they negate those practices that had been acceptable or even desirable cultural practices, and then they endow those practices with positive value by placing them within the framework of female subjectivity. It is of equal importance that these books overthrow the tradition going back to the proclamations of Elizabeth and James and, by a second inversion, situate subjectivity prior to the display of the body as the cause of unseemly female behavior. Thus we find the proclivity for self-display among certain woman represented as subjectivity gone awry: "Destitute of all *amusements with herself,* and incapable of perceiving her chief happiness to center at home, in the bosom of her family, a lady of this description daily sallies forth in quest of adventures" (italics mine).[28] The conduct books always use women who pursue amusement as examples to demonstrate why women lacking the conduct-book virtues do not make desirable wives. This other woman "is regularly seen in the ballroom or at the card-table, at the opera or in the theatre, among the numberless devotees of dissipation and fashion."[29] That, in a word, is her crime: she either wants to be on display or simply allows herself to be "seen." It is not that the conduct books disapprove of dancing, enjoying music, playing cards, or even attending theatrical performances when they are enjoyed in the sanctuary of one's parlor. This is a difference that both Austen and Burney scrupulously observe along with conduct-book authors. It is a woman's participation in public spectacle that injures her, for as an object of display, she always loses value as a subject. More than that, these books lump the woman of fashion together with "numberless" others who – in the conduct-book's terms – similarly lack the quality of subjectivity that makes a woman desirable. As it constitutes the female subject, then, such writing strips the body of the signs of identity that are essential to displaying female value according to aristocratic rules of kinship.

The production of female subjectivity entails the dismantling of the aristocratic body. In fact, the two must be understood as a single rhetorical move. So powerful was the effect of the critique of aristocratic behavior that by the end of the eighteenth century conduct books addressing words of advice to women of noble descent exhibit curious forms of stress and embarrassment. Written in 1806, Elizabeth Hamilton's *Letters: Addressed to the Daughter of a Nobleman on the Formation of Religious and Moral Principle* cannot assume there is any virtue in one's being a woman of wealth and position. She must take pains to argue such virtue back into being. But even in this she proceeds by defensive strategies as she protests that wealth, beauty, and an élite education do not necessarily cancel out a woman's domestic virtues. On the basis of her familiarity with people of nobility, Mrs Hamilton insists "that the consciousness of high descent, and elevated rank, and splendid fortune, does not necessarily give birth to pride; no, not even where, in addition to these advantages, nature has bestowed the most transcendent talents, and the charm of every personal attraction!"[30] In contrast to the ordinary run of conduct books, furthermore, this one must abandon the logic that links outward signs of humility and domestic value. Instead, the author resorts to metaphor. Poetry is apparently the only way she can imagine to counter a logic that pits the brilliant features of aristocratic beauty against the inconspicuous features associated with domesticity (and a women who wrote poetry could always be accused of indulging in a form of aristocratic display). So thoroughgoing was the condemnation of aristocratic display that Mrs Hamilton feels compelled to devise figures linking surface to depth so that the brilliance of the surface will not imply an underlying emptiness. "Such persons are to society," she explains, "not only the brightest ornament, but the most estimable blessing. Their influence, like that of the sun, extends not merely to the surface; it penetrates into the dark and hidden places of the earth" (108). By suggesting that a woman could have depth as well as surface, Mrs Hamilton argues that a woman could excel in both public and private spheres, that she could be the object of the gaze and still possess the subjective qualities required of a good wife and mother. For all her efforts, however, Mrs Hamilton's metaphors only direct the reader's attention to what could no longer be stated as truth.

It is a curious thing that even though conduct books represented aristocratic behavior as the very antithesis of the domestic woman, they never once exalted labor. They generally found women who worked for their living to be morally bankrupt too. The governess is an obvious case in point. Because her work was restricted to domestic duties, she belonged to the cast of respectable women, and hers was one of the few professions open to women of the gentry who had to support themselves. At the same time, the governess was commonly represented as a threat to the well-being of the household.[31] Whether she was in fact a person of breeding fallen from economic grace or someone of lower rank who hoped to elevate herself through a genteel education, she was marketing her class and education for money. The governess is particularly useful for purposes of my argument because she combines certain features of the aristocracy with those of the working woman. Yet that was clearly not the reason why authors and readers used her for drawing cultural lines. It was by fulfilling the duties of the domestic woman for money that she blurred a distinction on which the very notion of gender appeared to depend. She seemed to call into question an absolutely rigid distinction between domestic duty and labor that was performed for money, a distinction so deeply engraved upon the public mind that the figure of the prostitute could be freely invoked to describe any woman who dared to labor for money. One sweeping condemnation of female servants claimed that "Half the wretched beings of their sex, who live on the deplorable wages of iniquity, for the short time they live at all, are there being discharged out of service to pride."[32] The motivations of any woman who worked out of a desire for money were automatically in doubt, but it must have been particularly disturbing to think of such a woman supervising the young. The governess's transgression of the line distinguishing labor from domestic duty obviously lies behind such common assaults on her character as this: "Nor can we greatly wonder at the false position which governesses hold, when we consider how often they are induced by merely selfish and sordid motives to seek the employment which they ought to engage in only from a conviction of their fitness, mental and moral, for so important a post."[33]

As conduct books differentiated the woman's ideal role from both labor and amusement, they created a new category of labor. One finds that while these books elaborate all of the tasks that can be called domestic duty, they still represent the woman of the house as apparently having nothing to do. Ideally servants would perform most, if not all, of the work specified for maintaining the household. Yet the difference between the excesses that conduct books attributed to county-house life in an aristocratic culture and the domestic economy they envisioned for their readers has everything to do with the presence of the right kind of woman. To solve the enigma of what essential function this woman performed, I must refer back to the distinction between the woman as subject and the woman as the object of display. It is helpful to recall how the domestic woman comes into being as the notion of amusement is redefined within the framework of her subjectivity. In this way, hers appears to be precisely the power to turn behavior into psychological events. More than that, hers is the power to control and evaluate such events. To exercise this power, according to conduct-book logic, requires a passive and retiring woman. In 1798 the notably liberal thinker Erasmus Darwin held forth this kind of woman as the objective of his educational program:

> The female character should possess the mild and retiring virtues rather than the bold and dazzling ones; great eminence in almost anything is sometimes injurious to a young lady; whole temper and disposition should appear to be pliant rather than robust; to be ready to take impressions rather than to be decidedly marked; as great apparent strength of character, however excellent, is liable to alarm both her own and the other sex; and to create admiration rather than affection.[34]

Contrasting attributes shape each sentence, setting the mild-mannered woman of the conduct books against her flashier counterpart, the woman of high social station. Both characterizations are positive, yet one is definitely to be preferred over the other, and in purely semantic terms the domestic woman seems to be the less positive of the two. In other words, this author gives the traditional concept of female beauty its due in order to declare it obsolete. What he calls for is not a woman who attracts the gaze as she did in an earlier culture, but one who fulfills her role by disappearing into the woodwork to watch over the household. Thus Darwin concludes the introduction to his program for female education with this statement:

> Hence if to softness of manners, complacency of countenance, gentle unhurried motion, with a voice clear and yet tender, the charms which enchant all hearts can be superadded internal strength and activity of mind, capable to transact the business or combat the evils of life, with a due sense of moral and religious obligation, all is attained which education can supply; the female character becomes compleat, excites our love and commands our admiration. (4)

In quoting this passage, I simply want to call attention to the shift in diction that locates power in the mental features of the domestic woman where it was stripped away from the body in the preceding passage. So "compleat," this new woman commands "admiration" as well as "love" where before she deserved only "affection." In this comparison between two desirable women, we are witnessing the fact of cultural change from an earlier form of power based on sumptuary display to a modern form that works through the production of subjectivity.

The domestic woman's capacity to supervise was clearly more important than any other factor in determining the victory of this ardently undazzling creature over all her cultural competitors. For this reason, it appears, the peculiar combination of invisibility and vigilance personified in the domestic woman came to represent the principle of domestic economy itself. From *Thoughts in the Form of Maxims Addressed to Young Ladies on their First Establishment in the World* comes the advice, "Do not attempt to destroy his [the male's] innocent pleasures by pretexts of oeconomy; retrench rather your own expences to promote them."[35] The conduct books demonstrate how a woman who sought to enhance her value through forms of self-display would significantly diminish her family's possibilities for happiness, but more than her restraint from such behavior was required in order for the ideal domestic situation to be. The simple absence of domestic virtue would eliminate that possibility too. As one author writes:

> Vain are his [her husband's] labours to accumulate, if she cannot, or will not, expend with discretion. Vain too are his expectations of happiness if economy, order, and regularity, are not to be found at home; and the woman who has no feeling and principle sufficient to regulate her conduct in these concerns, will rarely acquit herself respectable in the more elevated posts of female duty.[36]

If "his" aim is "to accumulate," then "hers" is "to regulate," and on "her conduct in these concerns" depends the success of all "his labours." By implication, female "feeling and principle" increase male earning power by freeing up capital even as it is taken in and consumed by the household. The domestic woman executes her role in the household by regulating her own desire. On her "feeling and principle" depends the economic behavior that alone ensures prosperity. So conceived, self-regulation became a form of labor that was superior to labor. Self-regulation alone gave a woman authority over the field of domestic objects and personnel where her supervision constituted a form of value in its own right and was therefore capable of enhancing the value of other people and things.

ECONOMY THAT IS NOT MONEY

Because it suppressed economic differences, particularly concealing the ever widening gulf between rich and poor, this new form of value made sense to people with widely varying incomes in the old society. Despite its association with wealth and leisure, the country house also carried with it some of the cultural residue of a self-sufficient economy. True to their roots in the domestic economies of an earlier period, conduct books represented such an economy in opposition to one based on money. The conduct books invariably reformulated this opposition as their way of mounting an attack on what they saw as the excesses of a corrupt aristocracy. The recipes comprising the bulk of *The Compleat Housewife or, Accomplished Gentlewoman's Companion* reveal some rather costly ingredients – partridge and venison, for example – that average Englishmen obviously could not afford to enjoy without becoming either gentlemen or poachers. Insisting nonetheless on their suitability "for a frugal as well as for a sumptuous table," the author does not mean to imply that his is a subsistence diet. His intention is that of a reformer: to combat the evils of the dominant standard of good taste. "There are indeed already in the World various books that treat on the Subject and which bear great Names, as Cooks to Kings, Princes, and Noblemen," his preface declares, but "many of them to us are impracticable, others whimsical, others impalatable, unless to depraved Palates" (2). By representing the more privileged table as an object of disgust, such handbooks invest the frugal table with superior value.

Material differences appear to have little to do with determining the quality of life one can enjoy. As *The Compleat Housewife* situates the ideal table in opposition to meals that display wealth and title, it calls attention to qualities of mind observed in the objects under consideration, qualities that include practicality, wholesomeness, steadiness, and concern for health. The frugal table nourishes the social body, just as aristocratic taste corrupts it. Unlike that which enforces hierarchical distinctions, the more moderate standard of living extends to a wide spectrum of individuals within the economy. But if the conduct-book rhetoric did not exclude those at the bottom of the economic ladder from the good life, it never suggested the poor could live life as well as those who had plenty of money. Although relatively few felt compelled to say it in so many words, it was always assumed, as one of the more outspoken authors explains, that "where the blessings of independence and fortune are liberally bestowed, sufficient time may easily be found for all the purposes of mental improvement, without neglecting any of the more important and sacred offices of active virtue."[37] Such virtue evidently belonged to the woman who had neither suffered economic scarcity nor indulged in extravagance. As another conduct book explains, one's wife is much more likely to be frugal "if she has always been used to a good style of living in her father's house."[38] This subordination of money to a higher standard of value distinguished the ideal household from family life both at the top and at the bottom of the social ladder where – in each case – people were known for their profligate spending.

All these examples either suggest or openly state that without the domestic woman the entire domestic framework would collapse. From the beginning, her supervisory presence was a necessary component of its cultural logic. The consistency with which such terms as "modesty," "frugality," "regularity," and "discretion" recur cannot be ignored. The more practical conduct books address quite different local readerships concerning the constitution of the household, the nature of its objects, the number and kinds of its servants, the manner of its table, the style of its occupants' dress, and the conduct of their leisure activities, often down to the smallest detail in one category or another. But by the time the eighteenth century was well underway, the general categories of a domestic domain had been established and linked to qualities in the female. She brought these qualities to the sexual contract. At the same time, they were qualities that became demonstrably hers as she ran the household according to the taste that one acquired through a female education. This is to say the female character and that of the home became one and the same as she translated her husband's income into the objects and personnel comprising his household. Such an exchange at once enacted an economic contract and concealed the particular nature of the transaction because it fulfilled the sexual contract.

It must have been a remarkable moment when this way of representing kinship relations took hold. For the first time in history a view was put forth – admittedly a minority view – that appealed to people from radically different backgrounds, with substantially different incomes, and with positions in different chains of social relations. Any number of people in the middle ranks could thus believe that the same ideal of domestic life was available to them. To imagine this was to imagine an order of political relations that was substantially different from the one in force at that moment of history. To explain why the new mode of political thinking depended on the production of a certain kind of woman, I have chosen *The Compleat Servant*, a handbook from 1825, to demonstrate just how precisely codified – and hence reproducible – the sexual contract had become by the time the new middle classes were beginning to assume cultural ascendancy.

Identifying himself as "a servant who had passed time in the homes of the great," the anonymous author of *The Compleat Servant* shows how the principles of domestic economy might be translated into a precise calculus for the good life that could be extended to people of various incomes. Such is the claim of his preface: "As no relations in society are so numerous and universal as those of Masters and Servants – as those of Household Duties and performers of them – so it is proportionately important that they should be well defined and understood."[39] His idea of how the domestic economy relates to economy *per se* is so precise he can graphically represent the conversion of the one into the other.[40]

Net annual income	Household expense	Servants and equipage	Clothes and extras	Rent and repairs	Reserve
£1 000	333	250	250	125	42
£2 000	666	500	500	250	84
£3 000	1 000	750	750	375	126
...	...	...	...	...	...
£10 000	3 333	2 250	2 500	1 250	420

Most striking is the way in which this graphic representation translates the economic contract into a sexual one. The first column, or amount of income, represents what the male brings to the exchange. Although this way of designating male value distinguishes one individual from another according to the amount of money each brings to the household, it is important to note that the figure of sexual exchange has already translated the vertical organization of the old society into terms that nearly destroy its heterogeneity. As a result, the figure behaves much like any other representation of the social contract; it creates the very differences it proposes to unify. The chart specifies income as an amount rather than as a form of labor, trade, or service in relation to those whom one serves and who in turn serve him. Value is cut free from its source in human labor, and merely quantitative differences replace the qualitative distinctions of status and rank that held together the old society. In this purely relational system, income alone has come to represent the male party of the sexual exchange.

The transformation of male identity is only one half of an exchange between gender-specific systems of value. The chart cited above records two separate semiotic moves that together implicitly transform the whole organization of British society. The first strips the male of his traditional political identity, which was based on privileges of birth and proximity to the crown. The second converts income (the left-hand column) into the categories of the household. If we have to read vertically to gather the information concerning the male, then the chart requires us to read horizontally for the female. Under her supervision, income is taken into the household where it becomes a field of information organized according to the categories of domestic economy. The female operates in this sexual exchange to transform a given quantity of income into a desirable quality of life. Her powers of supervision ensure the income will be distributed according to certain proportions designed to meet certain domestic criteria, no matter what the amount of the husband's income may be. This double translation of one's social value – from a concept of quality based on birth to a quantity of income, which then materializes as a certain quality of domestic life – creates the economic basis for affiliation among competing interest groups. It creates an ideal exchange in which the female alone can perform the necessary economic transformation. Such a representation implies that people with incomes ranging from £1000 to £10 000 per year could share a world of similar proportions and therefore aspire to the same quality of life. There was also the implication that this world was available to those higher (as indeed the author's exemplary gentleman was) as well as lower on the social ladder, provided they chose to observe the categories comprising the economy of the ideal country life.

But *The Compleat Servant* does not leave it at that. It goes on to elaborate each category of objects, services, and personnel down to the microlevel of the individual item and its value in guineas. So even as this model of good country living has near universal applicability, it also makes quite specific recommendations. To demonstrate how representation can be at once so highly generalized and yet specialized for the individual case, I include the following list, which explains how money should be distributed to personnel:[41]

	Guineas
Housekeeper	24
Female Teacher	30
Lady's Maid	20
Head Nurse	20
Second Ditto	10
Nursery Maid	7
Upper House-Maid	15
Under House-Maid	14
Kitchen Maid	14
Upper Laundry Maid	14
Under Ditto	10
Dairy Maid	8
Second Ditto	7
Still Room Maid	9
Scullion	9
A French Man Cook	80
Butler	50
Coachman	28
Footman	24
Under Ditto	20
Grooms	
Nursery Room Boy	
2 Gamekeepers	
2 Gardeners	

Only a very few of the author's possible readers could hope to meet all the expenses on the list. But in order to create the same household on considerably less, he explains, one need only begin at the top of this list, omit the dittos, and consume in proportion to the amount of one's income. Thus we see why he has included basic housekeepers and childcare personnel at the top of the list, while relegating to the bottom, as least necessary, those servants whom only people of privilege can employ. The vertical system of relationships based on the quantity of the man's income is therefore preserved, but this quantitative standard is also inverted as it is enclosed within a female field of information where qualitative values ideally dominate. The author insists that, even so, anyone can observe the correct proportions and, within proportioning categories, the correct exercise of priorities. In his view, only the exercise of these personal qualities – elsewhere known as "discretion," "modesty," "frugality," and "regularity" – could ensure domestic happiness.

This handbook offers an unusually systematic representation – a grammar, really – of what was by that time in history a common language of objects and domestic personnel. It is fair to say that from the mid-eighteenth century on, every female conduct book presupposed such a grammar just by focusing on one or more of its categories. The principle of translation demonstrated in the above-cited text was at work in most conduct books from the beginning of the eighteenth century. By the early nineteenth century when *The Compleat Servant* appeared, then, this principle had transformed the material surface of social life to the point where such a descriptive grammar could be written. It was not that English homes underwent wholesale redecoration. I think it more likely that the texture of the household changed as people started reading it differently, that is, as people began to regard household in the terms of a written representation. At least it is quite plausible that domestic life first became an autonomous text when its objects and personnel, which appeared to have little relation to region and the local labor conditions external to them, achieved identity according to an internal force – a psychological principle – that held them all together. By means of this principle of reading, too, the household ceased to display the value of the man's income and instead took on the innermost human qualities of the woman who regulated the domestic economy.

As a world of objects thus invested with meaning, the household could not be invoked and used arbitrarily any more by authors of fiction than by those who wrote conduct books. Domestic fiction proceeded from the assumption that a similar interpretive mechanism could be put in motion merely by representing these objects in language. Such language would be governed by the very same rule that converted material differences into psychological ones, or male values into female norms. Before Richardson wrote *Pamela*, the feminized household was already a familiar field of information, but it had yet to be written as fiction. By the time Austen's novels appeared, the sophisticated grammar organizing that field evidently had so passed into common knowledge that it could simply be taken for granted. If Austen's writing proceeds with a kind of unprecedented economy and precision, it is at least in part owing to this intertexuality. In her world, one could not only extrapolate a man's net worth from just a few household objects, but also place his wife on a psychological scale. In *Emma*, for example, Frank Churchill's capricious purchase of a piano for Jane Fairfax represents an intrusion of male values into the exclusively female household of her Aunt Miss Bates. The mere appearance of an object that violates the proportions and priorities of such a household is enough to generate scandalous narratives implying that Jane has given in to seduction. Or Augusta Elton's failure to appreciate Emma's modest style of wedding dress – "Very little white satin, very few lace veils; a most pitiful business!"[42] – is sufficient to brand her own taste as hopelessly bound to materialistic values that contradict the metaphysics of domesticity dominating Austen's ideal community.

Later on, Mrs Gaskell extended this code of values into the households of the laboring poor. In *Mary Barton* she describes this scene in order to demonstrate how a woman's devoted application of domestic economy might enhance the value of a man's meager wages:

> In the corner between the window and the fire-side was a cupboard, apparently full of plates and dishes, cups and saucers, and some more nondescript articles, for which one would have fancied their possessors could find no use – such as triangular pieces of glass to save carving knives and forks from dirtying tablecloths.[43]

The Brontës, on the other hand, would carry the same ideal forth into the Yorkshire countryside where the apportionment of space within a house and the objects that fill it always describe the coming into being of this object world and the clash between its values and those of the traditional country house. But Dickens would carry the art of this object language to its logical extreme by creating a totally fetishized world. One need not think only of the junk shops that reappear here and there throughout his fiction. Nor even of Wemmick's castle in *Great Expectations*, which Lévi-Strauss took as his example *par excellence* of bricolage, or a second-hand object language.[44] More important even than these curious set pieces are Dickensian representations of the household inhabited by new money. Here one watches objects enter into a demonic exchange with their owners whereby things acquire human qualities and the people who live in a relationship with such things become as objects regulated by the very things they have endowed with human value. As Dorothy Van Ghent has noted, this particular form of exchange between subject and object permeates the Dickensian world and generates its distinctive character, which is that of a world all of surface where individuals convey the absence of depth.[45] There is, for instance, the well-known passage from *Our Mutual Friend* where Dickens allows a piece of the Podsnap plate to pass for commentary on the people assembled around it:

> Hideous solidity was the characteristic of the Podsnap plate. Everything was made to look as heavy as it could, and to take up as much room as possible. Everything said boastfully, "Here you have as much of me in my ugliness as if I were only lead; but I am so many ounces of precious metal worth so much an ounce; – wouldn't you like to melt me down?" A corpulent straggling epergne, blotched all over as if it had broken out in an eruption rather than been ornamented, delivered this address from an unsightly silver platform in the centre of the table.[46]

One should note that this critique of Podsnappery aims not at those who fulfill the conduct-book code, but at those who use objects to display wealth and power. Dickens's affection for cultural inversion leaves unmolested the whole idea of the household as a purely relational system of objects that includes people among them. The appearance of this world of objects that is free of labor distinguishes the home from the world of work and binds individuals together by forms of affection rather than by any need for economic survival. To construct and preserve this world without labor requires unflagging concern and vigilance, however, and this is where the female ideally figures in. She and not the male, as Dickens proves better than anyone else, should endow things with her docile features of character.

THE POWER OF FEMINIZATION

From the beginning of the eighteenth century conduct books had always presupposed the existence of a gendered self, a self based on the existence of positive female features, rather than on the lack or even the inversion of certain qualities of the male. In writing *The Character of a Good Woman, both in a Single and Married State* (1697), for example, the author Timothy Rogers feels he should defer to a feminine readership on religious matters despite the fact he is speaking as their religious instructor. "To you we are beholden," he says, speaking both as a male and as a member of the clergy, "for the Devotion and Numerousness of our Assemblies, for you are without flattery, generally more serious than Men, and you helpt to make them so."[47] By the end of the eighteenth century, however, such statements of deference not only represented the essential qualities of female nature, but they did so in a way that endowed this representation with the power of behavioral norms. As conduct books transformed the female into the bearer of moral norms and socializer of men, they also changed the qualities once attributed to her nature and turned them into techniques for regulating desire. These techniques aimed at nothing so clearly as producing gender-differentiated forms of economic behavior. Conduct books of the mid-nineteenth century thus completed a circular process that would also change the economic practices considered most natural and desirable in a male.

Written in the United States in 1853, T. S. Arthur's *Advice to Young Ladies on their Duties and Conduct in Life* extends the principle of female virtue into the rationale for a form of economic behavior that became known as the doctrine of enlightened self-interest. This doctrine represented the principle of female education in a way that made it applicable to men as well as to women, as the author's diction implies:

> We are all lovers of ourselves more than lovers of God, and lovers of the world more than lovers of our neighbors; and it is hard for us to conceive how there is any real pleasure to be found in denying our own selfish desires in order to seek the good of another. A very little experience, however, will make us plainly see that the inward delight arising from the consciousness of having done good to another is the sweetest of all delights we have ever known. (13)

This passage first attacks the Christian notion of self-sacrifice on grounds that it violates the facts of human nature over which self-interest holds sway. The Christian ethos is dismissed by the first sentence, however, only to be slipped back in through the second. Once banished, conventional theological doctrine returns in a thoroughly secularized form, as a quality that is considered by the author to be necessary in a woman and that has universal application as well. If conduct books habitually opposed their feminine ethos to aristocratic self-indulgence, then they did so in order to transform man's acquisitive instincts to serve the general good. They did not try to suppress those instincts. Represented as qualities inherent in sexuality, which were then differentiated according to gender, the two forms of desire – acquisitiveness and altruism – posed no contradiction. The sexual exchange converted male acquisitiveness into objects that diffused gratification throughout the household.

The logic of the contract had so thoroughly reorganized sexual relations by the beginning of the nineteenth century that the principle of domestic duty could be extended, then, beyond the middle-class household to form the basis of a general social policy. The reformist platform of Hannah More and her colleagues was founded on this principle. "Even those who admit of the power of female elegance on the manners of men," she argues, "do not always attend to the influence of female principles on their character."[48] If it is given to women to regulate the desires of men, then domestication constitutes a political force of no meager consequence, according to More. As she explains in the opening to her *Strictures on the Modern System of Female Education*,

> The general state of civilized society depends, more than those are aware who are not accustomed to scrutinize into the springs of human action, on the prevailing sentiments and habits of women, and on the nature of the estimation in which they are held. (313)

Dr Gregory similarly assures his many readers, "The power of a fine woman over the hearts of men, of men of the finest parts, is even beyond what she conceives."[49] With a kind of relentlessness, nineteenth-century authors picked up the language that would identify supervisory skills with a woman's sexual appeal. Written in 1822, *The New Female Instructor or, Young Woman's Guide to Domestic Happiness* cites "instances of the ascendancy with which

WOMEN OF SENSE have always gained over men of feeling."[50] Invoking the belief that specific powers adhered to gender, the author promises to elaborate "all those qualities which will enable you to attain the much desired art of pleasing, which will entitle you to the character of a WOMAN OF SENSE, and which will bestow on you all the power of which I have just spoken" (2).

As such writing turned sexual pleasure into a regulatory power, it also endowed the power of surveillance with all the characteristics of a benevolent parent. The new practical curriculum adopted the strategy formulated by conduct-book authors as it set out to produce a self-regulating individual. It would introduce practical mathematics and science into the standard curriculum, to be sure, but throughout the first half of the nineteenth century and well into the second, the educational reformers – reformers of all kinds for that matter – concentrated inordinate energy on controlling the peripheral activities of the individual's leisure rather than on ensuring one's economic survival.[51] Pedagogical concern seemed to fix upon novels, newspapers, and conversation and not upon the seemingly more practical areas of knowledge. Many conduct-book authors seemed to feel a woman's education amounted to little more than instilling good reading habits and cultivating conversational skills. They appeared to feel confident that such an education would establish the basis for her effective management of the home.

This notion of women's work as the regulation of information lies behind a fable included in T. S. Arthur's handbook. It should therefore give us some idea of how the strategies of domestication would be turned into a broad-reaching – and inherently colonial – policy in the United States. The fable states that its purpose is to prove that "No matter how many and great may be the advantages under which a young girl may labor, – she may yet rise, if she will, very much above the point, in external condition, from which she started in life."[52] At the same moment when the popularity of self-help philosophy was peaking,[53] in other words, the conduct books declined to show that a working woman could elevate herself socially through industrious labor. To the contrary, we are told,

> Out of the young girls in the work-room where Ann [the heroine of the fable] learned her trade, all with no better advantages than she had possessed, seven married men of low minds and

vulgar habits, and never rose above their original condition. Two were more like Ann, and they were sought by young men of a better class. One of them did not marry. (76)

To the degree that her desires conform to the conduct-book standard, Ann becomes the exception to the working-class rule; she becomes a woman whom "a better class" of men will desire. As far as this story is concerned, all that is necessary for a woman to rise above her "original condition" is to resist the temptations of idleness and become a kind of conduct book in her own right, a vessel of sexual norms. Having established this as the grounds for her sexual appeal to the male, the tale concludes with a description of the reward Ann earns for so nearly embodying the female standard: "And in proportion as she thus rises will she find a higher degree of happiness and be able to do more good than otherwise would have been possible to her" (76). If by internalizing the conduct-book norms, Ann can marry above her station, then altruism is both the reward for this effort of self-regulation and her obligation as the wife of a prosperous man. The tale concludes, in other words, by exalting a form of labor that is no labor at all, but a form of self-regulation that serves as an end in itself.

This principle would be extrapolated from the household and applied to society at large where it offered a way of displaying aristocratic largesse – or benevolent paternalism, as it is more appropriately called – in relation to those groups who had suffered most from the changes brought about by England's industrialization. The political application of this new idea of labor becomes instantly apparent if one observes how the principle organizing the household was extended outward to provide the liberal rhetoric for representing the relationship between one social group and another. In devising a curriculum for a boarding school run by his two illegitimate daughters, Erasmus Darwin tried to think of a way of installing in women the idea that their work was its own reward. "There should be a plan in schools to promote the habit as well as the principle of benevolence," as he calls it. With this in mind, he suggests that "each lady might occasionally contribute a small sum, on seeing a needy naked child, to purchase flannel or coarse linen for clothes, which they might learn to cut out, and to make up themselves; and thus the practice of industry might be united with that of liberality."[54] In allowing women to produce goods for charity when it was no longer respectable for them to produce goods for their own kin, much less for purposes of trade, the conduct books fostered a certain form of power relations that would flourish later as the welfare institutions of a modern culture developed.

It was their acknowledged aptitude for performing acts of charity that first enabled women to move out of the home and into the political arena. As Martha Vicinus has argued, "The public debate about conditions among the urban poor gave reformers the opening they needed."[55] On the basis of a need for charitable work among these newly impoverished social elements, women began carving out territory for domestic work in the larger social arena. Vicinus offers a particularly telling quote from Frances Power Cobbe, an advocate for celibacy among single women, to illustrate this line of argument:

> The private and home duties of *such women as have them* are, beyond all doubt, their first concern, and one which, when fully met, must often engross all their time and energies. But it is an absurdity, peculiar to the treatment of women, to go on assuming that all of them *have* home duties, and tacitly treating those who have none as if they were wrongly placed on God's earth, and had nothing whatever to do in it. There must needs be a purpose for the lives of single women in the social order of Providence . . . she has *not* fewer duties than others, but more extended and perhaps laborious ones. Not selfishness – gross to a proverb – but self-sacrifice more entire than belongs to the double life of marriage, is the true law of celibacy.   (13–14)

Translating Cobbe's statement into the terms of my essay, one can see the notion of charity was inexorably linked to the female role of household overseer. One can see, too, how the same logic that allowed women to carry the skills they possessed as women into the new world of work would eventually provide the liberal rationale for extending the doctrine of self-regulation and with it, the subtle techniques of domestic surveillance beyond the middle-class home and into the lives of those much lower down on the economic ladder. It was not uncommon for nineteenth-century conduct books to put forth a rather explicit theory of social control, as exemplified in the following statement:

> Take a mind at the lowest possible grade, the little outcast of the streets, abandoned by parents from whom even nature's

humanizing instincts had disappeared, exposed to every influence of evil, and knowing none for good; the first steps to
reclaim, to humanize such a mind, would be to place it in a
moral atmosphere, to cultivate and raise its intelligence, and to
improve its physical condition.[56]

I simply want to take note of how educational theory places all the
stress on psychological rehabilitation. The "physical condition" of
the "little outcast of the streets" comes as something of an after-
thought.

The sexual division of labor may have begun by allowing two
different ways of understanding the social reality to coexist side by
side, rather like the Puritan model of marriage. But the insertion of a
new idea of work into the field of social information would eventually make the sexual division of labor serve as a way of reconceiving
the whole. Because they confined themselves strictly to matters of
domestic economy, the conduct books may seem less noteworthy in
themselves than the other writing characterizing the eighteenth and
nineteenth centuries. But what I have been tracing by circling
backwards and forwards in time across this relatively ignored yet
utterly familiar body of data is the formation of a specialized
language of sexuality. In suppressing chronology, my point has been
to show how this language – by circulating between the psychological and the economic, as well as between the individual and the state
– separated and reconstituted each in relation to the other and so
produced a discourse, a new way of packaging cultural information
that changed the entire surface of social life. Such a change could not
have occurred in a single moment or through the effort of any
particular person, even though some kinds of writing clearly enjoyed
more currency than others during this period of time. More likely,
the change worked through the persistent use of certain terms,
oppositions, or figures until sexual differences acquired the status of
truth and no longer needed to be written as such. Taking on the
power of a metaphysics, then, these categories had the power to
influence not only the way people understood work, but also how
they viewed, and thus experienced desire for, the world of objects.

Despite noticeable changes in the stress and terminology of the
conduct books, which point us outside the household to the vicissitudes of economic life, to social history and the affairs of men, as well
as to the sequence of events that have come to comprise literary

history, I have for the most part regarded these quite different texts as a single voice and continuous discourse. My purpose in doing so has been to show how I think domestic culture actually worked as a principle of continuity that pervaded the social surface to provide a stable conceptual framework within which these "outside" changes appear as so many variations on the sexual theme. Although a female genre, often written by women and directed at female readers, conduct books of the eighteenth and nineteenth centuries – or for that matter, earlier female conduct books – were attuned to the economic interest that they designated as the domain of the male. By virtue of its apparent detachment from the larger economy of which it was an instrumental part, domestic economy provided the fables in terms of which economic relations would also be rethought. Furthermore, as I have argued, sexual relations could shape this new master narrative precisely because its power seemed to be so restricted.

As conduct books rewrote the female subject for an eighteenth-century audience, they shifted the whole strategic intention of the genre from reproducing the status quo – an aristocratic household – to produce an ever retreating future. If it preceded the formation of a coherent set of economic policies associated with capitalism, this reformist rhetoric anticipated even the establishment of marriage as a social institution. The conduct books always saw the domestic world as one that ought to be realized. When passage of the Marriage Act, 1754, institutionalized the household and placed it more firmly under state control than ever before, the sense of its futurity did not vanish for authors and readers of conduct books. With the wild demographic shifts of the late eighteenth century and the violent labor disputes of subsequent decades, the sexual division of labor rapidly became a *fait accompli*, but the conduct books preserved their rhetorical edge of a promise yet to be realized. Even today this promise apparently cannot be distinguished from the form itself. Such handbooks still offer the power of self-transformation. The illusion persists that there is a self independent of the material conditions that have produced it and that such a self can transform itself without transforming the social and economic configuration in opposition to which it is constructed. This transformational power still seems to arise from within the self and to effect upon that self through strategies of self-discipline, the most perfect realization of which is perhaps anorexia nervosa. What we encounter in books of instruction for women, then, is something in the order of Foucault's productive hypothesis that continues to work upon the material body unencumbered by political history because that body is the body of a woman. On grounds that her sexual identity has been suppressed by a class that valued her chiefly for material reasons rather than for herself, the rhetoric of the conduct books produced a subject who in fact had no material body at all. This rhetoric replaced the material body with a metaphysical body made largely of words, albeit words constituting a material form of power in their own right. The modern female body comprised a grammar of subjectivity capable of regulating desire, pleasure, the ordinary care of the body, the conduct of courtship, the division of labor, and the dynamic of family relationships.

As such, the writing of female subjectivity opened a magical space in the culture where ordinary work could find its proper gratification and where the very objects that set men against one another in the competitive marketplace served to bind them together in a community of common domestic values. If the marketplace driven by male labor came to be imagined as a centrifugal force that broke up the vertical chains organizing an earlier notion of society and that scattered individuals willy-nilly across the English landscape, then the household's dynamic was conceived as a centripetal one. The household simultaneously recentered the scattered community at myriad points to form the nuclear family, a social organization with a mother rather than a father as its center. The very fact of its interlocking symmetries suggests that the doubled social world was clearly a myth before it was put into practice, as was indeed the case for almost a century.

NOTES

* This essay is adapted from the second chapter of *Desire and Domestic Fiction: A Political History of the Novel* (1987) New York, Oxford University Press. We would like to thank Oxford University Press for permission to reprint this material.

1 There have been conduct books ever since the Middle Ages. From medieval to modern examples, they almost always imply a readership that desires self-improvement and for whom self-improvement promises an elevation of social position. In addition to the essays in this volume by

The Rise of the Domestic Woman

Kathleen M. Ashley and Ann Rosalind Jones, see also S. M. Hull (1982) *Chaste, Silent and Obedient: English Books for Women 1475–1640*, San Marino, Calif., Huntington Library; R. Kelso (1956, 1978) *The Doctrine for the Lady of the Renaissance*, Urbana, Ill., University of Illinois Press; L. B. Wright (1935) *Middle-Class Culture in Elizabethan England*, Ithaca, NY, Cornell University Press, 121–227; and J. E. Mason (1935) *Gentlefolk in the Making: Studies in the History of English Courtesy Literature and Related Topics from 1531 to 1774*, Philadelphia, Pa., University of Pennsylvania Press. The eighteenth-century conduct book has been discussed by J. Hemlow (1950) "Fanny Burney and the courtesy books," *PMLA*, 65, 732–61; M. Butler (1972) *Maria Edgeworth: A Literary Biography*, Oxford, Clarendon; and M. Poovey (1984) *The Proper Lady Woman Writer: Ideology as Style in the Works of Mary Wollstonecraft, Mary Shelley, and Jane Austen*, Chicago, Ill., University of Chicago Press, 3–47.

2 F. Whigham (1984) *Ambition and Privilege: The Social Tropes of Elizabethan Courtesy Theory*, Berkeley, Calif., University of California Press; J. L. Lievsay (1961) *Stefano Guazzo and the English Renaissance, 1575–1675*, Chapel Hill, NC, University of North Carolina Press; and R. Kelso (1929) *The Doctrine of the English Gentleman in the Sixteenth Century*, Urbana, Ill., University of Illinois Studies in Language and Literature, 14.

3 See, for example, Hull (1982) 31–70.

4 For a discussion of such writing produced by women during the seventeenth century, see P. Crawford (1985) "Women's published writings 1600–1700," in M. Prior (ed.) *Women in English Society 1500–1800*, New York and London, Methuen, 211–81.

5 B. Makin (1673) "An essay to revive the antient education of gentlewomen", cited by Crawford (1985) 229.

6 Hemlow (1950) 732.

7 See Crawford (1985) appendix 2, 265–71.

8 Commenting on a later surge in the publication of conduct books, M. Poovey (1984) claims that "conduct material of all kinds increased in volume and popularity after the 1740s" (15).

9 R. Williams notes that the failure to renew the licensing act in 1695 resulted directly in the growth of the press, in his (1961) *The Long Revolution*, London, Chatto & Windus, 180–1.

10 Mason (1935) 208. *The Whole Duty of a Woman . . . Written by a Lady* (1695) should not be confused with the later *The Whole Duty of Woman* (1753) written by W. Kendrick.

11 H. Perkin (1969) *The Origins of Modern English Society 1780–1880*, London, Routledge & Kegan Paul, 24. Citations of the text are to this edition. Perkin follows a line of argument similar to P. Laslett (1971)

The World We Have Lost: England Before the Industrial Age, 2nd edn, New York, Charles Scribner's, 23–54. R. S. Neal has faulted Perkin and Laslett for offering an historical representation of society that does not reveal the makings of a class conflict, in his (1981) *Class in English History 1680–1850*, Totowa, NJ, Barnes & Noble, 68–99. See as well E. P. Thompson (1978) "Eighteenth-century English society: class struggle without class?", *Social History*, 3, 133–65. Perkin responds to Thompson in "The condescension of posterity: middle-class intellectuals and the history of the working class," in his (1981) *The Structured Crowd: Essays in English Social History*, Sussex, Harvester Press, 168–85. Both Perkin and Laslett rely heavily on the manner in which social relations were represented to formulate histories of those relations. In citing Perkin for certain kinds of information, I am not interested so much in how he says things really were as I am in the representations he uses. I am interested in the struggle among such representations to define a social reality. It is in relation to the data that modern historians consider as history that I position "female" information, which represents, in my opinion, this nascent capitalist thinking.

12 I. Watt (1957) *The Rise of the Novel*, Berkeley, Calif., University of California Press; and R. D. Altick (1957) *The English Common Reader: A Social History of the Mass Reading Public 1800–1900*, Chicago, Ill., University of Chicago Press.

13 T. Rogers (1697) *The Character of a Good Woman, both in a Single and Married State*, London, 3. Citations of the text are to this edition.

14 *The Young Ladies Companion or, Beauty's Looking-Glass* (1740) London. Citations of the text are to this edition.

15 E. Smith (1734) *The Compleat Housewife or, Accomplished Gentlewoman's Companion*, London, 2. Citations of the text are to this edition.

16 T. S. Arthur (1853) *Advice to Young Ladies on their Duties and Conduct in Life*, London, 12. Although this is an American conduct book, its inclusion in the Fawcett Library collection – whose other holdings in this area are British – suggests that it was among the few that were popular in England as well as abroad. It is possible that the more active duties required of New England women at this time were deemed appropriate for English women of the lower-middle classes.

17 T. Broadhurst (1810) *Advice to Young Ladies on the Improvement of the Mind and Conduct of Life*, London, 4–5.

18 J. Donzelot writes that "wealth was produced to provide for the munificence of states. It was their [the aristocracy's] sumptuary activity, the multiplication and refinement of the needs of the central authority, that was conducive to production. Hence wealth was in the manifest power that permitted levies by the state for the benefit of a minority," in

his (1979) *The Policing of Families*, trans. R. Hurley, New York, Pantheon, 13. In this manner, the display of wealth as ornamentation of the body was a sign of social rank that could be read by one and all.

19 For a discussion of the country-house poem, see G. R. Hibbard (1956) "The country-house poem of the seventeenth century," *Journal of the Warburg and Courtauld Institutes*, 19, 159–74; C. Molesworth (1968) "Property and virtue: the genre of the country-house poem in the seventeenth century," *Genre*, 1, 141–57; W. A. McClung (1977) *The Country House in English Renaissance Poetry*, Berkeley, Calif., University of California Press; D. E. Wayne (1984) *Penshurst: The Semiotics of Place and the Poetics of History*, Madison, Wis., University of Wisconsin Press; and V. C. Kinny (1985) *The Country-House Ethos in English Literature 1688–1750: Themes of Personal Retreat and National Expansion*, Sussex, Harvester Press. D. E. Wayne argues that it is nostalgia for the ideals of the old but now vanished aristocracy that the new country house was always supposed to summon up; even today the surviving country homes retain, in his words, "a vestige" of "the theater for the enactment of a certain concept of 'home'" (11).

20 P. L. Hughes and J. F. Larkin (eds) (1969) *Tudor Royal Proclamations, The Later Tudors: 1588–1603*, vol. III, New Haven, Conn., Yale University Press, 175. Citations of the text are to this edition.

21 L. S. Marcus (1978) "'Present occasions' and the shaping of Ben Jonson's masques," *ELH*, 45, 201–25.

22 C. H. McIlwain (ed.) (1918) *The Political Works of James I*, Cambridge, Mass., Harvard University Press, 343. Citations of the text are to this edition.

23 H. Payne (1979) "Elite *vs* popular mentality in the eighteenth century," *Studies in Eighteenth Century Culture*, 8, 110.

24 *The Compleat Servant, Being a Practical Guide to the Peculiar Duties and Business of all Descriptions of Servants* (1825) London, 4.

25 M. Girouard (1978) *Life in the English Country House: A Social and Architectural History*, New Haven, Conn., Yale University Press, 270.

26 Broadhurst (1810) 8.

27 ibid. 12–13.

28 ibid. 18.

29 ibid.

30 E. Hamilton (1806) *Letters: Addressed to the Daughter of a Nobleman on the Formation of Religious and Moral Principle*, London, 109. Citations to the text are to this edition.

31 On this point, see M. J. Peterson (1972) "The Victorian governess: status incongruence in family and society," in M. Vicinus (ed.) *Suffer and Be Still: Women in the Victorian Age*, Bloomington, Ind., Indiana University Press, 3–19.

32 *The Young Woman's Companion (Being a Guide to Every Acquirement Essential in Forming the Character of Female Servants, Containing Moral and Religious Letters, Essays and Tales, also Valuable Receipts and Directions, Relating to Domestic Economy)* (1830) London, 32.

33 Mrs Pullan (1861) *Maternal Counsels to a Daughter: Designed to Aid Her in the Care of Her Health, Improvement of Her Mind, and Cultivation of Her Heart* London, 227.

34 E. Darwin (1798) *A Plan for the Conduct of Female Education in Boarding Schools*, Dublin, 3. Citations to the text are to this edition.

35 The Countess Dowager of Carlisle (1789) *Thoughts in the Form of Maxims Addressed to Young Ladies on their First Establishment in the World*, London, 4.

36 Mrs Taylor (1818) *Practical Hints to Young Females on the Duties of a Wife, a Mother, and a Mistress to a Family*, London, 18.

37 Broadhurst (1810) 5.

38 T. S. Arthur (1853) 191.

39 *The Compleat Servant* (1825) 1.

40 ibid. 4.

41 ibid. 270.

42 J. Austen, *Emma*, ed. S. M. Parrish (1972) New York, W. W. Norton, 335.

43 E. Gaskell, *Mary Barton, A Tale of Manchester Life*, ed. S. Gill (1970) Harmondsworth, Penguin, 49.

44 C. Lévi-Strauss (1973) *The Savage Mind*, Chicago, Ill., University of Chicago Press, 150.

45 D. Van Ghent, for example, writes: "This general principle of reciprocal changes, by which things have become as it were daemonically animated and people have been reduced to thing-like characteristics – as if, by a law of conservation of energy, the humanity of which people have become incapable had leaked out into the external environment – may work symbolically in the association of some object with a person so that the object assumes his essence and his meaning. . . . This device of association is a familiar one in fiction; what distinguishes Dickens's use of it is the associated object acts not merely to *illustrate* a person's qualities symbolically – as novelists usually use it – but that it has a necessary metaphysical function in Dickens's universe: in this universe objects actually usurp human essences; beginning as fetishes, they tend to – and sometimes quite literally do – devour and take over the powers of the fetish worshipper," in her (1961) *The English Novel: Form and Function*, New York, Harper & Row, 130–1.

46 C. Dickens, *Our Mutual Friend*, ed. M. Engel (1960) New York, Random House, 136.

47 Rogers (1697) 3.

48 H. More (1848) *Strictures on the Modern System of Female Education, The Works of Hannah More*, vol. I, New York, 313.

49 Dr J. Gregory (1808) *A Father's Legacy to his Daughters*, London, 47.

50 *The New Female Instructor or, Young Woman's Guide to Domestic Happiness* (1822) London, 2.

51 I am indebted on this point to T. Laqueur's discussion of the Sunday schools as an instrument of social control by virtue of their ability to appropriate leisure time, in his (1976) *Religion and Respectability: Sunday Schools and Working Class Culture 1780–1850*, New Haven, Conn., Yale University Press, 227–39. For a different account of the use of leisure time in the nineteenth century, see H. Cunningham (1980) *Leisure in the Industrial Revolution, 1780–1880*, New York, Croom Helm.

52 Arthur, 76.

53 Concerning the popularity of Samuel Smiles' *Self-Help* (1859), a book that represented self-regulation as the key to success in the business world, historian Asa Briggs notes that 20,000 copies were sold within a year of its first appearance, in his (1959) *The Age of Improvement 1783–1867*, London, Longman, 431.

54 Darwin (1798) 63.

55 M. Vicinus (1985) *Independent Women: Work and Community for Single Women 1850–1920*, Chicago, Ill., University of Chicago Press, 15. Citations to the text are to this edition.

56 Madam de Walend (1847) *Practical Hints on the Moral, Mental and Physical Training of Girls at School*, London, 64.

5

Educating women: Laclos and the
conduct of sexuality

THOMAS M. KAVANAGH

C'était toujours le mensonge, mais on n'adorait pas son semblable. On le *trompait*, mais on *se trompait* moins soi-même. (Baudelaire)

Taken from Baudelaire's long-planned but never completed study of *Les Liaisons dangereuses*,[1] the above statement represents his answer to the provocative question of "Comment on faisait l'amour sous l'ancien régime." Baudelaire's two sentences elegantly underline the way Laclos's novel presupposes almost mathematical proportions between, on the one hand, *lies* and *esteem*, and, on the other, *deceiving others* and *deceiving oneself*. More importantly, the whole of Baudelaire's observation, from its opening statement of the question to his final resolution, concentrates our attention on the role within this novel of the generalized, unspecified, supra-individual *on* appearing here as the unique subject of his sentences. *On*: one, people, they, society in general. Grammatically singular, yet semantically plural, the all-encompassing and distinctly socialized register of the *on* is a force primordial to the functioning of this novel.

Les Liaisons dangereuses is an epistolary novel. Each of its 175 letters is written and signed by a specific character. All of these voices, however, speak as they do with an acute awareness that their intelligibility depends on a far more generalized, impersonal, and society-wide voice of *opinion, reputation,* and *judgment* in terms of which their individual statements must define themselves. Valmont and Merteuil are among the most singular, the most resolutely and even painstakingly individualistic characters to be found within the eighteenth-century French novel. At the same time, however, it is difficult to conceive of two characters who depend more completely for their identities upon the society against which they set out to so singularly define themselves. Valmont and Merteuil may violate, with a cynicism and method rarely seen before or since, the mores of their society. At no point do they set out to overturn the reign of convention within their world. To do so would place them in the predicament of the proverbial dove which, lamenting the air's resistance, wished to fly in a vacuum.

Just as it is within a novel portraying the devious exploits of the *picaro* that we find the most realistic representation of the conventions marking the *picaro* as *picaro*, so also it is to a novel like *Les Liaisons dangereuses* that we might look for the most explicit representation of those conventions regulating sexual conduct against which its major characters seek to define themselves. It is logical, then, that the analysis of Laclos's novel has enjoyed a privileged position in those readings which posit an opposition of gender roles, of men and women locked in predetermined dramas of desire, as the organizing paradigm of eighteenth-century fiction. If, as these critics would have it, there is a definable literary femininity which is both produced by and sustains the conventions governing sexual conduct, we should certainly find it at work in this novel. No other text of that period presents its readers with characters (Valmont and Merteuil) who are more completely engaged in a constant and self-conscious attempt to define themselves ironically against the repertory of gender identifications operating within their society.

   In its most ambitious form, one kind of gendered reading argues that a novel can have meaning, can become *significant* for its audience, only when it presents situations obeying the semantic constraints traced out by the all-important opposition between a triumphant virility and a victimized femininity:

According to the ideological matrix out of which the novel arises – the preformed text the novel reproduces – the sign of a positive male character (in terms of gender-specific traits) *assumes* the dynamic exercise of sexuality. Virility must triumph. . . . The sign of a sym-pathetic female character pre-supposes, on the contrary, sexual inactivity (integrity). And since the pertinence of any sign depends upon a context of opposition, meaning (in this limited sense) is generated only when polarization occurs. In other words, if a *significant* drama is to be created, (positive) *femininity* must be challenged; innocence must be threatened. Hence the crucial importance of the sexual encounter and its consistent exploitation of the feminine.[2]

This combat of active and passive within an ever repeated allegory of seduction can, for the female character, result in only one outcome: suffering, victimage, and immolation. Given these conventions, the eighteenth-century novel must portray *all* female desire expressed outside the paternally regulated exchange of marriage as a movement toward dishonor and death.

The problems posed by *Les Liaisons dangereuses* for this kind of reading are obvious. While the Présidente de Tourvel and her destruction by Valmont might be seen as confirming the operative status of such a model, the novel's primary female character, the Marquise de Merteuil, acts in ways which are obviously asymptotic to that model. Might she not, we are forced to ask ourselves, represent Laclos's attempt to imply that the "gender polarization" is itself a function of other forces, of specifically *political* structures which extend beyond the sexual as such, and which use its polarities much as they do any number of other demarcational oppositions? Merteuil is a woman, yet Merteuil is able to act outside the conventions dictating the woman's conduct. Through the figure of Merteuil, the unwomanly woman, Laclos questions this polarization of gender and, with it, our understanding of the contrastive terms, male and female.

The anthropological seriousness of Laclos's concern with the question of woman, its presence as one of the organizing principles of his fiction, is confirmed in a series of texts he wrote beginning in March of 1783, one year after the publication of his novel. Although grouped together in the Pléiade edition under the collective title of "De l'éducation des femmes," that designation is clearly a misnomer.[3] The first and shortest of these texts is a three-page introduction to an essay he intended to write for the Academy of Chalons-sur-Marne's *concours* on the subject of "What are the best ways to perfect the education of women?" Laclos begins his remarks by denouncing the question as an absurdity. It is logically impossible, he contends, to perfect something which cannot exist: "Wherever there is slavery, there can be no education. In every society women are slaves. Therefore socialized woman can in no sense be educated" (405). The brash simplicity of Laclos's syllogism attacks the very posing of such a question as an exercise in mystification. Pushing this position as far as it will go, he breaks off his text with the observation that "without freedom there can be no morality, and without morality there can be no education" (405).

The second of Laclos's texts, by far the most articulated and the most pertinent to an understanding of his novel, might be described as a contrastive analysis of woman as she once existed within the state of nature and of woman as she now exists within society. Laclos here sets out to depict, first, how "natural woman" must have lived and, second, how she has degenerated to her present condition within society. Laclos's goal in this essay can justifiably be described as an attempt to provide for women the same kind of integrative historical synthesis which Rousseau elaborated for mankind as a whole in his *Discourse on the Origin of Inequality* of 1755.

Natural woman, like Rousseau's natural man, exists in a state of total independence. Able to fulfill her needs for food and shelter without anyone else's help, she lives in a state of isolation excluding all reliance on other human beings. Laclos's portrayal of woman within the natural state differs most markedly from Rousseau's by reason of the prominence he gives to her first sexualized encounters with man. In his chapter entitled "On puberty," Laclos offers an extended portrait of the natural adolescent as she becomes aware of her desire as a need equivalent to biological instinct:

Already her form is more rounded, her bosom larger. Her generative parts tighten and cover themselves with a budding down. Many times before our young woman has, on a hunting expedition or some other outing, been in the company of men without inspiring or experiencing any particular feelings. A new occasion brings her once again into their company. Scarcely has she touched one of their hands when a sweet trembling spreads throughout her body. She pulls back her hand involuntarily; she blushes – not from shame, but from perplexity. She desires, but fears to approach. . . . Her head grows heavy; signs of fullness appear in her breasts and in the other parts of her body concerned with generation. This state continues until her first menstrual flow brings her relief as it prepares the laboratory of nature. . . . Her discomforts disappear, but in their place comes a devouring fire which only pleasure will extinguish. . . . Her short and heavy breathing, the precipitous movement of her breast – everything betrays the troubles of her soul. Then, in the distance, her eyes come upon a man. A powerful instinct of involuntary movement forces her to run toward him. Approaching, she grows timid. She stops. Carried forward again, she joins him and grasps him in her arms. . . . Delicious pleasures! [*jouissances*] Who would dare to describe you! (414–15)

Experiencing her desire as a force over which she exercises little control, Laclos's natural woman nonetheless lives her newly awakened sexuality as a need whose fulfillment poses no threat to her independence. Once having satisfied herself with the male she has grasped in her arms, she leaves him and regains her solitary, self-sufficient status: "The natural woman retains full possession of those three benefits whose privation is the source of all our modern woes: freedom, strength, and health" (416). Insisting that the natural woman lived her sexuality as an experience of the most complete pleasure, Laclos anticipates his reader's objection that, since these pleasures exclude all continuity, they are nothing more than a "*jouissance sans amour.*" Cautioning his reader that any such reference to "love" brings with it all the vitiating evils of a mystified sexuality, Laclos points out that the one truly positive aspect of "love," its modulated progression from lesser to greater intensities of feeling, was indeed a part of the natural woman's experience:

Certainly there can be no sustained passion between two people who have come together for the first time and who will shortly forget each other. But this moment itself is not indivisible and, if we examine it closely, we discover within it all the different nuances of feeling. The couple's first caresses take the place of a declaration. The woman will then by turn draw back and provoke. Desire intensifies. Soon at its height, it gives birth to a rapture which expresses itself not in elegant phrases, but in the humid glances and burning sighs which are part of every language. Both know this language well enough to take their pleasure in perfect concert. What perhaps most distinguishes this couple from ourselves is that they leave each other without disgust. . . . Sincere women, I ask you: is there even one among you who has known a pleasure which is so constantly without fear, without jealousy, without remorse, and without the wearisome burdens of duty and uniformity? (417)

As Laclos's closing question to his reader shows, his portrait of natural woman is, like that of Rousseau's natural man, an indictment of the insipid substitutes through which his contemporaries live their own desire.

It is not long after her apprenticeship to this beatific sexuality that the natural woman conceives and gives birth to a child. In describing the way natural woman's life will be affected by this event, Laclos is careful to preserve her status as an independent and solitary being. She has long since, as we saw, forgotten the father. Mother and child, on the other hand, will remain together only so long as the infant is incapable of fending for itself. Self-sufficiency for the child comes, Laclos insists, no later than the age of three or four: that one-thirtieth of a species' normal lifespan which is everywhere observed by nature. At this point, as Laclos sees it, mother and child mutually choose to go their separate ways. The mother no longer feels a physiological need to nurse the child with her milk; the infant is anxious to free itself from the mother and surrender to the tutelage of a beneficent nature. By the age of four the natural child's existence has taken the form of a self-sufficient dialectic of movement, appetite, and sleep which nature will reward and consolidate:

Movement gives birth to appetite, appetite in turn leads to movement, and both of these, once they are satisfied, bring on sleep. . . . Each day the child learns a new lesson from nature; each prey he pursues is a subject of study, each of his meals a reward for his skill or his reflection. (410–12)

It is important to note that in so defining woman's natural sexuality, in limiting the mother–child relationship and in excluding the father from any participation in it, Laclos is setting the foundation for what is perhaps the most subversive premise of his anthropology. Laclos is in effect refusing any "natural" status to the family unit as a form of human conviviality preceding mankind's socialization. The family cannot, in other words, be seen as the natural building block from which a given society will construct itself. This implies that the specifically sexualized relation of male with female will not be a *given* of the socialization process, a *status quo ante* from which and in terms of which more complex structures will develop. Instead, the very possibility of a continuing male–female relation will be the first and determining *problematic* which any nascent social order will have to address and resolve. The enduring union of male and female is not, for Laclos, part of a scenario determined by the male's drive toward patriarchy. To the contrary, it is the conflict of male and female as equally free and independent beings which represents the first and structuring problematic of any society which would survive beyond the existence of its constituent members.

Having thus redefined the starting-point of nature, it remains for Laclos to explain how woman's situation has passed from one of freedom, strength and independence to one of indisputable vassalage. Proclaiming as a universal law that "Nature creates only free beings, society creates tyrants and slaves" (433), Laclos insists that it is the coercive *contract* at the basis of every society which incites each member of that society to sweeten his servitude by intensifying that of those weaker than himself. Laclos enunciates here a law which he sees as applying to all individuals within society regardless of their sex: "If the oppression of the weak by the strong is not a natural law in the sense moral philosophers give to that term, it is nonetheless a law of nature – or rather it is the first vengeance violated nature takes on socialized man" (433). No matter how eloquent the lip-service paid to such ideals as mutual protection and respect, "every convention entered into by two subjects of unequal strength will produce, and can only produce, a tyrant and a slave" (433).

At this point in his argument Laclos introduces what he sees as the biological fact of woman's lesser physical strength in relation to man's. This implies that, whenever women become part of a society, they quickly find themselves enslaved. The first societies were, for Laclos, exclusively masculine: groupings of single men who, because they are more or less equal in strength, were able to overcome an innate fear of their fellows. These men, however, "soon felt a need for women, and set out either to force or to persuade them to join their union" (434). It is at this point, because of the men's attempt to satisfy their sexualized desires, that woman's fate will be decided: "Be it by force or by persuasion, the first woman who gave in to them forged the chains for her entire sex" (434). After a first stage during which women were held in common by the group [*toutes étaient à tous*], Laclos sees the greater physical strength of the men as a force allowing them to heap upon their weaker female counterparts all work and drudgery. This state of affairs in turn initiates a general debasement of women's status to the point where men find themselves tempted to apply to these women the newly discovered and eminently seductive notion of "property" which they first developed in relation to their lands and chattel. Weaker and therefore vulnerable, women could only acquiesce. Laclos confirms his description of these early stages of society's development through a long list of references to the way women are treated in such primitive societies as those of the Lapps, the Koreans, the Lebanese, and the Hottentots. Drawn from the immensely popular travel literature of his period, each of these groups provide Laclos with examples of a common contempt for and enslavement of women within those societies considered as remaining closest to their origins.

At this point in his essay Laclos carries out a radical shift in the nature and intent of his argument. Still in the chapter entitled "Concerning the first effects of society," Laclos's focus moves away from an anthropological consideration of origins to an almost pedagogic reflection on the precise lessons contemporary women might draw from an understanding of their disadvantaged position within society's organized oppression of the weak by the strong. Having completed his inventory of primitive societies, Laclos must now close the gap between those far away lands and the France to which he writes. Yes, here, like there, women are "slaves" to their male "tyrants." Yet, it is clear, their actual condition has taken on quite different appearances. How is it, the question becomes, that from their starting-point as tribal drudges women have, here and now, produced obvious exceptions to a tyranny of the strong over the weak based only on sexual identity? "Oppression and contempt were, therefore, and must generally have been the lot of women in newly formed societies. This state continued in all its force until the experience of many centuries had taught women to substitute skill [*adresse*] for force" (435).

It is this axial substitution of skill for force, the saving jujitsu with which objectively weaker women have turned the greater strength of their male oppressors against them, which will allow Laclos to devote the rest of his essay to a series of practical counsels quite outside any inspiration drawn from a Rousseauian concern with the lessons of nature. "Women at last sensed that, since they were weaker, their only recourse was to seduce. They learned that, if force dictated their dependence on men, pleasure might dictate man's dependence on them" (435). Compelled by exploitation to develop their powers of thought and reflection long before men, women meditated upon the universal truth that "The pleasure we experience is always less than the idea we had formed of it. Imagination always surpasses nature" (435). Pondering this inevitable surplus of desire's promise over possession's fulfillment, the physically weaker women came to see that, in addition to the law of force, there is a second law: a law dictated by those pleasures men will imagine yet never attain. Whoever, the reflective women concluded, can control the power of the imagination will likewise control all the force that might be placed in its service.

What is most fascinating about Laclos's treatment of these questions is the way he draws from his portrait of the enslaved woman discovering the power of the imagination a series of practical counsels, almost a conduct book, concerning the way in which women might suspend the rule of force which has enslaved them. By such practices as "veiling their charms so as to excite curiosity," and "refusing men even when they wish to yield," women can "learn to ignite man's imaginations, to foster and direct his desires" (436). It is thanks to the exercise of these feminine skills that there will be generated the eminently imaginary concepts of "beauty" and "love" – concepts which, Laclos insists, will allow women to redefine the oppression to which they are otherwise condemned: "In the state of perpetual war between the sexes, women have, thanks to the caresses they invented, been able to resist valiantly, sometimes to triumph, and often, for the most skilled, to gain an advantage from the very forces directed against them" (436).[4]

Having so abruptly shifted the concerns of his essay from the anthropological to the strategic, Laclos devotes his closing chapters to a detailed consideration of the two most important tactics with which women may reverse the rule of force: the tactics of "beauty" and "ornament" (*parure*).

Understanding beauty and how men perceive it is, Laclos argues, essential for any woman living in our post-lapsarian, socialized world. Yet this is no easy task. Beauty is, even the slightest reflection tells us, a relative value which changes with every society and every individual. The woman whom a Frenchman or an Englishman finds beautiful will not be so for an American Indian or an Oriental. Is it possible, in spite of this diversity, to arrive at a general definition of beauty, one applicable to all societies and all individuals? Yes, Laclos responds, beauty is, no matter where it exists, "that appearance which is most favorable to sexual pleasure [*jouissance*], that way of being which leads the beholder to hope for the most delicious sexual pleasure" (437). While this physical semiology of promised pleasure may have been unambiguous in an age when women went naked and their entire bodies were visible to the male's eye, modern customs have produced a very different situation: "When women began to clothe themselves, imagination was obliged to supplement what the eye could no longer see. And imagination is easily seduced. Curiosity awakens desire, and desire always embellishes its object. . . . Men grew accustomed to desiring before they knew . . . and illusion was born everywhere" (439). Since clothes and corsets can give the body an appearance different from its reality, those still uncovered parts, primarily the face, take on an immense importance in this quest of an imaginary pleasure. The face becomes the one veridical space in terms of which the male might imagine the quality of sexual pleasure promised by the body as a whole.

The perception of beauty consists, however, in a reading of signs whose meanings are redefined by the specific values of the society in which they appear. The displacement of fleeting sexual encounters by marriage led to a second semiology of beauty, a semiology of moral as opposed to physical values. Each nation, Laclos points out, valorizes certain moral traits in the women it privileges as partners. This brings with it quite different ways of reading the same facial signs. The ancient Romans looked to the faces of their women for signs of an enthusiasm for liberty, a greatness of soul, and a severity of virtue. The Swiss and the English prefer a beauty tempered with mildness and reserve. The French seek out an expression of vivacity and pleasure.

This perception of beauty, be it physical or moral, is, it must be emphasized, always dependent upon an act of the imagination. To behold beauty is to read a limited field of signs and to deduce from the visible part an as yet unseen whole. The signs of beauty are therefore subject to simulation, to adornment, to *parure*. It is in the so entitled closing chapter of his essay that Laclos offers his most coherently developed series of practical counsels as to how women might best exploit the art "not only of profiting from the gifts of nature, but of lending to them those charms of imagination . . . which make them a stimulant to *volupté*" (444). Laclos's suggestions are numerous: never confuse dressing sumptuously with dressing well; follow a careful diet to preserve an appearance of freshness; avoid excesses of alcohol and sun, both of which destroy the complexion. Women must also understand, Laclos cautions, that their feelings and emotions will always inscribe themselves on their faces:

> If you do not restrain too frequent movements of anger, your muscles will acquire a dangerous mobility and soon your every expression will be a grimace. . . . Beware, too, of a fury for pleasure and the fatigue which follows it. Your tired eyes, your crushed lips, your irritated cheeks will never inspire desires you yourself are clearly in no condition to share. (446)

These counsels relative to *parure* concern not only the face as it mirrors the soul, but also the various artifices through which women may manipulate the messages their faces address to the beholder's imagination of the hidden body. Within this category of adornments there lurks, however, a real danger: that of fabricating a facial sign too radically removed from the reality of the body. To indulge oneself in such extreme breaks between signifier and signified is to practice a baroque illusionism which can lead only to disappointment. The intelligent woman never confuses the function of the part with that of the whole: "The face attracts, but the body holds. The first is the net, the second the cage. The prudent fowler sees to keeping the catch before setting her traps" (447).

What is most surprising about Laclos's essays on women is that, in spite of his Rousseauian starting-point in a portrait of natural freedom, he recognizes woman's socialized status as an incontrovertible fact. Her enslavement may be the arbitrary product of a past history, it nonetheless functions as an inevitable starting-point for any understanding of her present. Woman's condition within society is not a tragedy to be lamented, but an ongoing drama whose resolution is subject to both rectification and remedy. Whereas the Rousseau of the *Discourse on the Origin of Inequality* remains entirely within a paralyzed denunciation of the evils the human race has wrought upon itself, Laclos suggests a series of precise strategies through which women may reverse the tyranny of their male masters. The difference between these two positions is clearest in their respective treatments of "imagination." For Laclos, imagination is, as we have seen, an illusory prolongation of desire which women are able to solicit and direct within the consciousness of the male. Rooted in an inevitable surplus of desire over fulfillment, it opens up a space of manipulation potentially reversing the positions of tyrant and slave. For Rousseau, on the other hand, recourse to the imagination can, from the point of view of nature, only be a prelude to monstrosity and depravation: "So many speak of love, yet so few know how to love. Most take for its pure and sweet laws the vile maximes of an abject commerce. Soon repleted with itself, such love has recourse to monsters of imagination which deprave it to sustain it."[5]

Laclos's essays can be read as a conduct book because of what Emile Dard has aptly described as their abrupt transition from "pure reason" to "practical reason."[6] Laclos's counsels to women are based on his accepting as biological fact both a relation of mutual desire between the sexes and the lesser physical force of woman as compared to men. These two "facts" constitute what he sees as the natural foundation of sexual distinction. They determine the ways in which sexualized men and women are both similar (in being linked by reciprocal desire) and different (in that women are less strong than men). Laclos's real intent is to show how the reality of *sexual* difference (stronger and weaker) has been transformed, under the pressures of a specific social order, into a very different *political* difference (tyrants and slaves). Laclos, in other words, is offering his female readers an understanding not so much of their sexuality as of those arbitrary social designations which attempt to naturalize themselves through a fallacious equivalence to the reality of sexual difference.

This distinction is crucial. Rather than pointing to a "polarization of gender" which, it follows, would be as immutable as gender itself, Laclos asks his readers to look to those strategies of force which have perverted and extended the gender polarization of male/female into the political polarization of tyrant/slave. To the male's strategy of force, Laclos insists, the female is perfectly capable of opposing a strategy of imagination: an adroit manipulation of desire's surplus able to counter-balance and even reverse the gender-based domination implied by the first.

Laclos speaks to his reader not of the sexual, but of the political. And, like everything political, it is subject to change, compensation, and reversal. Yes, the male has greater physical strength than the female. Historically, he has used this to effect his tyranny over her. Yes, too, however, the female is the potential mistress of an imagination capable of exploiting the force of the male's desire in such a way that his tyranny be held in check if not eliminated. Everything, it would seem, is a question of strategy rather than sexuality. Both male and female are armed for the battle. The fact that these arms are different in no way dictates the result of the conflict. Gender determines strategy, not outcome.

Once Laclos's position within these essays has been understood, we can return to his novel and consider the implications these texts hold for its interpretation. Earlier in this study I pointed out how by positing a strict "polarization of gender" as the guiding paradigm of the eighteenth-century novel, one would be led to argue that it is the sincerely enamoured Madame de Tourvel who functions as the prototypical woman within Laclos's universe. Madame de Merteuil, on the other hand, becomes a grotesque illustration of the horrible fate awaiting any woman who would claim for herself the prerogatives of the male. Merteuil, by daring to desire, has violated that fundamental grammatical rule of sexuality dictating that women may be the object, but never the subject of desire. Merteuil's punishment for so grievous a transgression involves her expulsion not only from the society of letter writers, but also from all meaning and significance within the novel: "Disfigured, dispossessed and displaced," Nancy Miller claims, "the punishment fits the enormity of the crime: alienation is complete. Merteuil is ejected/rejected outside the community of value, hence meaning."[7]

No matter how we look at it, this is a strange way to interpret the novel's ending. On the most literal level, an impoverished Merteuil may well have left Paris for Holland with a bad case of smallpox, but this is hardly so definitive a punishment as Valmont's death at the hands of Danceny, as Danceny's exile to Malta, or as Cécile's entombment within the convent. Madame de Volanges's fastidious condemnation of Merteuil in the novel's closing letter makes it clear that Merteuil has been unmasked, but it can hardly be seen as annulling the very different effect of the 174 letters preceding it. In his April 1782 issue of the *Correspondance littéraire* Grimm offers an indication as to how the contemporary reading public evaluated Merteuil's place within this novel:

> As sublime as he [Valmont] may be in his genre, that character is still only a subordinate to the Marquise de Merteuil who inspires him, guides him, surpasses him in every way, and who joins to so many other talents that of conserving her reputation as the most virtuous and respectable woman in the world.[8]

As to the importance of virtue's eventual triumph, Grimm cautions that: "All the circumstances of this rather abruptly imposed ending take up scarcely four or five pages. In all conscience, can we presume that this is enough morality to destroy the poison secreted by four volumes of seduction?" (700).

For many who read this novel through the prism of gender, Merteuil's sin is to have attempted to change sexes, to become a man, and in so doing to have become a monster.

The question of sexual roles, and the penalties for stepping outside them, has long been a favorite theme of Laclos criticism.[9] In terms of his essays, we recall, Laclos's definition of the respective sexual strategies was clear: while men may be predisposed to rule by reason of their greater physical strength, women can reverse this imperium through a manipulation of the male's imagination. In light of this, it becomes clear that the "sex changes" in this novel are hardly simple. On one level, it is Valmont, the seducer, the purveyor of passions previously unsuspected by his naive victim, who effectively changes sexes, who adopts as his own a strategy which is eminently feminine. At the same time, if there is a woman who finds herself in the position of the male in this novel, it is Madame de Tourvel. In allowing herself to be seduced by Valmont, by actually believing in the illusions he creates, she finds herself in the position of the male who always runs the risk of being brought low by the feminine wiles of a manipulated imagination. Mystified by Valmont's pose as the languishing lover, Tourvel becomes the victim of an illusion originally fashioned by women for the control of men.

Merteuil, on the other hand, consciously and consequently acts as the most womanly of women throughout this novel. Unlike the mystified Tourvel, Merteuil insists above all on that complete lucidity toward herself and toward the society around her which Laclos sees as the prerequisite for the woman's triumph. Few documents display as firm a commitment to such lucidity as the famous eighty-first letter in which she relates to Valmont the various stages of her carefully self-imposed "education" as a woman who, while avenging her sex, has only contempt for the manipulated women she sees everywhere around her. If readers of this novel have consistently shuddered at the inhuman coldness of Merteuil's self-portrait, it is because she insists on the most unflinching vision of sexuality and desire as a politics to be pursued within a carefully determined strategy of retaliation. While some critics may see in Merteuil a woman who is monstrous because she dared to desire a man, Paul Hoffman comes closer to the mark when he points out that Merteuil's desire is in fact always directed at a particular image of herself. The men she desires are never more than pawns in a game she plays only with herself:

> The unforgiveable error is to lack lucidity. What a woman must demand of a man is . . . an unpunished pleasure which is the sign of her superiority, an occasion for domination, a pleasure for the intelligence as much as for the senses.[10]

From another perspective, it was Madame Riccoboni, the venerably prudish novelist Laclos rather hypocritically set out to convince of the morality of his intentions, who best described how Merteuil was seen through conventional eyes. Rather than a woman who became a man, she is, Riccoboni insists in one of her letters to Laclos, a whore:

> a vile woman determined from her earliest youth to educate herself to vice, to espouse principles of baseness, to fashion for herself a mask hiding from everyone her determination to adopt the morals of one of those unfortunate creatures whom poverty has obliged to live from their infamy.[11]

Laclos, interestingly enough, does not so much reject this judgment as he nuances it by insisting that everything Merteuil did was a function of her social position, of the options available to her within a specific symbolic order. Merteuil's are, he answers, "the morals of those women, even more vile, who are perfectly able to calculate what their rank and their fortune will allow them to add to their infamous vices" (697).

In *Les Liaisons dangereuses* Laclos confronts his readers, male as well as female, with the fundamental choice he saw every woman obliged to make between the two positions available to her within a symbolic order dominated by men. On the one hand, and everything invites her in this direction, she can subscribe to the mystified belief that desire can lead to fulfillment, that we can return to an untroubled Eden allowing the innocent transparency of body and soul. This, it is important to note, is not only Tourvel's mistake, but the implicit premise sustaining the position taken by those critics who would impose on Laclos's text that vision of women as inevitable victims, as the always seduced daughters, which he explicitly rejects. On the other hand, and this is what Baudelaire underlined so eloquently with his insistence that in a world given over to lies there is an inverse proportion between deceiving others and deceiving oneself, women can, like Merteuil, refuse this mystification. They can recognize that all mythical escapes from the conflict, opacity, and solitude of the individual within society come only at the highest of prices. To pine for an illusory Eden is to become the victim not only of the symbolic order, but also of that very imagination which the truly lucid woman can manipulate as victor rather than as victim.

The "facts" of force, of desire, and of the social order exist. Wishing they did not will never make it so. As an infinite concatenation of tyrants and slaves, society, as Laclos saw it, presents us, male and female, with constraints which cannot be eluded. To the male prerogatives of force and convention, the female must oppose not the delusory consolations of an impossible communion, but a strategic exploitation of desire and imagination redefining a servitude which can never be abolished.

Merteuil's downfall comes not because loving women must triumph over lucid women, but because even her commitment to an always self-conscious and self-sufficient lucidity is compromised by a lingering need to constitute herself as spectacle, to perform before an audience capable of beholding and applauding the quality of her deceptions. Tzvetan Todorov has perceptively remarked that *Les Liaisons dangereuses* really tells two stories: that of the characters who exchange the letters we read and that of the letters themselves and how they came to be gathered together in a collection offered to the reading public.[12] These two stories, he points out, are in fact the same story. All the characters in this novel meet the fates they do *because* their letters have begun to circulate, *because* letters Merteuil and Valmont intended only for each other are now read by those from whom they must remain secret.

Why, the question becomes, does Merteuil send Valmont a letter in which she states: "From that moment on my thoughts were for me alone to know, and I have revealed only what it was useful for me to make known. . . . These precautions, and that of never writing . . . may seem excessive. To me they have never seemed sufficient."[13] The conflict between what is said and the act of saying it is complete. Merteuil violates her cardinal rule even as she proclaims it. If she does this, if she unwittingly arms Valmont for the battle in which she will be defeated, it is because she herself, at a second level, has fallen victim to the mystification she so consistently denounces in the women around her. Delivering to Valmont the blue prints for her planned domination of every other character within the novel is a rational act only when it is predicated on her still harbored, but never consciously avowed belief that an absolute lucidity in the deception of others can become the basis of a higher sincerity between the two most adroit deceivers. Merteuil is undone, in other words, not because she wished or tried to become a man, but because she has deluded herself into believing that Valmont, her partner in deception, is a man with whom she need no longer employ the strategies of a woman. Merteuil loses because, having chosen this feminized figure of the male seducer as the privileged audience of her life-performance, she forgets that she is a woman living in the society of men. She forgets that her success depends on her acting as a woman with every man: as the mistress of his manipulated imagination.

NOTES

1 These notes, for the most part in the form of short paragraphs, are contained in the Pléiade edition of the *Oeuvres complètes de Laclos*, ed. M. Allem (1951) Paris, Gallimard, Bibliothèque de la Pléiade. My epigraph appears on p. 903.

2 This quotation is taken from N. K. Miller (1976) "Female sexuality and narrative structure in *La Nouvelle Héloise* and *Les Liaisons dangereuses*," *Signs*, 1, Fall, 612. This article, in an expanded form,

became part of chs 7 and 8 in N. K. Miller (1980) *The Heroine's Text*, New York, Columbia University Press.

3 *Oeuvres complètes de Laclos*, 403–58. In this study I discuss the first two of these essays, those first published by Edouard Champion in 1903 under the title *De l'éducation des femmes*. There is also a third essay of some eight pages which was first published by Dagnan-Bouveret in the *Revue Bleue* of 23 May 1908 and which Allem includes with the other two. Unlike the wide-ranging philosophical speculation of the first two, this last text consists of little more than a reading program suggested for a young woman of gentle birth. While it contains some echoes of the readings listed by Merteuil in Letter 81, it has little to say of woman's position within society.

4 Laclos does, however, see it as possible for men to turn the power of imagination back against women. This happens when women fall victim to "jealousy" for the beauty or love accorded another woman: "Jealousy was born of beauty and love. These three illusions have completely changed the respective statuses of men and women. They have become the basis and guarantee of all contracts between them" (436). It is, as we shall see, this pre-emption by men of arms first fashioned by women which makes possible both "the seducer" and "the woman in love."

5 *Julie ou la Nouvelle Héloïse* in B. Gagnebin and M. Raymond (eds) (1964) *Oeuvres complètes de Rousseau*, Paris, Gallimard, Bibliothèque de la Pléiade, vol. II, 138.

6 *Un acteur caché du drame révolutionnaire, Choderlos de Laclos* (1905) Paris, Perrin, 102.

7 N. K. Miller (1975) "The exquisite cadavers: women in eighteenth-century fiction," *Diacritics*, 5, 4, Winter, 42. This article, too, as a closing chapter separate from the analysis of Tourvel, became part of *The Heroine's Text*.

8 This excerpt is cited in the Allem edition of Laclos's *Oeuvres complètes*, 699.

9 For one of the most provocative recent studies of this question, see R. Roussel (1986) "*Les Liaisons dangereuses* and the Myth of the Understanding Man," in *The Conversation of the Sexes*, New York, Oxford University Press.

10 P. Hoffman (1963) "Aspects de la condition féminine dans *Les Liaisons dangereuses* de Choderlos de Laclos," *L'Information littéraire*, 15, March–April, 50.

11 This correspondence is contained in the Allem edition of Laclos's *Oeuvres complètes*, 686–98. This quotation is from p. 693.

12 T. Todorov (1967) *Littérature et signification*, Paris, Larousse.

13 *Les Liaisons dangereuses*, in *Oeuvres complètes*, 176–80.

6

Wild nights:
pleasure/sexuality/feminism*

———◆———

CORA KAPLAN

till women are led to exercise their understandings, they should not be satirized for their attachment to rakes; or even for being rakes at heart, when it appears to be the inevitable consequence of their education. They who live to please – must find their enjoyments, their happiness in pleasure!

(Mary Wollstonecraft, 1792)

> Wild Nights – Wild Nights!
> Were I with thee
> Wild Nights should be
> Our luxury!   (Emily Dickinson, 1861)

I had been a hopeful radical. Now I am not. Pornography has infected me. Once I was a child and I dreamed of freedom. Now I am an adult and I see what my dreams have come to: pornography. So, while I cannot help my sleeping nightmares, I have given up many waking dreams.   (Andrea Dworkin, 1981)[1]

How difficult it is to uncouple the terms pleasure and sexuality. How much more difficult, once uncoupled, to re-imagine woman as the subject, pleasure as her object, if that object is *not* sexual. Almost two centuries of feminist activity and debate have passed, two hundred years in which women's understandings have been widely exercised, yet most of Mary Wollstonecraft's modest proposals for female emancipation are still demands on a feminist platform. Most distant, most Utopian seems her hesitant plea that the social basis for woman's sexual pleasure be "dignified" after "some future revolution in time."[2] Too near, too familiar, is her temporary expedient, the rejection of woman's pleasure as inextricably bound to her dependent and deferential status. Revolutions have come and gone, and sexuality is once more at the head of feminist agendas in the west, the wild card whose suit and value shifts provocatively with history. As dream or nightmare, or both at once, it reigns in our lives as an anarchic force, refusing to be chastened and tamed by sense or conscience to a sentence in a revolutionary manifesto.

In "the right to choose" the women's movement has reasserted the tenets of liberal humanism, laying claim to its promise of individual civil rights for women, and acknowledging the difficulty of prescription in the area of sexual politics. Yet female sexuality remains one of the central contradictions within contemporary politics, causing as much anxiety to feminists and their sympathizers as to their opponents. Within feminist debate, radical and revolutionary feminists argue with their liberal and socialist sisters around definitions of a correct, or politically acceptable sexual practice. The possible positions on this troubling issue which can be identified as feminist range widely from a pro-pleasure polymorphous perverse sexual radicalism, through cautious permissiveness, to anti-porn activism and a political lesbianism which de-emphasizes genital sexuality. This muddy conflict on the site of feminism itself, suggests, among other things, how profoundly women's subjectivity is constructed through sexual categories.

The negative meanings which have been historically associated with women's sexuality have been a major impediment in their fight for liberation. Historians suggest that the "ideological division of women into two classes, the virtuous and the fallen, was already well developed" by the mid-eighteenth century.[3] Certainly it received one of its major modern articulations at about this time in Rousseau's *Émile* (1762). In *Émile* the possibility of women's civil, economic, and psychological independence is rejected because it would also enable the independent and licentious exercise of her supposedly insatiable sexual appetite. Woman's desire is seen by Rousseau as both regressive and disruptive of the new liberal social order he proposed; women's emancipation would mean a step backward for rational and egalitarian progress. It is important to remember that the notion of women as politically enabled and independent is fatally linked to the unrestrained and vicious exercise of her sexuality, not just in the propaganda of the new right, but in a central and influential work of the very old left.

When feminists sought to appropriate liberal humanism for their own sex they had to contend with the double standard prominently inscribed within radical tradition, as well as with its suffocating and determining presence in dominant ideologies. Female sexuality is still the suppressed text of those liberal and left programs which are silent on the issues of women's subordination. This silence has had its negative effect upon feminism itself, which must always speak into other political discourses. Where both right and left sexual ideologies converge, associating women's desire with weakness, unreason, and materialism, it has been noticeably hard to insist on positive social and political meanings for female sexuality. Only its supposed disruptive force can be harnessed to revolutionary possibility, and then, perhaps, only for the moment of disruption itself. While most feminisms have recognized that the regulation of female sexuality and the ideological mobilization of its threat to order are part of women's subordination, it is not surprising that they have too often accepted the paradigm which insists that desire is a regressive force in women's lives, and have called for a sublimation of women's sexual pleasure to meet a passionless and rational ideal. Rousseau's formulation has cast a long shadow that cannot be dispersed by simple inversions of his argument. As long as the idea survives that a reformed libidinal economy for women is the precondition for a successful feminist politics, women can always be seen as unready for emancipation. The view, explicitly expressed in Mary Wollstonecraft's *A Vindication of the Rights of Woman* emerges in a different form in Adrienne Rich's radical feminist polemic, "Compulsory heterosexuality and lesbian existence" (1980).[4] This chapter explores *A Vindication* at some length, and "Compulsory heterosexuality" very briefly, as part of a longer project to understand how the sexual politics of feminism has been shaped.

Wild Nights

THE RIGHTS OF WOMEN AND FEMININE
SEXUALITY: MARY WOLLSTONECRAFT

The reputation of Mary Wollstonecraft's *A Vindication of the Rights of Woman* (1792), the founding text of Anglo-American feminism, generally precedes and in part constructs our reading of it. We are likely to look for, and privilege, its demands for educational, legal, and political equality; these are, after all, the demands that link Wollstonecraft's feminism to our own. If we give ourselves up to *A Vindication*'s eloquent but somewhat rambling prose, we will also discover *passim* an unforgettable early account of the making of a lady, an acute, detailed analysis of the social construction of femininity, which appropriates the developmental psychology of enlightenment and romantic thought. It is certainly possible to engage with *A Vindication* so far and no farther, to let most of its troubling historical meanings and contradictions drop away, so that we may take away from it an unproblematic feminist inheritance. How much use can we make of this legacy without a sense of the history which produced it? Read *A Vindication* for its historical meanings and another text emerges, one which is arguably as interested in developing a class sexuality for a radical, reformed bourgeoisie as in producing an analysis of women's subordination and a manifesto of her rights.

This part of Wollstonecraft's project deserves our attention too, for only by understanding why Wollstonecraft wanted women to become full, independent members of the middle class, can we make sense of the negative and prescriptive assault on female sexuality which is the *leitmotif* of *A Vindication* where it is not the overt subject of the text.

It is usual to see the French Revolution as the intellectual and political backdrop to *A Vindication*; it would be more useful to see it as the most important condition of its production. As Margaret Walters has pointed out, *A Vindication* sums up and rearticulates a century of feminist ideas,[5] but its immediate stake was in the political advance of a revolutionary vanguard – the middle class itself, as Wollstonecraft and others imagined it. Every opinion in the text is written in the glare of this politically charged and convulsive moment, and the area of Wollstonecraft's thought most altered and illuminated by that glare is sexuality. In her two attempts at fiction, *Mary, a Fiction* and *Maria or The Wrongs of Woman*, one produced a few years before *A Vindication* and the other incomplete at her death in 1797, women's feelings and desires, as well as the importance of expressing them, are valorized. But in *A Vindication* Wollstonecraft turned against feeling, which is seen as reactionary and regressive, almost counter-revolutionary. Sexuality and pleasure are narcotic inducements to a life of lubricious slavery. Reason is the only human attribute appropriate to the revolutionary character, and women are impeded from their early and corrupt initiation in the sensual, from using theirs.

Why is *A Vindication* so suffused with the sexual, and so projectively severe about it? This is the question that I will explore at some length below. Wollstonecraft's feminism and her positions on sexuality were, at this point in her life, directly bound up with her radical politics – they can be understood only through each other. In untangling the knotted meanings of the sexual in our own history, our own politics, it is useful to understand the different but recurring anxieties it has stirred for other feminisms, other times.

A Vindication of the Rights of Woman offers the reader a puritan sexual ethic with such passionate conviction that self-denial seems a libidinized activity. And so it was, in the sense that a reform of sexual behavior was Wollstonecraft's precondition for radical change in the condition of women; permitting the development of their reason and independence. The democratic imperatives – equality and liberty for all classes of persons – have been, for so long now, the well-worn staples of liberal and left rhetoric that it is hard to remember that they were being invoked in new ways and with unprecedented exuberance in the 1790s. When we try to puzzle out the meanings of *A Vindication* it is the negative construction of the sexual in the midst of a positive and progressive construction of the social and political which we must question. In that contradiction – if indeed it is a contradiction – our present conflict over sexual politics is still partly embedded.

Written in six weeks at the height of British left optimism about events in France, *A Vindication* came out early in 1792, the same year as the second part of Tom Paine's *Rights of Man*, a year before William Godwin's *Political Justice*. Each was, equally, a response to the political moment. All three were crucial statements about the social and political possibilities of a transformed Britain. An almost millenarial fervor moved British radicals in these years. Their political and philosophical ideas were being put into practice only a few hundred miles away; there were signs of reasoned and purposeful unrest at home among ordinary working people. The end of aristocratic privilege and autocratic rule in France was to be taken as a sign of universal change. The downfall of the Bastille, Thomas Paine exulted, included the idea of the downfall of despotism.

A Vindication engages with radical romantic politics at a moment when the practical realization of such a politics seemed as near as France itself. Wollstonecraft had already written one short pamphlet, *A Vindication of the Rights of Men* (1790), in support of the revolution, and was still to write a long piece on its behalf.[6] In this, her most important work, she took advantage of an open moment of political debate to intervene on behalf of women from inside the British left intelligentsia. Its message is urgent precisely because social and political reform seemed not just possible, but inevitable. The status of women as moral and political beings had become one fairly muted instance of the unresolved contradictions within the republican and democratic tendencies of the time. The overlapping tendencies of enlightenment and romantic thought emphasized the natural virtue rather than innate depravity of human beings, their equality before God, and the evils brought about by unequal laws and hereditary privilege. Arguments initially directed at a corrupt ruling class on behalf of a virtuous bourgeoisie inevitably opened up questions of intra-class power relations. With *A Vindication* Wollstonecraft challenged her own political camp, insisting that women's rights be put higher up on the radical agenda. Addressed to Talleyrand, taking issue with Rousseau, speaking the political jargon of her English contemporaries, *A Vindication* invited the enlightenment heritage, the dead and the living, to extend the new humanism to the other half of the race. With a thriving revolution under way, the political and intellectual credit of republican sympathizers was as high as their morale. It seemed like the right moment to ask them to pay their debt to women.

The opening pages of *A Vindication* share the aggressive, confident mood, and tone that had developed under the threat and promise of the revolutionary moment. Ridiculing the "turgid bombast" and "flowery diction" of aristocratic discourse, Wollstonecraft offers the reader instead "sincerity" and "unaffected" prose, the style and standards of the class of men and women to whom she was speaking – "I pay particular attention to those in the middle class, because they appear to be in the most natural [i.e. least corrupted] state." Her unapologetic class bias was shared with her radical contemporaries – it is hardly surprising that idealized humanity as it appears in her text is a rational, plain speaking, bourgeois man. Denying any innate inequality between the sexes except physical strength, she promises to "first consider women in the grand light of human creatures, who, in common with men, are placed on this earth to unfold their faculties," and addresses her sisters boldly as "rational creatures" whose "first object of laudable ambition" should be "to obtain a character as a human being, regardless of the distinctions of sex."[7]

How to attain this character? In Paine's *Rights of Man* the reader was told that inequality and oppression were the effects of culture rather than nature. The text itself is a politicizing event, first constructing and then working on an uncorrupted rational subject. Paine hoped, and his enemies feared, that some sort of direct political action to unseat despotic power would follow from a sympathetic reading of his pamphlet. The message and intention of *A Vindication* are very different. Nowhere does Wollstonecraft pose women, in their present "degraded" condition, as either vanguard or revolutionary mass. Like the corrupt aristocracy, to whom they are frequently compared, they are, instead, a *lumpen* group who must undergo strenuous re-education in order that they might renounce the sensual, rid themselves of "soft phrases, susceptibility of heart, delicacy of sentiment, and refinement of taste" . . . "libertine notions of beauty" and the single-minded "desire of establishing themselves – the only way women can rise in the world – by marriage."[8] Before the middle-class woman can join the middle-class man in advocating and advancing human progress she must be persuaded to become "more masculine and respectable," by giving up her role both as "insignificant objects of desire" and as desiring subject.[9]

Even in its own day *A Vindication* must have been a short, sharp shock for women readers. Men might be able to mobilize reason and passion, in them equitably combined, to change the world immediately; women, crippled and stunted by an education for dependence, must liberate themselves from a slavish addiction to the sensual before their "understandings" could liberate anyone else. At later moments of political crisis feminists could, and would, portray women as vanguard figures, subordinated members of the propertied class who understood more about oppression, as a result, than their bourgeois male comrades. Not here. Read intertextually, heard against the polyphonic lyricism of Paine, Godwin, and the dozens of ephemeral pamphleteers who were celebrating the fact and prospect of the revolution, *A Vindication* was a sobering read. Wollstonecraft sets out on a heroic mission to rescue women from a fate worse than death, which was, as she saw it, the malicious and simultaneous inscription of their sexuality and inferiority as innate, natural difference. This was how her political mentor and gender adversary Rousseau had placed them, too weak by nature to reach or be reached by sweet reason. Rousseau's influence was great, not least on Wollstonecraft herself. She accepts Rousseau's ascription of female inferiority and locates it even more firmly than he does in an excess of sensibility. Since lust and narcissism were evil they must belong to social relations rather than human nature; this was Rousseau's own position in relation to men. Accordingly, female sexuality in so far as it is vicious is inscribed in *A Vindication* as the effect of culture on an essentially ungendered nature. By tampering with the site of degrading sexuality without challenging the moralizing description of sexuality itself, Wollstonecraft sets up heartbreaking conditions for women's liberation – a little death, the death of desire, the death of female pleasure.

Even if *A Vindication* is preoccupied with the sexual as the site and source of women's oppression, why is woman's love of pleasure so deeply stigmatized as the sign of her degradation? In refusing to interpret women's unbounded desire as a natural mark of sexual difference or the appropriate preoccupation of her mediated place in the social, Wollstonecraft is resisting a whole range of bourgeois positions around gender sexuality, positions which were rapidly hardening into the forms of bourgeois morality which would dominate nineteenth-century ruling-class gender relations. Her debate with Rousseau is central, because, like her, Rousseau wished to harness his gender ideologies to radical social and political theories. Rousseau's *Émile* is the place where he spells out the theoretical and socially expedient premises which excluded women from equal participation in the enlightenment projects for human liberation and individual transcendence. Arguing for the sexual assymetry of natural endowment, Rousseau insisted that women's "first propensities" revealed an excess of sensibility, easily "corrupted or perverted by too much indulgence." In civil society women's amoral weakness must not be given its natural scope lest it lead, as it inevitably must, to adultery and its criminal consequence, the foisting of illegitimate heirs on bourgeois husbands. The remedy is borrowed back from the techniques of aristocratic despotism, elsewhere in Rousseau so violently condemned: women

> must be subject all their lives, to the most constant and severe restraint, which is that of decorum; it is therefore, necessary to accustom them early to such confinement that it may not afterwards cost them too dear. . . . we should teach them above all things to lay a due restraint on themselves.[10]

Acknowledging, with crocodile tears, the artificiality of the social, while insisting on its necessity, Rousseau invokes a traditionally unregenerate Eve partnered to an Adam who has been given back his pre-lapsarian status.

> The life of a modest woman is reduced, by our absurd institutions, to a perpetual conflict with herself: but it is just that this sex should partake of the sufferings which arise from those evils it hath caused us.[11]

Émile lays out, in fascinating detail, the radical project for the education and adult gender relations of an enlightened bourgeoisie, a project which depended for its success on the location of affection and sexuality in the family, as well as the construction of the bourgeois individual as the agent of free will. The struggle between reason and passion has an internal and external expression in Rousseau, and the triumph of reason is ensured by the social nature of passion. Since male desire needs an object, and women are that infinitely provocative object, the social subordination of women to the will of men ensures the containment of passion. In this way Rousseau links the potential and freedom of the new middle class to the simultaneous suppression and exploitation of women's nature.

Rousseau plays on the already constructed sexual categorization of women into two groups – the virtuous and depraved. By insisting that these divisions are social rather than natural constructs – all women are depraved by nature – Rousseau can argue for social and civil restraints on women. Michel Foucault points out that the process of constructing women first and foremost as a sexual subject was in itself a class-bound project:

> it was in the "bourgeois" or aristocratic family that the sexuality of children and adolescents was first problematized. . . . the first

figure to be invested by the deployment of sexuality, one of the first to be "sexualized" was the "idle" woman. She inhabited the outer edge of the "world", in which she always had to appear as value, and of the family, where she was assigned a new identity charged with conjugal and parental obligation.[12]

Mary Wollstonecraft stood waist-deep in these already established and emergent sexual ideologies. At the time she was writing *A Vindication* she was neither willing nor able to mount a wholesale critique either of bourgeois sexual mores or the wider areas of gender relations. Her life was shortly to go through some very rapid changes, which would, ironically, mark her as one of the "degraded" women so remorselessly pilloried in her text. A year and a half after her essay was published she was living with a young American, Gilbert Imlay, in France; two years later she was an unmarried mother. *A Vindication* is a watershed in her life and thought, but this crisis is marked in a curiously wilful way. The text expresses a violent antagonism to the sexual; it exaggerates the importance of the sensual in the everyday life of women, and betrays the most profound anxiety about the rupturing force of female sexuality. Both *Émile* and *A Vindication* share a deep ambivalence about sexuality. Images of dirt, disease, decay, and anarchic power run as a symbolic undertext in both works, too frequently located in women's sexual being rather than in any heterosexual practice. This distaste is pervasively articulated in *A Vindication*, adumbrated on the first page with an arresting description of French gender relations as "the very essence of sensuality" dominated by "a kind of sentimental lust" which is set against the ideal of "personal reserve, and sacred respect for cleanliness and delicacy in domestic life."[13] The images of sexuality throughout are so gripping and compulsive that it is hard to tear oneself away to the less vivid analysis which insists, with commendable vigor, that these filthy habits are a social construction, foisted on each generation of women by male-dominated and male-oriented society.

The place of female sexuality in *A Vindication* is overdetermined by political as well as social history. Like many of the progressive voices of the late eighteenth century, Wollstonecraft had built her dreams of a new society on the foundation of Rousseau's *Social Contract* and *Essay on Inequality*. Rousseau's writings, in so far as they spoke about human beings rather than men, offered cold reason warmed with feeling in a mixture that was very attractive to the excitable radical temperaments of Wollstonecraft's generation. Rousseau's writing, Paine wrote in 1791, expressed "a loveliness of sentiment in favor of liberty, that excites respect and elevates the human faculties" – a judgment widely shared. How unlovely then for Wollstonecraft to consider that in *Émile* Rousseau deliberately withholds from women because of the "difference of sex" all that is promised to men. Rousseau's general prejudices and recommendations for women – functional, domestic education, nun-like socialization, restricted activity, and virtual incarceration in the home – colluded with the gender bias and advice of more reactionary bourgeois authors, as well as society at large. The sense in which Rousseau's prescriptions were becoming the dominant view can be heard in the different imaginary readers addressed by the texts. In the section on women *Émile* slips in and out of a defensive posture, arguing, if only tactically, with an anonymous feminist opponent for the imposition of a stricter regime for women. Wollstonecraft too is on the defensive but her composite reader-antagonist was a society which believed in and followed Rousseau's novel advice to the letter. *Émile* offered its ideas as a reform of and reaction to liberal ideas on female education and behavior. Thirty years on, *A Vindication* suggested that female sexual morality had become laxer, operating under just such a regime of restraint and coercion that Rousseau had laid out.

The project of *Émile* was to outline the social and sexual relations of an idealized bourgeois society by giving an account of the education and courtship of its youth. *A Vindication* appropriates part of this project, the elaborate set of distinctions between the manners and morals of the aristocracy and those of the new middle class. The anti-aristocratic critique is foregrounded and set in focus by the French Revolution: its early progress exposed the corruption of the ruling classes to a very wide and receptive audience. When Wollstonecraft suggests that vain, idle, and sensuous middle-class women are to be compared with the whole of the hereditary aristocracy who live only for pleasure she strikes at two popular targets. When she identifies the aestheticized and artificial language of the ruling class – "a deluge of false sentiments and overstretched feelings," "dropping glibly from the tongue" as the language of novels and letters, she implies that it is also the language of women, or of the society adultress. At one level she is simply producing a gendered and eroticized version of Paine's famous attack on Burke's prose style and sentiments, in *Rights of Man, Part I*. At another, the massing of these metaphors of debased and disgusting female sexuality, even when they are ostensibly directed at the behavior of a discredited class has the effect of doubling the sexual reference. Paine's comment – "He pities the plumage and forgets the dying bird" – already carries sexual and gendered meanings. Because a naturally whorish and disrupting female sexuality was so profoundly a part of traditional symbol and reference, used to tarnish whatever object it was applied to, it became extremely difficult for Wollstonecraft to keep her use of such images tied to a social and environmental analysis. She herself is affected by the traditional association.

In *A Vindication* women's excessive interest in themselves as objects and subjects of desire is theorized as an effect of the ideological inscription of male desire on female subjects who, as a result, bear a doubled libidinal burden. But the language of that sober analysis is more innovatory, less secure, and less connotative than the metaphorical matrix used to point and illustrate it. As a consequence, there is a constant slippage back into a more naturalized and reactionary view of women, and a collapse of the two parts of the metaphors into each other. Thus Wollstonecraft tries to argue *against* restraint and dependence by comparing the situation of women to slaves and lap-dogs:

> for servitude not only debases the individual, but its effects seem to be transmitted to posterity. Considering the length of time that women have been dependent, is it surprising that some of them hug their chains, and fawn like the spaniel.[14]

But it is the metonymic association of "slave," "women," "spaniel" that tends to linger, rather than the intended metaphoric distance, the likeness and unlikeness between them.

The same effect occurs when Wollstonecraft borrows a chunk of contemporary radical analysis of the mob to support her position that women need the same freedom and liberal educations as men. In enlightenment theory a libidinal economy is brought to bear on subordinated groups: mass social violence is seen as the direct result of severe repression which does not allow for the development of self-control or self-governance. The mob's motive may be a quasi-rational vengeance against oppressors, but the trigger of that violence is the uncontrolled and irrational effect of sudden derepression. Sexual symbolism is already prefigured in this analysis, so that when Wollstonecraft draws on it as a metaphor for women's uncontrolled sexual behavior she reinforces the identification of loose women and mob violence. "The bent bow recoils with violence, when the hand is suddenly relaxed that forcibly held it" – the sexual metaphor here, as elsewhere, is top-heavy, tumbling, out of control, like the imaginary force of female sexuality itself. Here, and at many other points in the text, *A Vindication* enhances rather than reduces the power of female sexuality, constructing it, unintentionally, as an intimate and immediate threat to social stability, nearer than the already uncomfortably near Parisian mob. It is no wonder that many nineteenth-century feminists, for whom the mob and the French Revolution were still potent symbols of disorder, found the book, for all its overt sexual puritanism, disturbing and dangerous.

The blurring of sexual and political metaphor so that sexuality is effectively smeared all over the social relations under discussion emphasizes Wollstonecraft's deliberate privileging of sensibility and pleasure as the ideological weapons of patriarchy. Picking up on the negative vibes about female sexuality in *Émile*, she beats Rousseau with his own stick (as it seems) by making the sensual both viler and more pervasive in women's lives as a result of his philosophy of education put into practice. Wollstonecraft too wishes bourgeois women to be modest and respectable, honest wives and good mothers, though she wishes them to be other things as well. Yet only by imagining them *all*, or almost all, crippled and twisted into sexual monsters by society as it is can she hope to persuade her readers to abandon a gender-specific and deforming education for feminity.

Yet the most incisive and innovative elements of *A Vindication* are deeply bound into its analysis of the construction of gender in childhood. The book gives us a complex and detailed account of the social and psychic processes by which gender ideologies become internalized adult subjectivity. This account is spread across the two-hundred-odd pages of the book and is extraordinary both as observation and as theory. Here is the childhood of little girls brought up, *à la* Rousseau, to be women only:

> Every thing they see or hear serves to fix impressions, call forth emotions, and associate ideas, that give a sexual character to the mind. False notions of beauty and delicacy stop the growth of their limbs and produce a sickly soreness, rather than delicacy of

organs. . . . This cruel association of ideas, which every thing conspires to twist into all their habits of thinking, or, to speak with more precision, of feeling, receives new force when they begin to act a little for themselves; for they then perceive that it is only through their address to excite emotions in men that pleasure and power are to be obtained.[15]

It is exaggerated; it is even fantasy up to a point. Yet reading this passage, I was both shaken by its eloquence and pricked by its accuracy.

Only an unusual "native vigor" of mind can overturn such a vicious social construction, for:

So ductile is the understanding, and yet so stubborn, that the associations which depend on adventitious circumstances, during the period that the body takes to arrive at maturity, can seldom be disentangled by reason. One idea calls up another, its old associate, and memory faithful to first impressions . . . retraces them with mechanical exactness.[16]

Here, in part, is the romantic theory of the unconscious, its operations laid bare to draw a particularly bleak conclusion about the fate of women.

The need to exaggerate the effects of a gender-biased rearing and education led Wollstonecraft to overemphasize the importance of sexuality in women's lives. A Vindication is hardly a realistic reconstruction of the day-to-day activities and preoccupations of bourgeois women, the author herself not excepted. Rather it is an abstract formulation of the sort of social and psychic tendencies that a one-sided reactionary socialization could produce. It is unfortunate that Wollstonecraft chose to fight Rousseau in his own terms, accepting his paradigm of a debased, eroticized femininity as fact rather than ideological fiction. Woman's reason may be the psychic heroine of A Vindication, but its gothic villain, a polymorphous perverse sexuality, creeping out of every paragraph and worming its way into every warm corner of the text, seems in the end to win out. It is again too easy to forget that this suffusing desire is a permanent male conspiracy to keep women panting and dependent as well as house-bound and pregnant. What the argument moves towards, but never quite arrives at, is the conclusion that it is male desire which must be controlled and contained if women are to be free and rational. This conclusion cannot be reached because an idealized bourgeois male is the standard towards which women are groping, as well as the reason they are on their knees. Male desire may be destructive to women, but it remains a part of positive male identity. A wider education and eros-blunting forays into the public world of work and politics keeps the rational in control of the sensual in men, and is the recommended remedy for women too. Wollstonecraft thought gender difference socially constructed but she found practically nothing to like in socially constructed femininity. With masculinity it was quite different – "masculine" women are fine as long as they don't hunt and kill. Yet there could be nothing good about feminized men, since the definitions of the feminine available in *A Vindication* are shot through with dehumanizing and immoral sensuality. It's not surprising that women together – girls in boarding schools and women in the home – can only get up to unsavory personal familiarities, "nasty, or immodest habits." This description backs up an argument, possibly forceful in its own time, for mixed education and a freer association of adult men and women; it rounds off the indictment of women's world in *A Vindication*.

Ironically, it is the revolutionary moment, with its euphoric faith in total social transformation which permits Wollstonecraft to obliterate women and femininity in their unreformed state. Although *A Vindication* outlines a liberal and unsegregated program for female education and a wider scope for women's newly developed reason in the public and private world, it has nothing complimentary to say about women as they are. Their overheated sensibility is never seen as potentially creative. One can see how the moral analysis and the social description in *A Vindication* could be appropriated for a more conservative social theory, which might advocate a degree of exercise for women's adolescent bodies and minds, but would confine them to a desexualized domestic sphere as wives and mothers.

The novels of Jane Austen, Wollstonecraft's contemporary, are the most obvious immediate example of a conservative recuperation of Wollstonecraft. *Northanger Abbey* paraphrases Wollstonecraft on the dangers to the young female reader of the gothic and sentimental novel, and *Mansfield Park* reads in many places like a fictional reworking of *A Vindication*. Possibly influence, partly mere convergence, the voices of the two women whose politics were deeply opposed, echo each other. It is Wollstonecraft who writes that "while women live, as it were by their personal charms, how can we expect them to discharge those ennobling duties which equally require exertion and self-denial," but it might as easily be Austen on Mary Crawford. In the same sentence, and in much the same terms, Wollstonecraft denounces hereditary aristocracy. The appropriation of much of Wollstonecraft's writing for conservative social and political ideologies went unacknowledged because of her outcast social status and her revolutionary sympathies.

Nevertheless, mid-century women writers and feminists, looking for ways to legitimize their feminism and their sexuality, as well as their desire to write them both out together, found small comfort in *A Vindication*, where the creative and the affective self are split up and separated. In fiction and poetry, that discursive space open to women but sheltered from the harshest judgments of Victorian morality, late romantic women writers, as sick of Wollstonecraft's regime, if they knew it, as she had been sick of Rousseau's, tentatively began to construct the idea of a libidinized female imagination and, through it, women's right to reason and desire. Authority for such an unmediated and eroticized relation to art and life had to be sought in and stolen from male romantic manifestos. Nothing suggests more unequivocally how deep the effects of separate gender sexualities went, than a quick look at the 1802 introduction to *Lyrical Ballads* after a long look at *A Vindication*. The bourgeois poet was the romantic radical incarnated. Here is Wordsworth, like Mary Wollstonecraft a supporter of the revolution, telling the reader, as she never could, that the poet is a man "endued with more lively sensibility, more enthusiasm and tenderness" than other men, "a man pleased with his own passions and volitions, and who rejoices more than other men in the spirit of life that is in him."[17] The appropriate, democratic subjects for his art were "moral sentiments and animal sensations" as they existed in everyday life.[18]

We must remember to read *A Vindication* as its author has instructed us, as a discourse addressed mainly to women of the middle class. Most deeply class bound is its emphasis on sexuality in its ideological expression, as a mental formation, as the source of woman's oppression. The enchilding of women – their relegation to the home, to domestic tasks and concerns, while men's productive labor was located elsewhere – was a developing phenomenon of middle-class life in the eighteenth century. The separation of home and work in an industrial culture affected the working class too, but it was not the men only who worked outside the home: nor was the sexual division of labor along these lines a working-class ideal until well on in the nineteenth century. The romantic conception of childhood, already naturalized in *A Vindication*, had no place in working-class life. Nor did female narcissism and a passion for clothes have the same meanings for, or about, working-class women, who, as Wollstonecraft observes in *Maria*, were worked too hard at "severe manual labor" to have much time or thought for such things. The ideal of education, opening up wider fields for the exercise of the mind, was part of a bourgeois agenda for social improvement that would "lift" the poor as well as women. Sequential pregnancies, exhausting child care in the grimmest conditions, the double yoke of waged and unpaid domestic labor, none of these are cited in *A Vindication* as the cause of women's degradation. *Maria* includes an honorable if genteel attempt to describe the realities of life for working-class women. *A Vindication* is more class bound and more obsessive; a brief though not unsympathetic passage on the horrors of prostitution, and a few references to the dirty backstairs habits which female servants pass on to ladies is the selective and sexualized attention that working-class women get in *A Vindication*.

Most of Wollstonecraft's difficulties are with the obviously binding power of the binary categories of class sexuality. Rather than challenge them, she shifts her abstract women around inside them or tries to reverse their symbolism. The middle-class married adultress is magically transformed by liberty and education into the modest rational wife. If women in public and in promiscuous gatherings, whether schoolroom or workplace, were considered sexually endangered, Wollstonecraft would eroticize the safe home and the all-girls establishment, so that these harems and not the outside world are the places where modesty is at risk. It doesn't work, but it's a good try. It doesn't work because Wollstonecraft herself wishes to construct class differentiation through existing sexual categories. The negative effects of the text fell on the middle-class women which it is so eager to construct and instruct.

In *Sex, Politics and Society, The Regulation of Sexuality since 1800*, Jeffrey Weeks, summarizing and extending Foucault, reminds us that:

the sexual apparatus and the nuclear family were produced by the bourgeoisie as an aspect of its own self-affirmation, not as a means of controlling the working class; that there are class sexualities (and different gender sexualities) not a single uniform sexuality. Sexuality is not a given that has to be controlled. It is an historical construct that has historical conditions of existence.[19]

If we apply these comments, we can see that the negative gender sexuality which Wollstonecraft constructs was one of several competing gender sexualities of the late eighteenth century. As Margaret Walters indicates, contemporary femininity grips Wollstonecraft even as she argues against it: a sexually purified femininity was equally a precondition for any optimistic, liberal re-ordering of intra-class gender relations, or female aspiration. But Walters is wrong in seeing this struggle as one between feminism and femininity. There is no feminism that can stand wholly outside femininity as it is posed in a given historical moment. All feminisms give some ideological hostage to femininities and are constructed through the gender sexuality of their day as well as standing in opposition to them. Wollstonecraft saw her middle class, for a few years at least, as a potentially revolutionary force. The men and women in it would exercise their understandings on behalf of all mankind. It was important to her that the whole of this class had access to reason, and that women's liberation was posed within a framework that was minimally acceptable to popular prejudices. That is why, perhaps, she finds herself promising the reader that the freedom of women was the key to their chastity. Within the enlightenment and romantic problematics, reason was always the responsible eldest son and sensibility – emotion, imagination, sensuality – the irresponsible rake, catalyst of change. Class differentiation through the redefinition of sexual mores was a process so deeply entrenched, in Wollstonecraft's time that the moral positions around sexual behavior seemed almost untouchable. Feminists of her generation did not dare to challenge them head on, although Wollstonecraft was beginning to work over this dangerous terrain, in her life and in her fiction at the time of her death. The combination of equal rights and self-abnegating sexuality in *A Vindication* had special attractions for feminists who led very public lives, and found it terrifying and tactically difficult to challenge too many prejudices at once. As a livable formula for independent female subjectivity though, it never had much going for it – not because an immanent and irrepressible sexuality broke through levels of female self-denial, but rather because the anti-erotic ethic itself foregrounded and constructed a sexualized subject.

As long as the double standard survives, gender sexualities will be torn by these contradictions. When Wollstonecraft's ideas for mixed education and wider public participation for women began to be put into practice, women started to query and resist the gender ideologies in which they had been raised. With some help from a popularized psychoanalytic theory, pleasure and sexuality were written into a reworked version of female romantic individualism. Both individualism and these new gender sexualities are, quite properly, heavily contested areas within feminism. Wollstonecraft's project, with its contradictory implications, suggests some of the problems involved in the moralization of sexuality on behalf of any political program, even a feminist one.

FEMINISM AND COMPULSORY HETEROSEXUALITY: ADRIENNE RICH

Between the two texts I have chosen to discuss lie nearly two centuries in which successive feminisms have engaged with recalcitrant issues surrounding women's sexuality. Yet while the specific issues have changed, many of the terms in which they are debated would be familiar to Mary Wollstonecraft. In the 1980s the independent sexuality that seems most threatening to the dominant culture as fact and symbol of women's escape from patriarchal control is lesbianism. Lesbian feminists, in the various political tendencies in the women's movement have for many years now been insisting that the cultural constraints on their sexual expression are central to women's subordination as a whole. Sexuality has never been a hidden issue in modern feminism, but its theorization has produced many painful if necessary disagreements, none more so than the place of lesbianism as a political stance within feminist practice. Adrienne Rich, the American poet and feminist theorist, has developed a range of arguments about the meaning of female sexuality in our culture. Her position on the sexual politics of feminism is powerfully stated in an article first published in the feminist journal *Signs* in the summer of 1980, and widely available soon afterwards in pamphlet form. "Compulsory heterosexuality and lesbian existence" challenges the normative heterosexist values and repressive liberal tolerance of a large section of the women's movement, arguing that an acceptance of the virtue and centrality of historical and contemporary forms of lesbian experience is the base line for a feminist politics. Like Wollstonecraft, if a trifle more tentatively, Rich also poses a reformed libidinal economy for women as the precondition for the successful liberation of women. It is the common element in their thinking about women's sexuality that I wish briefly to examine in this last section.

The foregrounding of sexuality as the source of women's subordination is the element that most obviously links Wollstonecraft's analysis with radical and revolutionary feminism in the distinct but linked tendencies that have developed in Britain, France, and the United States over the last fourteen years. These strands in feminism have taken the lead in privileging sexuality as the central fact and universal symbol of women's oppression. Radical feminism has built its theory and rhetoric around the ideological and actual violence done to women's bodies, while liberal and socialist feminism has been rather nervous of the sexual, working instead to define the specific forms which women's subordination takes in different class, cultural, and racial groups, at discrete historical moments. These projects and strategies frequently overlap, but it is roughly fair to say that radical feminism emphasizes the identity of gender oppression across history and culture. Revolutionary feminism pushes this analysis farther, posing a monolithic patriarchal tyranny, with sexuality as its weapon. Both tendencies have located the universal truth of gender oppression in a sadistic and insatiable male sexuality, which is empowered to humiliate and punish. Any pleasure that accrues to women who take part in heterosexual acts is therefore necessarily tainted; at the extreme end of this position, women who "go with men" are considered collaborators – every man a fascist at heart. While Wollstonecraft acknowledged that a depraved sexual pleasure for both men and women was the effect of unequal power relations between them, radical feminism underlines the unpleasure of these relations for women. Where women have no choice over the aim and object of their sexuality, heterosexuality, in the words of Adrienne Rich, is "compulsory" – an institution more comprehensive and sinister than the different relations and practices it constructs. Worse, compulsory heterosexuality is part of a chain of gender-specific tortures, both medical and conjugal: hysterectomy, cliterodectomy, battering, rape, and imprisonment are all elaborations of the sadistic act of penetration itself, penetration the socially valorized symbol of violence against women. Men use these torments to shore up their own subjectivity. Their pleasure in them is a confirmation of male power. Pornography, in this analysis, is emblematic of all male sexuality, the violent fantasy behind the tenderest act of intercourse.

Rich defines heterosexuality as an institution "forcibly and subliminally imposed on women" who have "everywhere . . . resisted it." Although she admits that there are "qualitative differences of experience" within heterosexuality, these differences cannot alter the corrupt nature of the institution, since a good partner is rather like a good master in slavery, a matter of luck not choice. While Wollstonecraft believed, cynically, that all women took pleasure in their slavery, Rich backs off from admitting that coercion, however, subliminal, can produce pleasure. Binary categories, historically differentiated, are operating here. Bad women in 1792 experienced bad pleasure; good women in 1980 experience no pleasure. In both cases the effect is punitive.

Rich's abstract women – they are no nearer to real, historical women than the incredibly lascivious ladies of *A Vindication* – are neither masochists nor nymphomaniacs, they are simply women whose natural sexuality has been artificially diverted, from their real object, other women. Women's long struggle against heterosexuality took, according to Rich, a wide variety of forms which she calls the "lesbian continuum," as distinct from "lesbian existence" – the natural sexuality of women. Rich has shifted the terms in the nature/culture debate without really altering the paradigm around women and sexuality. In her scenario female heterosexuality is socially constructed and female homosexuality is natural. As in Wollstonecraft, what is bad goes on the outside, what inheres is neutral or good. In Rich's formula, women's libidinal drive is made central, transhistorical, and immanent where dominant sexual ideology had constructed it as accidental and/or pathological. Political lesbianism becomes more than a strategic position for feminism; it is a return to nature. In this new interpretation of sexuality a fairly crude libidinal economy is asserted:

> Woman identification is a source of energy, a potential springhead of female power, violently curtailed and wasted under the institution of heterosexuality. The denial of reality and visibility

to women's passion for women, women's choice of women as allies, life companions, and community; the forcing of such relationships into dissimulation, their disintegration under intense pressure, have meant an incalculable loss to the power of all women *to change the social relations of the sexes*, to liberate ourselves and each other. The lie of compulsory female heterosexuality today afflicts not just feminist scholarship, but every profession, every reference work, every curriculum, every organizing attempt, every relationship or conversation over which it hovers. It creates, specifically, a profound falseness, hypocrisy and hysteria in the heterosexual dialogue, for every heterosexual relationship is lived in the queasy strobelight of that lie. However we choose to identify ourselves, however we find ourselves labelled, it flickers across and distorts our lives.[20]

The saturating power of this socially enforced – as opposed to naturally lived – sexuality represses, in Rich's view, all creative expression and all radical and revolutionary process. It is eerily like Wollstonecraft's totalizing view of sexuality. Both Rich and Wollstonecraft believe that heterosexuality as it is and has been lived by women is an ideological distortion of the possibilities of female sexuality. At one level *A Vindication* is highly prescriptive: it asks women, at the very least, to resist the appeal of a pleasure which will put them at the sexual and emotional mercy of men. Wollstonecraft stopped short of defining an innate form of female sexuality – she understood after her encounter with *Émile* that arguing difference from nature was ultimately reactionary. Rich, on the other hand, has no qualms about constructing female sexuality as naturally different. She uses her analysis, in the passage cited above, to interpret conflicts within feminism today. The result is that these crucial differences, on whose working through the future of feminism depends, are collapsed into the denial of *some* women of the universal sexuality of *all* women. Any failure of energy or strategy can be reduced to the frustration and anxiety around a denied or feared sexuality. Difficulties between women are no longer about age, class, race, or culture. All the legitimate problems that inhere to an emergent politics are whittled down to a repressed but supracultural sexuality. In "Compulsory heterosexuality" the solution for a better politics is contained in the appeal from bad culture back to good nature.

The theme of Rich's revision of female sexuality is the possible construction of a specifically *feminist* humanism. Benign nature is female – affectionate and sensual as well as creative, revolutionary, and transcendent. In its political inflection it opposes an innately vicious male nature whose ascendency has produced the bad dream of phallocratic culture. According to Rich,

> heterosexuality as an institution has been organized and maintained through the female wage scale, the enforcement of middle-class women's leisure, the glamorization of so-called sexual liberation, the withholding of education from women, the image of "high art" and popular culture, the mystification of the "personal" sphere and much else.[21]

These rather heterogeneous, class-specific, and ethnocentric devices support heterosexuality rather than capitalism or patriarchal relations. Take away these and other cultural supports and heterosexuality would presumably wither away. Destroy heterosexist culture at any historical moment and lesbian/feminism would emerge triumphant from its ashes. Rich's simple belief in the all-embracing political possibilities of lesbian existence, her rejection of the political integrity of heterosexual feminism constitutes a denial both of the specificity and variety of female sexuality and the specificity and variety of feminism.

The identification of the sources of social good or evil in the sexual drive of either sex, or in any socially specific sexual practice is a way of foreclosing our still imperfect understanding of the histories of sexuality. The moralization of desire that inevitably follows from such an analysis colludes with those dominant practices which construct human sexuality through categories of class, race, and gender in order to divide and rule. The sexuality constructed by a feminist revolution will be a new social relation, with new contradictions and constraints. The dream of an autonomous sexuality, not constructed through the desire of the other, male or female, is a transcendental fantasy of bourgeois individualism. It poses a subject who can stand outside the social. Perhaps, considering its political difficulties in the past, feminism should resist appropriating such a subject, or at least refuse to hang our hopes for sexual pleasure round its neck.

The walls and doors of the women's lavatories at the University of Sussex library were, and are, covered with women's writing. From this lowest seat of high learning a polylogic testament to women's entry into discourse can be read in the round. There is, inevitably, a euphoric temptation to read too much out of these expressive inscriptions. For if young women can shit *and* write, not for some patriarchal pedant, but for each other's eyes only, what vestiges of Victorian constraints remain? It is true, of course, that the vast majority of contributors to this particular public/private debate are young, white, and middle class, but not all women's lavatories so decorated are quite so class and race bound. In the smallest rooms of this academy politics and intellectual matters are informally debated, but sex as the preferred topic wins hands down.

"How do I get an orgasm?" prompted a booth-full of replies and commentary in the mid-1970s, showing off the range and ingenuity of women's sexual practices and theories. Advice included detailed instructions to be relayed to a male partner as well as the succinct, laconic recommendation to "Try Women." There was an address for suppliers of vibrators and an illustration, definitely not erotic, to help one find the elusive clitoris. In the wide variety of responses one was noticeably absent – no contributor contested the importance of the question. No one queried the centrality of orgasm for women's sexual practice or the importance of sexual pleasure itself. No anachronistic bluestocking suggested that intellectual and sensual pursuits were incompatible. No devout Christian was moved to tell her sisters to wait until marriage. Only now, from a different time and place in the feminist debate over sexuality does that apparently unanimous agreement among young educated women that sexual pleasure, however achieved, was an unproblematic desire seem curious. About the means of arriving at pleasure there was plenty of disagreement; if anything that cubicle was a telling reminder that there has never been a single femininity, and that within feminism sexuality and the meaning of pleasure have most frequently been the site of anger, contradiction, and confusion, too often illuminating class, cultural, and racial division between women. Now, when female sexuality is indisputably centre-stage in feminist debates but pleasure is too rarely its subject and eros rampant is more likely to conjure up a snuff movie than multiple orgasm, that lavatory wall remains with me as an important event in the history of feminism, a moment whose appearance and significance we must work to understand.

NOTES

* This essay originally appeared in Formations Editorial Board (1983) *Formations of Pleasure*, London, Routledge & Kegan Paul.
1 M. Wollstonecraft (1792) *A Vindication of the Rights of Woman*, repr. (1975) New York, W. W. Norton, 119. E. Dickinson (1861) *The Complete Poems of Emily Dickinson*, repr. (1977) London, Faber & Faber, 114. A. Dworkin (1981) *Pornography: Men Possessing Women*, London, The Women's Press, 304.
2 Wollstonecraft (1792).
3 J. Weeks (1981) *Sex, Politics and Society*, London, Longman, 30.
4 A. Rich (1980) "Compulsory heterosexuality and lesbian existence," *Signs: Journal of Women in Culture and Society*, 5, 4, 631–60.
5 M. Walters (1979). "The rights and wrongs of women: Mary Wollstonecraft, Harriet Martineau, Simone de Beauvoir," in J. Mitchell and A. Oakley (eds) *The Rights and Wrongs of Women*, Harmondsworth, Pelican, 304–78.
6 *Historical and Moral View of the Origin and Progress of the French Revolution* (1794).
7 Wollstonecraft (1792) 9–10.
8 Wollstonecraft (1792) 10.
9 Wollstonecraft (1792) 11.
10 J.-J. Rousseau, *Émile*, trans. B. Foxley (1974) London, J. M. Dent, 332. Passages from *Émile* can all be found in Book V of this edition. However, I have followed the translation used by Wollstonecraft who cites large chunks of Book V in *A Vindication*.
11 Rousseau (1974) 332–3.
12 M. Foucault (1979) *The History of Sexuality: Volume 1: An Introduction*, London, Allen Lane, 121.
13 Wollstonecraft (1792) 3–4.
14 Wollstonecraft (1792) 82.
15 Wollstonecraft (1792) 117.
16 Wollstonecraft (1792) 116.
17 Wordsworth and Coleridge, (1976) *Lyrical Ballads*, London, Methuen, 255–6.
18 Wordsworth and Coleridge (1976) 261.
19 Weeks (1981) 10.
20 Rich (1980) 657.
21 Rich (1980) 659.

7

Modes of modern shopping: Mallarmé at the *Bon Marché*

RACHEL BOWLBY

Women shop: this statement, clear at one level, calls for explanation, or at least for further specification. It might mean any, or all, of the following (and more): that women, and not men (or children, or caterpillars) go shopping; that all shoppers are women; that all women (or some women) shop (and so do some men or all men); that women do nothing but shop; that women can be defined by the fact that they shop.

Leaving aside the question of what is a woman (in this statement or elsewhere), there are also problems about the definition of shopping. "To go shopping" or "to do the shopping:" is it an open-ended leisure activity or a finite, specifiable task? Is it fun or is it functional? If it is true that "a woman's work is never done," shopping might indeed turn out to straddle both these categories, or to fit into neither.

I start from the proposition that women shop is a problem as much as a premise. Empirically, it is the case that in modern industrialized countries women, more than men, spend time and money on an activity known as shopping. It is also the case that this social fact is often taken in a supplementary sense, as implying that something in the nature of women predisposes them to shopping; and reciprocally, that something in the nature of shopping makes it more likely to appeal to women than to men. The fact that women shop demands explanation on more than one level, and not least because it immediately raises the issue of the relation between "historical" and "natural" categories of interpretation. In the yoking of women and shopping, it might further appear that while shopping is generally taken as an historical variable, women are thought to do it as part of their nature. In this essay I try to show that the analysis of historically specific articulations of women and shopping can also elucidate questions about what is taken as woman's nature.

"Women shop" is not a random starting-point: it is meant to recall the way in which Nancy Chodorow's book, *The Reproduction of Mothering*, takes its cue from another statement about women whose empirical truth and apparent obviousness seem, however, to require analysis.[1] "Women mother:" biologically women (not men) have babies; socially women (not men) "mother" children in the sense of rearing them. The slide between these two propositions, the literal naturalness of the first lending support to the presumed naturalness of the second, is what Chodorow undertakes to question. Like the question of why women shop, the question of why women mother is one which engages problems about the relation between the natural and the social or historical; and about how such oppositions are constructed in the first place.

That women mother seems to follow as a law of nature, a law of the species. Chodorow's investigation of the "reproduction" of mothering polemically points out that this reproduction of the social practice is not as inevitable as it sounds. Shopping, too, is linked to the metaphorical "reproductive sphere" of the social order, within which, according to Marxist historical analyses, women perform the task not only of a literal reproduction of the workforce in the form of babies, but also of rearing the future workers and servicing the existing ones. Shopping, and mothering in the extended sense of rearing, would both fall into this area.

Shopping and mothering are both, in a certain sense, part of women's "reproductive" roles, but the definitions of woman's nature implied by the assignment of each as a "naturally" feminine task are in fact not the same. Motherhood is associated with self-denial and deferral to others' needs. Shopping, while in one way regarded as an indispensable task, is also regarded as a field for the exercise of self-indulgent pleasures which are nonetheless taken to be "feminine" in the same way as are the different, responsible qualities attributed to the mother.

The presumèd connection of women and shopping is inseparable from the nineteenth-century development of fashion as an organized system, which was hailed at the time as "the democratization of luxury." Partly through the invention of the sewing machine and the consequent possibility of mass-produced clothing, the regular purchase of fashionable goods now became possible for the bourgeoisie as well as for the upper classes and it was pre-eminently women, not men, who became their avid consumers. This might seem to follow "naturally" from women's imagined liking for pretty things and novelties, and the nineteenth-century construction of consumption certainly built on the assumed existence of such a disposition. But it is important to point out that just as fashion had not always been a middle-class phenomenon, so its exclusive focus on a female clientele, as opposed to one of both sexes, was relatively new. Ostentatious dress was an accepted feature of the fashionable male aristocrat of the eighteenth century, but the scandalous appearance of the late-nineteenth-century dandy operated against a norm according to which men were now expected to cover themselves with a uniform anonymity quite distinct from the colorful variations of female clothing. Equally new was the fact that the making and selling of fashion was now almost entirely in the hands of men, where previously these professions had been open to both sexes.

High-turnover fashion implies change and transitoriness rather than stable or permanent criteria of quality: "the latest" rather than "the best." But this indeterminacy is in striking contrast to the regularity of the mechanism for the continuous production of new things on which fashion is based. Given this oddly double structure, and the coincidence between the systematization of fashion and its sexual polarization, the French word *mode* has an interesting history. Meaning "fashion," the word is feminine (*à la mode*), but the masculine noun, *le mode*, has a rather different set of meanings. In Littré's nineteenth-century dictionary of French, the following definitions appear:

MODE, *sm.* En Philos. Manière d'être qui ne peut exister indépendamment des substances, quoiqu'elle puisse être conçue à part abstraitement. Forme, méthode. Mode de gouvernement.

II. Nom donné aux différentes formes du verbe employées pour exprimer les différents points de vue auxquels on considère l'existence ou l'action. // En mus. Disposition des sons de la gamme, déterminée par la place du demi-ton, qui occupe le troisième degré dans le mode majeur, et le second dans le mode mineur.
MODE, *sf.* Manière, fantaisie. // Usage passager qui dépend du goût et du caprice. // A la mode, dans le goût du jour. // *Au pl.* Ajustements, chapeaux, parures à la mode. // Marchande de modes, faiseuse de chapeaux.[2]

On the one hand, then, a technical term used in analytical fields: philosophy, grammar, music theory. On the other, feminine hand, "fantasy" as opposed to method, the concrete (things or persons) as opposed to the abstract; variation rather than continuity; a "temporary practice" which is itself derived from "taste" and "caprice."

This distinction between the two genders of *mode* is thus practically one of contrary terms. But it was not a historical constant. In Bloch and von Wartburg's etymological dictionary, we find:

Empt. du lat. *modus*, "manière", prop. "mesure", qui s'employait aussi comme terme de musique et de grammaire. Dans tous les sens féminin jusqu'au XVI s.; le masc. a été rétabli au XVII s. pour des sens techniques.[3]

And further in the OED:

The F. *mode* remained fem. in all cases until the 17th cent., when the masc. gender was adopted for the uses, chiefly technical, that belonged to L. *modus*. For the sense of "fashion" the fem. gender was retained.

Perhaps it is not by chance, this separation between *le* and *la*, between masculine and feminine modes. But without wishing to choose between viewing history as accidental or determined, capricious or methodical, it might be interesting to consider how far this modern division of labour between technical and other *modes* is substantiated by some texts in which the fabrication of female shoppers would seem to be the point.

My first example is the series of *agendas*, or appointments diaries, produced for their clientele by the Paris *Bon Marché*, and which are briefly discussed in Michael Miller's history of this department store and its relation to the development of French consumer culture.[4] The diaries were produced at least from 1880 (the earliest example that survives). Very little is known about their production or distribution: who wrote them, whether they were free to regular customers, how many were printed. Nor is it known whether other stores also produced diaries. The survival of the (incomplete) *Bon Marché* collection is something of a historical fluke; but it supplies some useful evidence for the way in which one of the new institutions of fashion and shopping presented itself to its prospective female public.[5]

Zola's novel *Au Bonheur des Dames* (1883) is partly based on the *Bon Marché*.[6] It pictures the department store as a "cathedral of commerce" providing occasion for the ecstasies of a female congregation devoted to the *consommation* of fashion and sexuality rather than that of the outmoded church whose function it usurps. Of necessity, the consumer, so that she keep coming back, keep spending more, keep finding new things to want, must be anything but "rational:" her "mode" is that of caprice rather than order. In this context, it might be expected that the diaries would reinforce the store's generalized invitation to *extravagance*, to wanderings or vagaries outside the bounds of deliberation or thrift. But in fact its promotion does not work in such a straightforward manner.

In format, the *agendas* are much the same as present-day desk diaries; there are up to 150 pages, most of them divided into four spaces for different days, with ruled lines for filling in lists or appointments. But the proportion of editorial matter is much higher, and it is oddly disparate in content. There are pages of information about Paris public transport, about postal services, the *Bon Marché* mail order system, theatres, railway excursions. Particular care is taken to present the bus, and later metro, timetables in terms of how to get to the rue de Sèvres, where the store was situated; in general, the effect is to associate shopping with other elements of a leisured city lifestyle. That this should have been practically available to the bourgeois lady marks a significant break with the past: department stores were in fact the first public places – other than churches or cathedrals – which were considered respectable for her to visit without a male companion. But this also signified, at another level, a stepping out from domestic bounds – what the "feminine" writer of the text discussed below elliptically, if not euphemistically, designates "our double existence, street and drawing room."[7]

Apart from these metropolitan "pointers," the diaries contain articles of a light, informative type, not unlike the miscellaneous "factual" features produced for children's papers. Topics range from the history of old French towns to "Great Inventions," to a series on "*La Science amusante*" and a piece on jogging at the height of a craze for this *sport pédestre* in the 1890 edition. In addition, there are detailed monthly menu suggestions (including, once, the *diner maigre*, an early version of *cuisine minceur*), and sundry cartoons and comic strips. In relation to all these items, the reader is taken to be less a streetwise urban *habituée* than a potentially unruly infant to be kept amused or occupied by a heterogeneous spread of innocuous material. This random selection of articles and types of article assembled under no principle of unity other than the interest or entertainment value established by their mere presence in the diary, exactly reproduces the organization of the department store. There, an assortment of otherwise unrelated objects is gathered together under one roof, linked only by the characteristic of being merchandise and therefore presented as desirable objects of purchase. Between the store and the diary/magazine, there is a structural homology whereby a superficial variety of contents is offered in such a way as to make that variety and surface interest into self-supporting values. The distractable attention of the diary's reader, as she flips from one page to another, is of the same type as that of the impulse buyer drifting round the shop.

The diaries also contain portentous features about the *Bon Marché* itself. These consist for instance of celebratory biographies of the founders, Monsieur and Madame Boucicaut, with due attention given to the philanthropic, as opposed to profit-seeking, side of their work. There are artists' impressions of different parts of the store, including the working and dining quarters of its staff. The *Bon Marché* did not conceal the fact that behind the scenes of the consumer wonderland visible to customers, it was organized like an industry. With far more subtlety, the diaries describe with pride the provisions made for the comfort of employees, inviting readers to share in the vaunted self-congratulation. So there are details of the retirement plan and drawings of the fencing classes kindly provided by the management. The effect is to represent the commercial giant as more like the fairy godmother of a charitable institution. The store appears not as a factory, but as a large, well-ordered domestic establishment. In this way, the diary brings the store closer to home, suggesting its likeness to the (ideal version of the) setting in which the reader finds herself. She is addressed as a responsible member of the middle class, naturally interested in the proper welfare of the class which serves her needs, and whose needs she serves in return. Sex does not enter the picture here: the reader and her servants are distinguished simply by class. Further, the responsibility attributed to the reader is of a quite different order to the childish capacity for distraction assumed elsewhere.

There are other modes by which the diaries make the connection between the worlds of the household and the department store. Most obviously, the housewife's domestic and culinary arrangements will be made in the context – on the very paper – of the store which by its physical presence and regular use in the form of the diary becomes an indispensable part of day-to-day life. But again, this is not primarily an incitement to erratic or capricious behaviour. Rather, it leaves the reader free to adapt the diary's pages to her own requirements, and equips her with a tool that is more appropriate to the manager of a domestic establishment than to the irresponsible, flighty character associated with the modern spending woman.

Since a diary is used or leafed through every day of the year, the store is not only a presence, but also a continuous presence in the home. Shopping for fashionable goods appears as a routine practice, "domesticated" from its possibly risky undertones of unruliness – which are themselves contained in another way by the address to the woman as child in search of random occupation. At the same time, though, the store is able to set itself up on a par with the ritual occasions which break the monotony of the quotidian. Along with saints' days and other religious festivals, the diary indicates the dates of commencement for the *Bon Marché*'s special sales: from "whites" in January through to toys in December, each month has its own particular feature – and this in addition to the two principal semi-annual sales. In this way, shopping takes on the attributes of a new religion of consumption, a new mythical cycle of seasons and red-letter days which is added to, without opposing, the existing one. The two orders sit side by side as complementary markers of an annual rhythm of prescribed activities and exceptional events, and the modern temptations of shopping are rendered innocuous by their neutral assimilation to the established moral authority of the church.

This comfortable accommodation of old and new in the pages of the household diary is all the more striking in view of the way that the new commerce which made shopping for fashionable goods a part of middle-class life promoted newness itself into a value. Starting with the *magasins de nouveauté* (novelty shops) which were the immediate precursors of department stores in France, the extended fashion system operated on the basis of a perpetual, regular "discovery" of new lines whose representation as "the latest thing" depended solely on the possibility of their differentiation, as new, from the previous fashion thereby rendered "out of date." It is not perhaps by chance that semiotics, based on a structuralist linguistics which situates meaning in the differences between signs rather than in their supposed independent meanings, should have taken the fashion system as a privileged field for analysis. (More tendentiously, it might also be suggested that the possibility or necessity of structuralist linguistics, developed at the beginning of the twentieth century, bears some relation to the development of the fashion system itself.)

The juxtaposition of religion and shopping, one the representative of a timeless, stable order of traditional values and practices and the other of a system founded on change and novelty as its governing principles, thus has the air of a minor scandal – or at least of an extraordinary feat of marketing finesse. Not only is something new grafted onto, and legitimized in terms of, something old, as a natural and non-contradictory passage from one to the other, but in the case of religion and shopping, it is the old and the new *par excellence* which are gently brought together. This simple unification seems to apply as well to the terms of other potentially incompatible pairings in the diary: the serious and the frivolous, the responsible *mère de famille* and the wayward child, the duties of regular commitments and the fun of play and naughtiness.

This account of the *Bon Marché* home diaries has emphasized the way that the new nineteenth-century habit of shopping was not represented or sold only in terms of an appeal to the female consumer as inherently pleasure-seeking and potentially extravagant. Yet it is in these terms that the connection between women and shopping, between *la mode* and femininity, has usually been made; and this is the aspect which seems to dominate my second example. *La Dernière Mode* (The Latest Fashion) was a Paris fashion journal which ran to eight issues edited and written in their entirety by Mallarmé during the last part of 1874. In addition to advertisements and illustrations of fashions, it included numerous articles on topics ranging from books and the arts, to recipes, to readers' letters and questions, and more, as well as on current fashion itself. The signatories to these features are numerous, and mostly feminine; all of them were in fact written by the poet.

In his (veiled) capacity as a man initiating his female readers into the world of fashion, Mallarmé looks at first (or second) sight like one more example, if a somewhat unexpected one, of the new masculine élite of fashion publicists: a brother, then, to leading department store owners and fashion designers. The acknowledged star of Paris *haute couture* at the time was an Englishman named Frederick Worth, whose phenomenal prestige is described by the historian Marylène Delbourg-Delphis in the following terms:

> In the reduced sphere of the affairs of "society", Worth has a role equivalent to that of Napoleon III in public affairs. In becoming the initiator of fashions, the grand *couturier* appears as the grand legislator, the grand organiser of the feminine universe.[8]

But it might be thought that this "feminine universe" of fashion and beauty would be attractive in a particular way to "men of letters" in so far as they, unlike most of their sex, have an interest in beautiful things. In this light, Mallarmé's enterprise would seem less one of legislation – dictating his taste to a powerless female readership – than one of identification, taking up the attractions of participation in a femininity that consists in the pleasures of self-adornment. A certain "Ix," writer of the *Chronique* on the contemporary cultural scene, starts his first number with this interesting defense:

> These products of the latest hour. . . . are they in fashion or are they to be? A frivolous critique, apparently? No, for it begins from this absolute point that all women like verse as well as perfumes or jewels or the characters in a story as much as themselves.[9]

According to this, the value of new books is to be judged solely by the criterion of women's random and diverse likings: the criterion substituted for the possible objection of a "frivolous critique" amounts to what is apparently a description or exemplification of a frivolous disposition.

It might then seem not unreasonable to imagine that in taking this reversal seriously for six months, Mallarmé was doing no more than engaging in a form of temporary distraction or relaxation. It would be as if for the time being he wanted to give a free rein to a lighter, more casual side to his character than the aspect of the austere devotee of pure poetry. This, at any rate, is the assumption made by some of Mallarmé's commentators. Guy Michaud, for instance, says of *La Dernière Mode*:

> At first sight a strange enterprise on the part of a poet, but one which will seem less surprising if one thinks of the feminine preciosity there was in the character of Mallarmé.[10]

Femininity is here taken as a recognizable attribute able to be predicated of a characteristic such as "preciosity." It is not, apparently, confined to the female sex, nor does the quotation pronounce it as necessarily a characteristic of all members of that sex. Whereas "Ix" makes a general hypothesis about "all women," Michaud invokes a notion of the feminine which can be part of the make-up of a man, and indeed is assumed to be part of the make-up of this man. Mallarmé's undertaking appears less strange or surprising when it is referred to this "feminine" element of which it would then be a natural expression. Far from being a deviation or addity, *La Derniére Mode* is then seen as complementary to works which manifest other elements of Mallarmé's character than "feminine preciosity:" it completes, rather than disrupts, the unity of his *oeuvre*, which is both presupposed and defended.

On this reading, the feminine frivolity of *la mode* could then perhaps be said to be necessary, whether for an individual or for society, as a harmonious counter-balance to a life that would otherwise seem too masculine and too serious. But Michaud takes as read a fixity to the identification of femininity, whether as man or woman, which Mallarmé's text does not itself substantiate.

At the opposite end of the spectrum of possible classifications, writing about fashion can be considered an eminently scientific undertaking. This is the position taken by the sociologist Pierre Bourdieu in the course of making a distinction between the two spheres of fashion and high culture which Mallarmé seems, seriously or not, to bring together. At the beginning of a paper entitled "Haute couture et haute culture," Bourdieu says:

Modes of Shopping

The title of this lecture is not a joke. I really am going to speak about the relationships between *haute couture* and high culture. Fashion is a subject with a great deal of prestige in the sociological tradition, at the same time as being a little frivolous in appearance. . . .

What I am proposing rests on the structural homology between the field of production of that particular category of luxury goods which are fashion goods, and that other category of luxury goods which are the goods of legitimate culture such as music, poetry or philosophy. This means that in speaking of *haute couture* I shall continually be speaking of high culture. . . . You will say: "Why not speak of it directly?" Because these legitimate objects are protected by their legitimacy against scientific scrutiny [*le regard scientifique*] and against the work of desacralisation which is presupposed by the scientific study of sacred objects.[11]

Instead of this "scientific look" of the sociologist, Mallarmé's look would seem rather to render sacred that which is normally looked upon as frivolous. Within the text of the journal, fashion is placed alongside high culture, and the eight issues are regarded as forming part of the *oeuvre* of someone considered to be a thoroughly serious poet. Where Bourdieu provocatively brings high culture down to the level of fashion, equalizing them both as objects to be regarded from the perspective of a sociological study which now takes over the position of seriousness, Mallarmé, as a "legitimate" representative of high culture, takes this identification seriously by entering into *la mode* and refusing or undoing the opposition on which its alleged difference is based. The frivolous and the serious can no longer be held apart.

This can be seen from parts of *La Dernière Mode* which would seem to resemble a project of analysis not dissimilar to that of Bourdieu. The fashion writer "Marguerite de Ponty" calls herself an *historiographe* and sets out to explain, not just to describe, the present state of her field of interest:

not just those touches necessary to the completion of a new harmony . . . but also where this comes from and where it will lead us, its origin, its results, and above all the transitions which have accompanied it.[12]

La Dernière Mode seems thus in a sense to combine two attitudes which are in principle contradictory. In treating fashion as worthy of serious consideration, the writer(s) take(s) it sometimes as an object demanding explanation from the outside, as with the *regard scientifique*, and sometimes as a personal matter, having no determinations apart from the tastes of those who take an interest in it. This personal aspect is itself, as we have seen, regarded elsewhere in the journal as characteristic of women, who like verses and jewellery as much as they like themselves. And this doubling perhaps bears some relation to the alternation of the two sexes in the text according to the diverse signatories of the articles. But Mallarmé's complication of the issue is sufficiently indicated here by the fact that "Marguerite de Ponty" is evidently not presented as a man.

The journal is addressed to women, who are invited to read it without giving it too much serious attention. "Ix" refers to taking "the time to leaf through it, and probably not to read at all the *Présentation* of Your Servant." The imagined life of the reader is one of distractions and novelties, in which she is forever seeking new *spectacles* to go and see, new books to look at, new clothes to buy. An apparently frivolous existence: according to the self-proclaimed *serviteur*, the woman, and her magazine, are interested only in pleasure:

> We will appear, everywhere, the same: attentive to the sum of pleasure which can be obtained by a contemporary person from these new practices.[13]

But there is also, it would seem, the fact that fashion is itself a kind of absolute that must be followed fairly rigorously by the reader who wishes to be recognized as this "contemporary person" of what the journal calls, in English, "*high society*:"

> Laws, decrees, projects, rulings, as the gentlemen say, all is now promulgated as far as Fashion is concerned; and no new Message from this sovereign (who, herself, is all the world) [*tout le monde*: also "everybody"], will come to take us by surprise for a fortnight or two.[14]

It is necessary, then, to be *au courant* with *la Mode* which, in this regard, looks more like a female Frederick Worth – a grand legislator – or, indeed, like *Le Mode* of a mode of government. Fashion's capriciousness is here raised to the level of an arbitrary power, a sovereign's decree, to be imposed or enforced upon her subjects thereby deprived of their own capricious likings in the matter. By the mediation of "Marguerite de Ponty," *porte-parole* of her queen, fashion is consecrated as an absolute feminine authority in the case of feminine preferences. The reader stands in need of a constantly renewed process of education with regard to the pleasures that are hers. She is placed in the position of a pupil learning her lessons – just as, in other parts of the journal she is pedagogically instructed by the *professeur de lycée* with respect to the education of her children. Schoolmaster, critic, and fashion adviser would seem to be united in their joint project of informing the reader of the choices her capriciousness will make.

All the same, "Marguerite de Ponty" seems at the end of this article to dispense with the alleged requirement to learn and obey the laws of fashion:

> These precepts should only be known in order to forget them; and better than them, I am presuming, Ladies, upon all the disobedient caprice which your Fantasy is already mixing with this reading.[15]

But it is just as much an exercise of authority to give the readers permission to indulge their "Fantasy." This "disobedient caprice" addresses them as small children whose silliness is both predictable and amusing, and has no significance for the survival of the law to which they fail to conform. Rather, it is that same law which grants permission to disobey, so that feminine fantasy comes under its decrees, as part of its project. The *mode* or technique of *la Mode* is precisely what constitutes it as caprice; and the form of the caprice is determined by what it disobeys, what it has "learned" to "forget."

But the legislative Fashion remains, in gender at least, a woman, suggesting, as with "Marguerite de Ponty" herself, a certain complexity in the fusion or confusion of law and caprice, masculine and feminine modes. There might seem to be an absolute distinction between the ruler of fashion and her subject followers; but the journal also gives reason to suppose not just that the sovereign might be a woman, but that all women are sovereigns. This is what "Ix" implies, in referring to a mirror, in which you would recognise yourself. You and others casting your eyes at it, when the rhythm of the winter dances brings you in your turn before the impartial mirror, all of you will seek the queen of the celebration by a look, which will go straight to your image; for in truth, what woman, always being this queen for someone, is not it a little bit for herself?[16]

In seeing herself as another, and as seen impartially, she will see herself as queen of the occasion and queen of herself. In doubling her by the image, the mirror reflects back or represents her as the unique sovereign; and in representing this process, "Ix" explicitly draws out the further irony: that the queen is any woman who happens to pass the mirror.

The uniqueness of the queen is thus undermined from the outset, both because it is reduced to pure generality and because it is recognizable only in the image which separates the woman from what she none the less views as herself. This implies not only that there is no queen (if every woman is a queen) but also that there is no woman (if a woman "recognizes" herself in the form of the mirror image which shows her what she is). It is not that the beautiful image is a delusion, but that there can be no woman (or queen) without the mirror which informs her (as it did Snow White's stepmother) that she is the most beautiful woman in the world.

"Ix" further describes the process of the reader's identification of herself as woman in terms not of recognition but of imitation:

This blossoming [*épanouissement*] of your two lips, I will note its grace, which other lips, following in a murmur [*tout bas*] this reading are already trying out for themselves. Things are thus, and rightly: does not the world have as it were a right of repetition [*reprise*] over the most profound manifestation of our instincts? it provokes it, it refines it. Everything is learned "live" [*sur le vif*], even beauty, and the carrying [*le port*] of the head, one takes it from someone, that is to say from everyone, like the wearing [*le port*] of a dress.[17]

What Mallarmé's, or Ix's, text reveals is that there is no identity, no unique self, before imitation. The structure of repetition or reply set in play by the manifestation of the instincts returns upon that manifestation itself, which must also, according to the logic of the second part of the description, be attributed to imitation: "everything is learned 'live'." There can be no possibility of distinguishing the imitation from the original, or the instinct from the "everything" which is learned.[18]

Not only are instincts always imitations, but it is also necessary that their manifestation occur by means of an interpreter or intermediary. Here it is a matter of a "smile" whose "grace" appears only because of the "reading" by the viewer. "Everything is learned 'live,'" including the instincts of the beautiful woman, but the life from which it is learned is here a reading or viewing of the woman by a man. The woman, following this trajectory, must read this reading, see this seeing, in order to know, to recognize, her own instincts.

As with the mirror image, the acquired instincts are not thereby unreal or falsified, as if there were some more original or genuine ones which they suppressed or from which they deviated. "Miss Satin," another fashion correspondent, advises her readers as to the value of department stores, which "contain all the dream . . . of a Parisian woman:"

> It is not only chance which makes us, before any other, write the name of the *Bon Marché*; but we are obeying an intimate conviction that never will the Reader [*Lectrice*] who has mounted her carriage and thrown out the words, "*rue du Bac*" or "*rue de Sèvres*" come home vexed [*contrariée*] by our advice or by her own personal movement [*son propre mouvement à elle*].[19]

"Our advice" and "her own personal movement" are one and the same.

If the woman's instincts are learned by a double *reading*, it is perhaps not surprising that they should also be available for reading or learning in literature itself. This would seem to be borne out by a reading of "Ix"'s reading of a newly published collection of poetry:

> From the solemn and unforgettable past, fable, legend, history, but which is now closed to the blossoming out [*éclosion*] of those miraculous types, Théodore de Banville, with the collection of *Princesses*, has resurrected the souls and bodies of Semiramis, Ariadne, Helen, Cleopatra, Salomé, the Queen of Sheba, Mary Queen of Scots, the Princess of Lamballe and the Princess Borghese. All there is of cruelty, pride, luxury and

candour inherent in Woman herself [*à la Femme même*] has been perpetuated through the long ages in precious examples until its reaching him, the only one capable of accepting such a treasure! the poet makes it live in a gallery of some extraordinary Sonnets. . . . It is up to you, Ladies, to plunge your eyes into these *tableaux* profound like mirrors, where you will always think a little bit that you are contemplating yourselves: for there is not one little girl seated on the school benches who does not carry in her a drop of this eternal and royal blood which made the great princesses of yore.[20]

Once again, it is a masculine reading (of a masculine reading) which gives the woman her image in the mirror. Here the image is not of an actual mirror, as at the ball, nor in the form of another woman, but in a literary text, written by a man, which requires a specific reading on the part of women, for whom it is to be transformed into "*tableaux* . . . like mirrors."

While still maintaining the reader in the position of pupil, the little girl at school, her teacher here teaches her to recognize a far more sublime or exalted image than that of the queen of the society ball. "All there is of cruelty, pride, luxury and candour inherent in Woman herself" seems very different from the kind of instinct that would find expression in a smile. Yet these aspects of Woman are first of all manifested not in images, but in a "treasure" preserved from time immemorial until its reaching the present, rightful heir. This multi-faceted Woman whom "the poet makes live" is thus a valuable property for those who have preserved her in the form of "examples." Her value belongs to, or is recreated by, the man who inherits her by means of a new literary text. The eternal "drop of blood" innate to Woman is pricked or made manifest only by the resuscitation or reinscription which gives it new life at the hands of its latest reader and rewriter.

This femininity, which varies but somehow always remains the same, seems further to need to be taught: the cruelty and candour that are "in" the woman have first of all to be inculcated in order that the *Lectrice*, the woman reader, will know them – know herself – when she sees them. The legendary "Woman" has no existence outside a text-mirror offered then to female readers as an image in which they will recognize themselves. The woman learns to read herself in the form of a perfect mutual reflection of subject and text/mirror image, via the interpretations (to be subsequently "forgotten" as nature takes over) of a teacher – or indeed of a poet: someone, according to "Ix," "whose authority in the matter of vision is not less than that of an absolute prince," and who "with thought alone maintains control over [*dispose de*] all earthly ladies."[21] Both the drop of that eternal, royal blood she "bears in herself" and the clothes and looks she wears on the outside depend, equally, on a masculine law – a "vision" and a writing – which resurrects or gives life to the difference of man and woman.

The reader of *La Dernière Mode* is addressed as "eternal and royal" and also as a pupil or little girl: an apparently contradictory combination which has some affinities with the disparity identified in the *Bon Marché* appointments diaries between the reader as honored lady and the reader as foolish child. According to Roland Barthes, this opposition, fairly constant in the language of fashion, can be linked to a polarity not dissimilar to that of the serious and the frivolous. In *Système de la mode*, Barthes describes

> a rhetoric which is sometimes sublime, giving to Fashion the guarantee of a whole nominal culture, sometimes familiar, carrying clothing off into a universe of "little things". It is however likely that the juxtaposition of the excessively serious and the excessively trifling [*futile*] which is the basis of the rhetoric of fashion only reproduces at the level of clothing the mythical situation of Woman in western civilisation: at once sublime and infantile.[22]

This takes us back to the quotation from Mallarmé's text in which the question of frivolity was juxtaposed with a universe of fashionable "little things" around the woman, and also with products of culture in the form of newly published books:

> These products of the latest hour, . . . are they in Fashion or should they be? A frivolous critique, apparently? no, for it starts from this absolute point that all women like verse as well as perfumes or jewels or again as characters in a story like themselves.

The criterion which will render the *critique* according to *la Mode* a serious enterprise and not a frivolous one is the love of women, founded, apparently, on their *amour-propre* which is an absolute given. The serious has no basis of coherence outside this seemingly random series of objects women like: perfume, jewels, fictional characters, themselves. It is an apparently frivolous set of criteria which justifies as serious the apparently frivolous critique.

Barthes's point about the alternation of the two "modes" of rhetoric in fashion writing can be connected with what he says about Mallarmé's text itself:

> If it was a matter of a dialectic of the serious and the silly, in other words if the silliness of Fashion was taken *immediately* as absolutely serious, then we would have one of the most elevated forms of literary experience: this is the very movement of the Mallarméan dialectic with reference to Fashion itself.[23]

In contrast to other fashion magazines, such as the *Bon Marché agendas*, in which the polarities of frivolous/serious, or sublime/childish are juxtaposed but never interrogated, Mallarmé's text would thus permit a kind of double vision or double reading. Further, the implications of these pairings for representations of masculinity and femininity turn out to be destabilized: the poet as "absolute prince" strips off the outer forms which provisionally cover his lack of total power in the arbitrary construction of the figure brought to life as that of eternal Woman. Mallarmé's interweaving and unweaving of sublime and infantile, masculine and feminine modes, seriously and frivolously divulges the process by which the image of a natural woman, in which women learn to recognize themselves, is sewn up into the apparently seamless text of a world in which women shop.

NOTES

1   N. Chodorow (1978) *The Reproduction of Mothering*, Berkeley, Calif., University of California Press.
2   Littré's dictionary was completed in 1872.
    "MODE, *masculine noun*. In philosophy. Manner of being which cannot exist independently of substances, although it can be conceived separately in the abstract. // Form, method. Mode of government. // Name given to the different forms of the verb used to express the different points of view from which one considers existence or action. // In music. Disposition of the sounds of the scale, determined by the place

of the semitone, which occupies the third degree in the major mode and the second in the minor mode.

MODE, *feminine noun*. Manner, fantasy. // Passing practice which depends on taste and caprice. // *À la mode*: according to the taste of the day. // *In the plural*. Decorations, hats, jewellery. // [Female] seller of *modes*: [female] milliner."

3 O. Bloch and W. von Wartburg (1968) *Dictionnaire étymologique de la langue française*, Paris, Presses Universitaires de France.

"Borrowed from the Latin *modus*, 'manner', properly 'measure', which was also used as a musical and as a grammatical term. Feminine in all senses until the 16th century; the masculine was restored in the 17th century for technical senses."

4 M. B. Miller (1981) *The Bon Marché: Bourgeois Culture and the Department Store, 1869–1920*, Princeton, NJ, Princeton University Press.

5 The *agendas* are currently kept with other archives in the attics of the store building. I would like to thank Michel Simonnot and Chantal Laquintat for generously allowing me access to these materials, and office space in which to examine them.

6 I have discussed this novel in relation to the construction of women as shoppers in my (1985) *Just Looking: Consumer Culture in Dreiser, Gissing and Zola*, London, Methuen.

7 "Notre double existence, rue et salon," S. Mallarmé, *La Dernière Mode*, in H. Mondor and G. Jean-Aubry (eds) (1945) *Oeuvres complètes*, Paris, Gallimard, 780. All further references will be to this edition. A facsimile edition of extracts from *La Dernière Mode*, including illustrations, was published by Ramsay in 1978. All translations from French texts are my own.

8 M. Delbourg-Delphis (1981) *Le Chic et le look*, Paris, Hachette, 47.

9 Mallarmé (1945) 716. "Ces produits de la dernière heure . . . sont-ils à la mode, ou doivent-ils l'être? Critique, apparemment, frivole? non, car elle part de ce point absolu que toutes les femmes aiment les vers autant que les parfums ou les bijoux ou encore les personnages d'un récit à l'égal d'elles-mêmes."

10 G. Michaud (1953) *Mallarmé: L'Homme et l'oeuvre*, Paris, Hatier, 94.

11 P. Bourdieu (1981) *Questions de sociologie*, Paris, Minuit, 196.

12 Mallarmé (1945) 831. "Non seulement ces touches nécessaires à compléter une harmonie nouvelle . . . mais aussi d'où celle-ci vient et où elle nous mènera, son origine, ses résultats, et surtout les transitions qui l'ont accompagnée."

13 Mallarmé (1945) 718. "Nous apparaîtrons partout, le même: attentif à la somme de plaisir que peut, de ces usages nouveaux, tirer une personne contemporaine."

14 Mallarmé (1945) 812. "Lois, décrets, projets, arrêtés, comme disent les messieurs, tout est maintenant promulgué, pour ce qui est de la mode: et nul Message nouveau de cette souveraine (qui, elle, est tout le monde!) ne viendra nous surprendre d'une quinzaine ou de deux."

15 Mallarmé (1945) 815. "Il faut ne savoir ces préceptes qu'afin de les oublier; et mieux que d'eux, je me prévaux, Mesdames, de tout le désobéissant caprice qu'à cette lecture mêle déjà votre Fantaisie."

16 Mallarmé (1945) 718. "Une glace, où vous vous reconnaissiez. Vous et d'autres y jetant les yeux, quand le rythme des danses d'hiver vous ramène à votre tour devant ce miroir impartial, toutes vous chercherez la reine de la fête par un regard, qui ira droit à votre image; car, de fait, quelle femme, étant toujours cette reine pour quelqu'un, ne l'est pas un peu pour elle-même?"

17 Mallarmé (1945) 719. "Cet épanouissement de vos deux lèvres, j'en noterai la grâce, à laquelle d'autres lèvres, suivant tout bas cette lecture déjà s'essaient. Ainsi les choses, et justement: le monde n'a-t-il pas comme un droit de reprise sur la manifestation la plus profonde de nos instincts? il la provoque, il la raffine. Tout s'apprend sur le vif, même la beauté, et le port de tête, on le tient de quelqu'un, c'est-à-dire de chacun, comme le port d'une robe."

18 For more on this in relation to Mallarmé, see J. Derrida (1972) "La double séance," in *La Dissémination*, Paris, Éditions du Seuil, 199–318; translated as "The double session" in *Dissemination*, trans. B. Johnson (1982) Chicago, Ill., University of Chicago Press.

19 Mallarmé (1945) 816. "Le hasard n'est pas le seul à nous faire, avant tout autre, écrire le nom du *Bon Marché*; mais nous obéissons à une intime conviction que jamais la Lectrice qui aura, montant en voiture, jeté ces mots! *rue du Bac* ou *rue de Sèvres*, ne reviendra chez elle, contrariée de notre conseil ou de son propre mouvement á elle."

20 Mallarmé (1945) 802–3. "Du passé solennel et inoubliable, fable, légende, histoire, mais qui est maintenant fermé à l'éclosion de ces types miraculeux, Théodore de Banville, avec le receuil des *Princesses*, a ressuscité l'âme et le corps de Sémiramis, d'Ariane, d'Hélène, de Cléopâtre, d'Hérodiade, de la reine de Saba, de Marie Stuart, de la princesse de Lamballe et de la princesse Borghese. Tout ce qui de cruauté, d'orgeuil, de luxe et de candeur inhérents à la Femme même, s'est à travers les longs âges perpétué en des exemples précieux jusqu'à sa venue à lui, seul capable d'accepter un tel trésor! le poète le fait vivre dans une galerie de quelques Sonnets extraordinaires. . . . À vous de plonger les yeux, Mesdames, dans ces tableaux profonds à l'égal de miroirs, où vous croirez un peu toujours vous contempler: car il n'est pas une petite fille assise aux bancs du pensionnat qui ne porte en elle une

goutte de ce sang éternel et royal qui fit les grandes princesses d'autre-
fois."

21 Mallarmé (1945) 803. "Le Poète (dont l'autorité en matière de vision
n'est pas moindre que celle d'un prince absolu) dispose avec la pensée
seule de toutes les dames terrestres."

22 R. Barthes (1967) *Système de la mode*, Paris, Éditions du Seuil, 246. This
book has now been translated by M. Ward and R. Howard (1985) as
The Fashion System, London, Jonathan Cape.

23 Barthes (1967) 246.

8

The beauty system *

---◆---

DEAN MacCANNELL
JULIET FLOWER MacCANNELL

In all societies, the arrangement between the sexes is an uneasy one involving tensions, separation, and segregation.[1] Institutionalized opposition between the sexes occurs in obvious ways as in some Australian aboriginal groups where males speak a language forbidden to females, or the urinary segregation of the sexes found in our society. There is also a set of oppositions that penetrate to the level of the subconscious so that males and females who associate intimately, sharing sex, toilet facilities, even language, can nevertheless inhabit separate phenomenal worlds and stumble around in quite different libidinal territories. Recent feminist writers have done much to remind us of our deficiencies in understanding the mind and social situation of women. But they may be closing the door on understanding the overall relationship between the sexes by pretending to open it. Feminists now speak of "hot pussy,"[2] rape, even rape fantasies, and other formerly tabooed topics of female public discussion. But in so doing, they carefully step over the *relationship between the sexes* considered as a totality in its everyday expression.

The discipline of social sciences blocks understanding of the arrangement between the sexes in a different way, by reducing relational matters to questions of gender or sex-role differences. The social sciences simply repeat, on a more sophisticated level, the same program followed by people in everyday life: boys are like this, girls are like that. The *form* of the relationship between the sexes is not studied directly and specifically, nor is it possible to do so without exceeding the limits of discipline theory and methods. In two pioneering studies, *Gender Advertisements* and "The arrangement between the sexes" ("ABS"), Erving Goffman directs our attention to this embarrassing gap in sociological knowledge, but he does not claim to have filled it. To the contrary, Goffman remarks

> [Gender role performance competency] might be said to be essential to our nature, but this competency may provide a very poor picture of the overall relationship between the sexes. And indeed, I think it does. What the relationship between the sexes objectively is, taken as a whole, is quite another matter, not yet well analyzed. . . . There is no relationship between the sexes that can be characterized in any satisfactory fashion.[3]

If we explore the terrain between the sexes, we find a pattern of expressive constraint in "masculine" self-portraiture, especially as this imaging is turned toward women. Men, in our Anglo-American society, are supposed to be "cool." This requirement operates on every detail of behavior, including language performance rules requiring men to flatten and draw out the ends of sentences in order to sound "masculine." There are prohibitions and injunctions, not against "showing off," but against *appearing* to be showing off. The man should wait for an opportunity to demonstrate his physical strength or co-ordination, and hope that his shirt sleeves are rolled up when the opportunity comes; he should not seek out such opportunities, or offer to show his muscles. He should be similarly cautious when it comes to other forms of self-expression-for-women, his behavior, speech, and dress, lest they be seen as *intentionally* produced for the purpose of being attractive to females. The woman is supposed to be attracted to the man for his social achievements (wealth and power) and simply because he is a man, not because of any special effort on his part to make himself attractive to her. He must avoid verbal admissions of interest in a particular woman, unless this admission can also be read as unserious, insulting, and so on. The main expression of masculine orientation toward women in our society is a non-reciprocal license to study, stare, examine, no matter what female in no matter what situation, a license which sometimes extends beyond the visual to verbal insolence. This male behavior is a component of an enormous complex of cultural practices that can be called the *feminine beauty system*. Although the men themselves would put it in cruder terms, what they are measuring is the degree to which the woman they are studying has subordinated herself to the beauty system, that is the degree to which she appears to be committed to making herself attractive to men.

The feminine beauty system, including the masculine appraisal of it, and attraction, is the main feature of the cultural terrain between the categories "male" and "female" in our society. There is no other cultural complex in modern society which touches upon individual behavior that is as rigorously conceived and executed, total, and minutely policed by collective observation and moral authority, than are feminine beauty standards. (For example, standards for mothering behavior are nowhere near as detailed.) Beauty standards apply to face paint color, body size and weight, breast shape, upper arm measurement, head and body hair texture, color and visibility, facial expression, garment and accessory selection and co-ordination.[4] A close examination of the beauty system reveals it to be an *ideology*, or a way of living a contradiction as if it were not a contradiction. The ostensible reason for attempting to make oneself beautiful is first to attract men, then to "get" or to hold a man in a marriage or other lasting relationship. The true hidden purpose of the feminine beauty system is to transfer the power of the female libido to men-in-general, not merely toward the end of maintaining male dominance over women, but "male" power in the abstract, or cultural power under a masculine sign, even that which is directed against other males and nature. Institutionalized separation and segregation of the sexes is not the cause of gender disorders but only a part of the system, its maintenance equipment. In short, the contradiction at the base of the beauty system is that prescribed feminine beauty practices are believed to attract males, or bring the sexes closer together, while their real effect is to keep the sexes separate and unequal, even, or especially, as they seem to be coming together.

THE MALE SET-UP

In our society, noted for its commitment to privacy, the assignment of human infants to one of two "sex classes" is done at birth on the basis of visual inspection of the genitalia. Goffman notes that the practice is not unlike "that employed in regard to domestic animals," and it is immediately followed by an appropriate alignment to gender-marked language terms: boy–girl, he–she, man–woman, and so on ("ABS," 302). After the original inspection, the genitals are covered for social occasions. There will only be a few more times in the course of a man's life when he will be asked to take it out and show it as proof of his sex: his seventh-grade physical education class showers, his military induction physical. Most of the time he will be on the honor system, as when he takes his Scholastic Aptitude Test and is permitted to check the appropriate box "male" or "female." In short, after the genitals are covered, gender is imputed, mainly on the basis of arbitrary signs: blue blankets for boys, pink for girls, hair length, etc. Visible so-called "secondary" sex characteristics may be used after adolescence, but this is also largely a matter of imputation as there is considerable overlap between the sexes *vis-à-vis* the actual development of these characteristics. And, of course, there has never been an aspect of our biological constitution subject to as much socio-cultural manipulation as our secondary sex characteristics which are routinely created and destroyed by cosmetic and surgical procedures. Without actually viewing another's genitals, we have no real *proof* of the other's sex. This, of course, is the way gender, or more properly "genderism," is born, from all the little details of "masculine" and "feminine" behavior, dress, appearance, from the signifiers that displace, hide, and otherwise obliterate the actual sex. The enormous complex of cultural practices we are calling the "feminine beauty system" flows from the literal and figurative absence of sex, and interestingly it is mainly the male sex that is being covered by the tokens of femininity. How can this work?

> Women seem to sit a different way to show their legs when they wear skirts instead of pants. You feel more like a woman. You look like a woman. . . . I never wear pants.
>
> (Diane von Furstenberg, 33)

> My conversion to pants at the start of the Seventies was slow but complete, accompanied by a sense of relief and relaxation.
>
> (Susan Brownmiller, 80)

Go back to the original moment of gender classification based on empirical observation. Of this original visual inspection, Goffman remarks politely only that the genitals are "visibly dimorphic." If we are to clarify the overall relationship between the sexes, it will be necessary to be a little less polite and more specific than Goffman. Infants classed as males have a penis and testicles where infants of the other class have a suture in the place of a penis.[5] There are three logical forms an opposition can take: A:B, in which objects of two merely different classes are distinguished; $+:-$, in which objects which are considered to be equal but opposite are opposed; and 1:0 in which objects are classed by the presence or absence of a crucial characteristic. The last form of opposition is called a negation, and it is the form of the original classification, male:female.[6] Males, as a class, do not need to dramatize their sexuality, because they are the only actual sex class. Females are in the other class, not because they possess anything positive, or even negative, of their own; it is only that they are not males, theirs is a residual class: 1:0.

The zero which is the base of the identity "feminine" is also the base of widely held notions that women have a vacuous consciousness, that they are not capable of shaping or forming thought itself. The form of the original classification is the ultimate grounds of the separation of femininity from serious cultural achievement, especially intellectual achievement, and the reason that women who are "accomplished" are given honorary male status. From the original emptiness of the category radiates a myriad of beliefs in the essential comparability of all females in entirely visual terms. Both men and women understand that a man may leave one woman for another simply because the other is "prettier."[7] The most pernicious form this belief system takes, the most self-sustaining achievement of genderism, is the normalization of *boredom* for women. In all beauty books, it is taken for granted that most women will be agonizingly bored most of the time; that when they are alone, they will occupy themselves preening and their heads will be empty. The Princess Pignatelli, a Beautiful Person from the 1960s, reports, "I . . . spent a whole year doing nothing at all. I was so bored I used to remove the hairs from my legs, one by one, with tweezers" (13–14).

Men in our society wear pants and women wear pants and skirts. Feminists have argued that men make women wear skirts that can be lifted on demand for sex, to remind them of their degraded status as the sexual property of males, and to maintain them in a state of vulnerability. From the perspective being developed here, the wearing of skirts has additional and more basic connotations. Women wear skirts to signify that they have nothing to expose, and so that men can wear pants and appear thereby to be covering something up. The real source of male power is in keeping the basis of their identification as males hidden away.[8] The covering of the penis itself precisely corresponds to the promotion of male power by means of a seemingly endless series of penis substitutes the "uncontrolled" use of which is justified on the grounds that they are not the real thing, and are therefore not a real application of male power, only a stand-in for it: knives, clubs, guns, sharp words, hard facts, and so on. A sports writer eulogizing a former golf champion comments, "46-year-old Nicklaus is still bigger than life (would you believe he is just 5–11?), more of a man with a club in his hands than most of the rest with a gun."[9] This game risks being called at the first moment of interpretation based on disclosure of the relationship of the instruments of power to the *veiled* penis. For as soon as a gun appears in this new frame it produces a kind of anxiety of impotence, an uneasy sense that the man might not be able to perform without the aid of a prosthesis. It is this fragility of masculinity which is protected in the overall arrangement between the sexes by shifting virtually all attention away from questions of masculinity to the feminine beauty system. The feminine beauty system is the Maginot Line around male power as it is currently set up.

The preservation of the male set-up depends upon several things. First, adult males must keep their pants on in public as any re-exposure of their claim to unique identity and power threatens the entire set-up by revealing the ridiculous basis for their claim. Second, representative women must on occasion be made to appear naked, or about to be exposed, and a little embarrassed, in public in order to remind us that they have no indexical qualities when it comes to sex class assignment. Diane von Furstenberg enthusiastically volunteers herself and her sisters for the role of the slightly exposed female:

> You should wear a dress that moves with your body, clings a little, and makes you feel sensual. It is fun to see a woman in a shirtdress with the buttons opened low, or a wrap dress that's loosely tied and somewhat décolleté. I like to see women who show their bodies because they are pleased with them. (33)

In this regard, it is interesting that some organizations, which have approved the wearing of pants by female employees, still do not approve of women wearing pants with fly fronts. The wearing of such pants on the part of women might force men to have to prove that *they* have something in there. Going beyond von Furstenberg, female frontal nudity is not necessarily a scandal even in prudish social circles, so long as everyone agrees there is nothing to see. One can note, for example, that the editing of the pornographic movies shown on the *Playboy* cable channel involves cutting all footage showing the male organ while leaving abundant footage of female frontal nudity. In *un*edited pornographic movies, the role of the female is to continue to cover the male member, mainly with their faces. The pornographic "violation" is only that it literalizes the real arrangement between the sexes, the same relationship metaphorically expressed outside the pornographic frame by "Cover Girl" facial make-up.

The female beauty system covers the social fact that men are not supposed to have to show or represent themselves in any way in order to be accepted as *men*. They are originally and authentically men in the first place. Men are real. Women are "made up." But this alleged authenticity of the male gender hides behind and is entirely dependent upon feminine self-characterization as fake, false, superficial, artificial, and the like. Now it should be possible to explore the contradictions at the heart of the ideology of feminine beauty in some detail.

BEAUTY IS ONLY UGLINESS IN DISGUISE

A recurring feature of the autobiographical beauty narrative is the confession to being ugly. Most writers put their ugliness in the past, as something they experienced as a child or especially as an adolescent. Laura Cunningham writing in the *Cosmo Girl's Guide* claims to be ugly underneath her make-up in the present:

> My *essentials* are: 1. Foundation – to cover grey skin and mini acne. 2. False eyelashes – to bolster my real lashes which are so sparse I cannot bat them. 3. The "primary line" – a line that I carve out with shadow in the hollow above my eyelids, and without which my eyes sink into my face like raisins in a rice pudding. 4. Dark pinkish-brown lip slicker – without this my lips are a shade darker grey than my skin. [etc. for nose and hair.] (27)

When the beauty narrative dwells upon self-alleged childhood ugliness, it usually includes some expression of anxiety concerning the breasts. The Princess Pignatelli states flatly:

> I was a lump and everyone knew it. To compound the dreariness, my parents sent me to a school run by nuns. All legs and big feet, thick at the waist and thick in the nose, with no breasts and droopy shoulders, I had only one dream – I would grow up to be madly sexy like the movie stars of the forties with their curves and cleavage. I longed for big breasts. (4)

Jane Fonda remarks:

> As a child, I was your basic klutz – awkward, plump and self-conscious. . . . Like a great many women, I am a product of a culture that says thin is better, blond is beautiful, and buxom is best. (9, 13)

And Susan Brownmiller confesses:

> I agonized that I was miserably flat-chested and wore my small breasts unnaturally high and pointed in a push-up bra with foam rubber padding. (26)

The centrality of concern about the breasts in these confessions may reflect an inchoate understanding that the only true sex is male, and until the recent invention of the female muscles, the breast is the most phallic feminine attribute, or the only real grounds for a claim to "feminine" sexuality. Of course they have to be *large*.

It would be easy to dismiss the general form of these complaints as a kind of hypocritical posturing to sell "beauty" books to readers who must think of themselves as plain or they would not consider buying the books in the first place. The ugly confession puts the writer in a necessary identification with the reader: "I was once mousy, flat-chested, and awkward like you, and look at me now." One suspects that Diane von Furstenberg, who can find precious little basis for her claim to have been plain, but makes it nevertheless, does not quite believe herself as she writes

[A]fter having had a simple childhood, I spent my teenage
years infiltrating into more sophisticated groups. Always
the youngest, the most awkward, the least experienced and
definitely the least glamorous, I kept looking around, wanting to
learn how to become one of those secure and glamorous women
across the room. (15)

But there is also often something heartfelt in these passages, a real
anxiety that would not go away even if the commercial reasons for
expressing it were removed. One cannot read this Lilly Daché
passage as anything but a statement directly from the heart:

Every little girl starts looking in the mirror almost as soon as she
can walk. And almost every little girl fears at some point that she
is hopelessly ugly, that nobody will ever admire her and that she
is doomed to be an old maid. I remember I used to look at myself
in the mirror and wonder if other people really saw how ugly I
was (or thought I was), and then I decided to fool them so that
they should never know. (116)

Daché's remarks notwithstanding, a young girl has a choice. She can
accept herself as she is, or she can enter the beauty system, motivated
by a belief in her own deficiencies as the taken-for-granted baseline
condition justifying the numerous and often bizarre operations
deployed against her body. Once in the beauty system, she must live
an absolute contradiction: beauty is proof of ugliness. For a young
girl to accept herself "as she is " is not an easy choice. She is drawn
into the beauty system by the force of her entire culture, by the design
of the overall relationship between the sexes. When she looks in the
mirror and sees ugliness reflected back upon herself, what she is
actually experiencing is the value that her society has placed upon her
gender category, that she has no value. And the approved cultural
response is to pick up pencil and paint and try to draw a human face
on this nothingness, a beautiful face.

Here it should be noted that the beauty system reflects the class and
ethnic standards of the entire society in its aesthetic formulas. The
Cosmo Girl's Guide mainly provides advice on how to pretend you
are a class or two above your actual station. Jane Fonda repeats the
way the beauty system veils its support of ethnic hierarchies by its
emphasis on "blonds." Black women are still not permitted to play in

the beauty system major leagues. Interestingly this also saves them from having to view themselves as essentially ugly. Barbara McNair, who is the Jackie Robinson of her gender, addresses black girls

> Honesty is the basic ingredient in any beauty plan, and it can be the most difficult. We all, to some extent, see ourselves as being great beauties, and we're right.   (15)

But "times they are a changing," and McNair goes on to advise her readers, in effect, that if they wish to compete on an equal footing with white women, they must adopt the attitude of white women, that is, come to regard themselves as essentially ugly, but "perfectable."

"NATURAL" BEAUTY

> No one, not even my husband, has seen my face *au naturel* in three years.
> (Laura Cunningham, writing in the *Cosmo Girl's Guide*, 26)

The originary "hidden ugliness" which serves as a psychological motivation for the beauty complex is precisely analogous to the male sex organ which must be covered. This is the reason that "beauty" as defined by the beauty system can never be natural beauty but must always involve covering and make-up, even when the desired end result is the appearance of being a "natural" beauty. Von Furstenberg remarks:

> Begin with an honest evaluation. Look in the mirror and really examine yourself. . . . Then think "what am I going to do about it?" That's the first step – to decide what you want to do about something unattractive. You have a choice. You can do nothing and accept yourself as you are. Or, you can choose to reshape your body, color your hair, even have plastic surgery. . . . My own feeling is that it is important to be as close to natural as possible; generally, being natural is really a great part of being beautiful.   (29–30)

The beauty complex charts a progression from a break with nature, through display craft and other artifice, often arriving back to "nature" or a constructed image which is ideally natural seeming. The Princess Pignatelli is aggressively candid on the relationship of beauty procedures to the face and body as given by nature:

> [W]hat nature skipped, I supplied – so much so that I cannot remember what is real and what is fake. More important, neither can anyone else. (3)

> Before, during, and after marriage, happy or unhappy, I underwent hypnosis, had cell implants, diacutaneous fibrolysis, silicone injections, my nose bobbed, and my eyelids lifted. I have tried aromatherapy, yoga, and still go to the best gymnast in Rome. Facials and pedicures are normal routine, as are frequent hair and makeup changes, I will try anything new in beauty. I could not bear not to try. I must have experimented with every gadget on the market. (11–12)

The beauty complex suppresses nature, even or especially as it appears to imitate nature.

> When you become deeply involved in any discipline – and beauty, above all, is discipline – it takes you outside yourself. First, you learn to see your own looks as a quality apart from self, as a symbol, "a thing." This leads to an immediate appraisal of other beauties and an understanding of the whole problem and phenomenon. In reaching out, you see that all other women can be in the game together. (Princess Pignatelli, 15)

STAGED AUTHENTICITY AND FEMININE SOLIDARITY

A great deal of the moral force of the beauty complex, the way it serves as a basis for feminine solidarity, derives from its simultaneous dissociation from, and imitation of, nature. Natural advantage or disadvantage can never be used as an excuse for success or failure within the beauty system. The central theme of every beauty manual is that any and every beauty flaw can be corrected by rigorous adherence to beauty discipline. The moral force of the system extends to override the process of aging itself. According to each of these writers, if you appear to age, it is because you have failed to follow their advice. And the parallel subtheme, that a great natural beauty can also flop if she fails to attend to her eyebrows, waist, or accessories, is also present. Again, the Princess Pignatelli comments succinctly:

> When you care about beauty, it may be all to the good if nature is not overgenerous. There is no chance then of living in a mythical past or in perpetual illusion. It does not matter what you start with, try and get on by nature alone past thirty and you are finished. (3)

In other words, a woman who does not play the "beauty game," at least on some level, even a woman who might pass as "naturally" beautiful, is admitting, in effect, that she has opted for a non-standard relationship with men and with other women, in fact, with society in general.

The double theme of suppression and imitation of nature is especially evident in contemporary guides to makeup application which stress (1) cleaning the face completely, (2) applying a layer of skin-colored foundation to the entire face and neck, (3) painting on a new face which resembles as much as possible a "natural" face, but one that is beautiful, and (4) (this step is optional, for evening wear, or for catching someone's eye) one or two, but not all of the following: high gloss lips, extra eyeshadow or liner, cheek blush co-ordinated with hair, eye, and/or dress color, purple or gold nails, and large or multiple (on the same ear), or mismatched, earrings. The goal of these procedures is to achieve a look of generalized natural seeming beauty that is accented by an unnatural beauty system cliché (perhaps a little extra dab on the eyes) which can serve as a personalized marker. These little, supposedly personalized, beauty markings are intended to make their bearer attractive to men. Sometimes men are attracted because of them, but not for the reason that they are, in-and-of-themselves, attractive. Rather it is because they are expressions of feminine desire to be attractive to men, and a willingness on the part of the woman to subordinate herself to the discipline of "beauty," which, within the framework of the beauty system, is the same thing.

When viewed from the perspective of the thesis of this paper, the beauty system appears as an amazing feat of cultural engineering. To the extent that the beauty system holds, in order to attract men the woman must make herself principally responsible for covering up the inadequate basis for the male claim to socio-cultural superiority. No one, neither males nor females, need be conscious of these forces in order to be caught up in them, in fact, it helps to be *not* conscious of them. But even when these things are not consciously understood, on some basic level, a woman who relates to men via the beauty system is always fundamentally stigmatized, or seen by herself and others as a half-person, if seen as a person at all.

STATUS DISORDERS

The beauty system is related to systems of class, status, and power in society, but they are not in perfect synchronization. Beauty system conventions are more widely accessible than are actual wealth, prestige, and power. At the point of intersection of the system of beauty and status, the powerless may appear to be powerful and vice versa. Pathological expression occurs throughout the social order when an individual comes to believe that his or her personal power derives entirely from appearances, when a woman believes her make-up, hair style, clothing is all that is important in shaping her relations with others, or the man thinks of his gun or Cadillac the same way.

There is evidence for substantial status disorders in the beauty system that takes the form of vicious competition for rank among women, based solely on physical appearances. This attitude is barely suppressed in most of the beauty manuals, and not suppressed at all in the *Cosmo Girl's Guide* or by the Princess Pignatelli who often take aim at Third-World women and menial laborers. A *Cosmo* writer remarks:

> Hairpiece – my bureau is stuffed with the hair of a thousand Orientals. I feel occasional pangs of remorse when I picture all those peasants going around half-bald in the hot sun. But it was either them or me. (27–8)

The Princess makes clear that competition for *rank* is more important to her than competition for men. Specifically she is willing to sacrifice a relationship with a man if he does not relate to her through her achieved "beauty," which, she believes is the basis of her power and prestige:

> [F]inding the wrong man is disaster. For example, the man attracted by your glamour who then proceeds to tell you that you would be much lovelier with your hair down and your eyes unmade; the man who cannot see why a few pounds (which sink straight to the rear) could possibly do any harm. It is such a boring attitude, and when heeded, leads always to the same boring result. You take away this, take away that, and in six months you look like a cook.   (12)

Given the contradiction at the heart of the beauty complex, it is not surprising that the perverse appeal of this passage is to cooks and to other women in the lower socio-economic classes who dream of being a princess. Beautification contains elements of "identifying up," desiring to be seen as among the rich and famous who are often represented in the popular entertainments as proponents of the beauty system. In the actual social order, a few people have more wealth and power than they can ever use, while most of the others do not have enough to maintain even minimal self-respect. Some moderns cannot control their own children or their neighbor's dog. Such people may understandably spend much of their lives longing for fame, wealth, or freedom from workplace constraints. Under these conditions, the working-class male may find escape in his phallic substitutes, guns, cowboy boots with sharp toes and heels, four-wheel drive vehicles with dual drive shafts, and so on. The woman may derive some pride and self-assurance from making herself beautiful.

If she tries too hard, of course she will fail. Too much, or obvious make-up or glitter in the clothing, is a universal sign of lower-class status. The *Cosmo Girl's Guide* cautions that this same principle applies to language use: that is if you want to appear to be from a higher class, you must learn to avoid the use of exactly those terms which working-class people believe that upper-class people use. Such glitzy language is the surest indicator of one's actual condition. The *Cosmo* language lesson for the girl who would appear to be upper-class "U":

You should say *car* (U), and not *limousine* (Non-U), even if it is a limousine. *House*, never *estate* or *mansion* (as in "I'm going to his ——"). *Boat*, not *yacht*. And you say my *coat*, not my *mink* or my *sable*, Even If It Is One. (52)

Saying "yacht" instead of "boat" is the linguistic equivalent to wearing too much mascara. A working-class girl who struggles for hours in front of her mirror to get her eye make-up to look like the eye make-up of a famous movie star affirms the existing hierarchies in the same way as a man who wears a jacket that says "Corvette Racing Team" on the back. Both gestures indicate subservience to the system of socio-economic values by those who are oppressed by the system. That this subservience manifests itself in behavior which may confer a sense of "identity," a little feeling of capacity for independent self-expression, makes it all the more effective and complete.

POWER FAILURES

Women can gain and wield personal power in a variety of ways having nothing to do with the beauty system. They can start social movements, amass wealth, teach, manage small and large "empires," write and publish, they can even be brilliant and accomplished wives and mothers. A woman's intellectual and emotional life need have nothing to do with her relationship to the beauty system. But to the extent that the woman believes her identity and power derives from her beauty, there is a complex linkage between beauty and the emotions. Given that beauty is only a cover for "original ugliness," the emotions will always vacillate between joy and depression. Human physiology has nicely adapted itself to these cultural arrangements: beautiful powerless women claim to suffer more from menstrual cramps than do powerful plain women.

Eleanore King subscribes to the thesis that improvement in appearance will produce an inner feeling of calm assurance, that is, beauty drives the emotions. She promotes the idea, common in the 1950s, that feminine beauty, or "charm," is intimately connected to strong fellow feelings in general, not just heterosexual love leading to marriage. And she assumes that such feelings do not occur in a natural state, but must be acted out.

Then, after their outward manifestations become habitual, they may actually be felt:

> You learn through doing. You move gracefully until that is your only way of movement. You incorporate radiant, sincere facial expressions until they become yours. You practice tactful, gracious conversation until any other kind would be foreign to you. . . . Soon your friends, your business associates, even your family notice, first, a subtle change, then a remarkable one. . . . "You're a glorious person. . . . Do you know that?" *And you are.* (11)

This "acting is becoming" thesis relating beauty to mood is also found in Lilly Daché's book written at about the same time:

> [A]s a paint company has pointed out . . . often "if you preserve the surface you preserve all." The consciousness of looking her best often touches off a woman's inner mainspring of joyous self-confidence and – presto – all of a sudden she is glamorous. (29)

Diane von Furstenberg, who lets us know that she can take her own beauty for granted, relates appearance to mood via a cybernetic feedback loop:

> I think make-up and fashion should not be taken that seriously. I've tried to make them fun. You should have fun making up for a party. You should have fun wearing a sexy dress. When you are beautiful it should give you pleasure. . . . You should always be as beautiful as you can be so you will be desired. And isn't being desired a part of being fulfilled? (31)

Von Furstenberg is confused about her own motives for accenting her beauty. It is somehow associated with pleasure for her. "Isn't being desired a part of being fulfilled?" We don't know. Is it? The Princess Pignatelli simply endures the depression which she knows is the constant companion of beauty which is used as the sole source of feminine power:

I now realize that happiness does not in itself guarantee that you will look marvelous – not unless you use that happy glow only as a starting point and then really work at it. . . . [The three way mirror] can be a shattering reflection when all one has to show is inner radiance. (11)

And quoting a model on the same relationship of mood and appearance:

If you never sleep, or smoke like crazy, or never go out in the air . . . it shows. But if you are not happy, that is what shows the most. Some evenings I can spend two hours in front of the mirror and nothing fantastic happens. . . . Other evenings I put a little black here and there – put a little black on my spirit – and I look great. (11)

RELATIONS WITH MEN

Imagine something that does not occur in real life but is theoretically possible, a relationship between a man and a woman that is framed entirely by convention. The only form it could possibly assume is one of reciprocal sadism. If the only power a man has derives solely from his "masculinity," and the power of the woman derives from her "attractiveness," the pure form of interaction between two such beings would involve pushing each other around with *mood* – or with their "looks." The man tantalizes and tortures by dangling his "thing" (and his feelings) just out of reach, literally and figuratively by sullen withdrawal, silence, and by preoccupation with phallic substitutes, his "things." The woman knows that his attraction to her has nothing to do with herself. Her attractiveness is only an assembly of conventions borrowed from the beauty system to cover up her emptiness and ugliness. His interest in her only serves to indicate that he is susceptible to being duped by the oldest, most widespread, and open cons around, that his balls are bigger than his brains. The more she is interested, and the more he reciprocates her interest, the less she can respect him. The only real personal power she will ever be able to wield is to deny or turn-off the men to whom she is attracted who are also naive or crude enough to be attracted to her false beauty. The man expresses his masculine power and "love" by coldness and silent withdrawal, sometimes punctuated by phallic rage at being trapped in a contradiction as final and absolute as this one. Or, if he really loves her, he may attempt to enter into an "intersubjective relationship" with the woman by insulting her, by telling her directly and indirectly that he sees through her feminine facade and knows how stupid and ugly, what a nothingness, she really is. Similarly, the woman can express herself, as an individual and as a woman, only by transforming all attraction into rejection. With her characteristic clarity on such matters, Mae West sums up succinctly, "If I find a man absorbs too much of my time and my mind, and makes me concentrate on him, I get rid of him. It's alright for a man to concentrate on me" (Quoted in Pignatelli, 13).

In the final accounting, "sex appeal," or the power to attract using beauty system clichés, becomes its opposite. If it works, it has no relational function except to put men and women into positions where they can express their individuality only by mutual rejection. While the man wields power *as a man* in every cultural arena, the beauty system provides the only cultural place where a woman can exercise power *as a woman* (as opposed to any power she might have as a "mother," an "executive," a "wife," and so on). That this power takes the form of pure denial follows logically from the original designation of "woman" as a genderless, zero category. If the man's attraction is purely physical, and he stays within the bounds of physical control, the woman's rejection can take the form of silent refusal. If, however, he is attracted to her "as a person," her denial will be verbal as well as non-verbal, perhaps assuming the form of petty self-assertion called "bitching" and going into "deep freeze." That uniquely feminine power is always wielded in the name of its opposite (beauty, love, and attraction) and ultimately serves to separate woman from man, rather than uniting them, is among the most basic contradictions and darkest secrets of the conventionalized arrangement between the sexes.

The beauty system provides the perfect formula for a "Rock-a-Billy" romance of the powerless. Fortunately it does not circumscribe the totality of actual cross-sex relationships. In real life, men and women, even beautiful women, manage to sustain cross-sex relationships. The interesting feature of these relationships is that they have *no basis* in the beauty system which, if we hold to strict anthropological definitions, is the only cultural complex specifically designed to structure the arrangement between the sexes as such.

(Marriage, for example, has sufficient additional economic, inter-familial, and other functions, that it can outlast any male–female relationship that might also occur within its compass, and it may be specifically engineered to operate in this way in opposition to the beauty system.) While the tendency in the beauty system is to destroy male–female relations, there are a variety of strategies for maintaining them. The most effective of these strategies are *ad hoc*, worked out by creative couples. Others involve mutual subordination to a system of external values, fear of authority, religious beliefs, or common interest in the raising of children. The most interesting strategies are those elaborated on the borders of the beauty system itself, under the heading of "How to hold on to your man."

Lilly Daché lays down the basic, most repeated, advice: prolong the moment of initial attraction by simple repetition of courtship behavior, flirting, clinging, wet-kissing, appearing to yield to his superior strength and the like.

> A husband expects the undivided attention of his wife when he is with her. . . . [Mine expects me] to be waiting eagerly when he comes home, to defer to his opinions and admire his strength, to be soft and clinging and feminine and to put him first, above any other person or any other interest. (19–20)

Similarly Coco Chanel quipped, "In love, what counts is to please a man. If it pleases him, paint yourself green" (quoted in *Cosmo*, 16). While it is true that Daché's marriage lasted over twenty years, her account of it, as contained within the beauty system, is highly fictionalized.

Madame Daché arrived in New York in the 1920s, alone at age 18, without enough English to get a job or enough money to get a hotel room. She set herself to making hats, at first for anyone who would pay her, eventually for Greta Garbo, the Queen Mother, and others. She made enough money making hats to put up her own building, "seven floors devoted to workrooms and salons and business offices," and above the "shop," a two-story penthouse apartment into which she moved her "very traditional" husband. In the 1930s she became the first transatlantic air commuter, flying between New York and shops in Paris, Rome, Cairo, Geneva, and London. One doubts that she was always "waiting eagerly for him when he came home." And one might also wonder if she always gave him her "undivided attention" and "deferred" to his opinion. Actually we need not wonder as she quickly contradicts herself on this point:

> [My husband] thought I was foolish when I insisted on putting up my own building in the heart of New York. It was toward the end of the depression, and it seemed a tremendous undertaking, but I was convinced it was the right step. It meant going into debt, and [his] business sense did not approve of this. But at last he agreed. (20)

So much for "clinging" and "feminine," although these adjectives continue to be essential for beauty-system love stories, and they might well have helped her get her way. But her husband obviously admired her building and drive (that is, her overtly phallic attributes) as much as her soft lips and build.

Daché's maintenance of the myth of feminine attraction in the face of her own business accomplishments (all in the name of "beauty," of course) is nothing short of heroic. Even though the comportment advice she proffers (as opposed to her example) could never actually serve as a basis for a lasting relationship with a man, within the beauty system, there is a compulsion to repeat a version of her advice as the *only* basis for a relationship. "Clinging" and "yielding" are graphically detailed in the *Cosmo Girl's Guide* to the unimaginative:

> A woman should freely practice kissing a man's hands. The back of the hand is acceptable. But . . . it's preferable to take his hand and lightly lick the palm and/or the index finger. And, of course, there is foot and shoe kissing – only recommended if you really enjoy it or *he* does, and you're more than anxious to please. (45)

> Sew on his buttons. . . . Hold his one *big* hand in your two little ones. . . . Rearrange his tie after you have both mussed it. . . . Polish and sort his cuff links. . . . Put your hands on his naked waist and stare at him. . . . Toy with his belt. . . . Feel his muscles. (241–2)

SINGLED OUT

During the decades since World War II the beauty system has undergone an evolution. Specifically there has been a progression away from heterosexual love as that which is represented as the underlying motive for the entire beauty complex. From the standpoint of this paper, the disappearance of Love as a category in beauty writing is not surprising, and may even reflect a partial coming to consciousness within the beauty system. But this disappearance is unmarked from within, no one seems to have noticed that Love is gone. So we cannot assume that the internal contradictions of the beauty system are about to be exposed to revolutionary action. Something like the opposite is happening, the system is moving in the direction of a more logical and rational elaboration of values around its contradictions.

Begin again with Daché. She enthusiastically embraces the love of a man as the primary goal of beauty discipline. In her chapter 19, titled "How to get – and keep – a husband," she states:

> As a flower needs sunshine, a woman needs love. . . . [N]o matter how much love a woman may have, she always wants more.

After 1980 Love will not be mentioned again. Interestingly Brownmiller is an exception, although there is an undisguised bitterness in her tone as she attempts to keep something like "love" alive: "But even those who earn their own living share a universal need for connectedness (call it love if you wish)" (17).

Sometime between Daché and Fonda, the goal of heterosexual love is replaced by the idea that the pursuit of beauty is a part of "self-discovery," and "self-assertion." The current definition of marriage within the beauty system is a *rite de passage*, a temporary, bounded event in the quest for "individualism," always a dangerous term, especially so when applied to women. Von Furstenberg comments on her divorce:

> We separated soon after that . . . and I began the painful process of rebuilding my life. I became more involved with my children and with my work. I started taking the first tentative steps towards discovering myself as a human being and a woman. (17)

Within this new framework of feminine individualism, the requirement of being beautiful in order to attract does not disappear. It becomes even more important. Being beautiful is the only socially acceptable cover for having no heterosexual relationships, for beauty alone can convey the impression that the woman is without a man by choice. Similarly, sexual intercourse loses most of its former connotations of intimacy, and becomes mainly a matter of expressive self-testing of one's attractiveness relative to other independent women in the new beauty system. Von Furstenberg claims to feel little need to test herself in this way:

> The only way for a relationship to survive, I think, is to have no sex at all. After all, you marry for friendship, for companionship – and passion after awhile . . . pffft. I mean, does it excite you when your left hand touches your right? (17)

The Princess Pignatelli comments: "I believe in separate bedrooms. . . . I am not about to point out the latest wrinkle, emotional or otherwise, to the man in my life" (13).

The Princess and the *Cosmo Guide* make clear that there is not merely a tension between beauty and the kind of intimacy once thought to be associated with heterosexual love, but they are now seen as in *opposition*. In other words, a contradiction is coming to the surface. A *Cosmo* writer complains:

> The man is a walking, talking, love-making make-up destroyer. . . . Virginity is not all that is lost in bed. More make-up disappears here than anywhere else. And the bed is where you need it the most. Every girl having an affair should have a magnifying mirror and her *essentials* make-up kit hidden under the bed. While her lover sleeps, she can make repairs. (29)

And the Princess complains:

> [W]hen you have to watch calories, it is much easier if you eat alone. This does not mean that you have to give up men's company, but ideally, you should have a man who is not always around. A man . . . loves to go out to eat. (25)

As long-term cross-sex intimacy declines, the approval of strangers is sought out as a replacement for the give and take that once characterized more lasting relationships. In order to obtain the approval of strangers in sufficient amounts to make up for long-term intimacies, however, it may be necessary to escalate one's involvement in the beauty system. The Princess comments:

> You want to be beautiful in the objective sense, with the beauty that no one fails to notice, envy, or admire. When you have it, men turn to look at you in the street. Often their appraisals are offensive, if harmless, and you could do without them – until they stop. (57)

In a parallel passage which connects several points (belief in original ugliness, the relationship of mood to beauty, desire for the approval of strangers) a *Cosmo* writer tells an interesting story:

> The happiest moment of my life . . . occurred on a sunny end-of-Saturday afternoon. . . . I was on my way to a post-shopping visit at my old friend Kenneth's. . . . As I waited for a light to change, a . . . delivery boy careered towards me on a bicycle-wagon, lurched frighteningly in my path, grinned insanely in my face, and shouted blissfully, "Hey, mama, you lookin' fine." Actually, I had imagined I was looking only middling; no makeup except eyeliner, clean but limp brown hair, [etc., this self-description goes on for several lines]. But if this cat said I was lookin' fine, then I was feelin' fine – and as we all know, *that* gives you a 90 percent advantage in the battle for beauty.
>
> I must have been glowing like an expectant mother when I reached Kenneth's apartment . . . and just this once didn't suspect that his inevitable "My dear you look *divine*" was the tiniest bit undiscriminating. For the truth is, there are some people in your life whose compliments become devalued, like Kenneth's. . . . So what happens when all the inputs you get about yourself come from somebody like Kenneth, whose "truth" puts you in a crazy . . . world where heads come up with every flip of the coin? What happens is that his compliments become devalued. (75–6)

(The writer's "old friend," Kenneth, is evidently inadequately socialized to the beauty system and might have been able to hold her interest by interspersing his compliments with an occasional insult.) The interesting part of the story is the encounter with the stranger. It is no accident that the valued compliment in the account was delivered in sub-proletarian black argot. It was valued not because it was "pure" as the writer claims in another passage. It is valued because she is excluded by social convention from any possible relationship with the utterer beyond the fleeting, one-sided exchange in the street. From the standpoint of emerging new beauty system ideology, this is a perfect male–female bond, completely contained in the immediate present, unencumbered by the emotional complexities of long-term relations. She even fantasizes that she was impregnated by her contact with this black stranger.

The Princess Pignatelli also valorizes male–female relationships which preclude any long-term physical intimacy: "Every woman over thirty needs a homosexual in her life. She needs someone who is genuinely interested in making her look better. . . . Husbands and lovers cannot be bothered" (13). Even Brownmiller, who in many ways is the most romantic of the writers reviewed here, has a soft spot in her heart for homosexual men: "'homosexual designers' cannot be blamed for the uncomfortable, unrealistic fashions they 'foist' upon women, for the whole show is produced for the approval of heterosexual men. Many gay men, as straight women often observe, are very attractive" (97–8). This particular development within the beauty system has dramatically increased the stakes in the game, cost of entry, and strategic requirements. In seeking the approval of *everyone* with the possible exception of actual and potential long-term intimates, the risk of failure and depression is enormously increased.

By the 1980s the development of the beauty system, which flows logically from its underlying contradiction, is almost complete. The woman is no longer advised to enter into lasting or fleeting relationships, not even with strangers. A new realism replaces the romanticism of the 1950s. Diane von Furstenberg remarks off-hand:

> The security of feeling more attractive can encourage your security as a woman. But don't allow yourself to think you can change a nose or get bigger breasts to get back a man you've lost. If you've lost him, that's not why you lost him. (196)

Susan Brownmiller specifically equates "beauty" (in this instance, a beauty system operation, a trip to the hairdresser) with getting out of a relationship, not into one:

A woman will often choose to "do something different" with her hair after a difficult crisis, for a new way of wearing the hair gives the impression of a new lease on life. A fashionable hair style can elevate the mood more successfully than any drug (although the effect may be equally temporary), a fresh look can sever emotional ties with a person who preferred it the old way, it can offer visible proof that this spunky lady is taking charge of her personal survival. (76)

In a mass transference, beauty discipline, once thought to be a means to an end, to get a man, becomes an end in itself with the same libidinal contours once thought to be the exclusive bounds of intimate physical and emotional adult cross-sex relations. In a brilliant pragmatic move, the loving care of a man (the beauty system promise that could never come true) has been replaced by the care one takes in making oneself beautiful. The Princess Pignatelli is a little bitter but articulate about this transition as she experienced it after the break-up of her marriage:

> For helping your looks, the emotional security and teamwork of a good marriage is unbeatable. The trick I had to learn early was to keep going no matter what. This takes a strong dose of ego – or just plain selfishness. If loving care is so good for people, one might as well lavish some on oneself. (10)

The logical progression of beauty system ideology arrives at its fullest expression in the writing of Jane Fonda. In the first equation, found in Daché, King, and other writers in the 1950s, appearance and mood were always connected through the man: classically,

$$BEAUTY \rightarrow MAN \rightarrow HAPPINESS$$

(It is the formula for fairy tales.) By the 1960s and 1970s, in the writings of the Princess, *Cosmo*, and others, the man is no longer the central term holding the system together. He is marginalized. His role is to generate beauty, not vice versa:

$$MAN \rightarrow HAPPINESS \rightarrow BEAUTY$$

This was the historical equation inherited by Fonda, and on which she worked her radical transformation of the system.

The Beauty System

Fonda does not promote "beauty" in the traditional sense, in fact, she opposes herself to beauty system abuses. Describing an early make-up session readying her for work as a beauty system exemplar, she comments:

> When they were through, I could hardly recognize myself in the mirror – winged eyebrows, false eyelashes, big pink lips, hair that looked as if it had been ironed, right off the Warner Brothers assembly line together with Sandra Dee, Connie Stevens. (17)

She renounces this approach to beauty in favor of one that is more authentic and more powerful – the workout:

> Working out has become a part of my life. . . . [W]hen I approach my Workout I play a game of "pretend." I am no longer Jane Fonda, the actress, wife, mother, activist. I am an athlete. I *have* to push myself to the limit and beyond because I'm preparing for competition. But the competition is with myself. (24)

As the quote implies, Fonda's book contains no attitude whatever on relationships with others, lasting or temporary, with men or women. In this regard, it is unique among beauty books. She is absolutely neutral on her marriages, divorce, and children, printing a photograph of herself with her first husband, and her infant child by him, next to a same-sized photograph of herself with her second husband and her infant child by *him*. These two interesting pictures appear face-to-face on pages 28 and 29 over the captions: "With Roger Vadim and our daughter, Vanessa," and "With Tom Hayden and our son, Troy."

Fonda is emphatic on the point that her beauty treatment is a valued end-in-itself. It is not to get a man, or even to achieve a possible fleeting effect on strangers, to draw a compliment from a man or an envious glance from a woman. Shaping the body is pursued for the sensations experienced while pursuing it, sensations described throughout the book in terms similar to those used to describe the release which some derive from sado-masochistic sex. For example:

[M]y co-workers would wonder why at the end of a fourteen-hour day on a stuffy sound stage I pushed myself . . . instead of joining them in collapsing with a drink. I certainly felt more like collapsing than working and sweating until I ached, but afterwards I would feel alive and revitalized. It was hard to explain this or describe how good I felt about being disciplined.   (21)

The underlying motive of the Fonda narrative is not to fall in love or even to get in touch with others. Rather it is to get in touch with herself, to become an entirely self-contained dialogic unit in which the only important relationship is with her own body. She recalls that she was able to break free from the alienation of the old beauty system only after "*I began consciously listening to what my body was telling me*" (27). The alchemy worked by this onanistic final expression of western individualism is intended to produce a new gender, the first to deserve to be called "woman," that is, an independent woman, one who is not defined entirely by her role in maintaining the cultural and other potency of males. But this cannot occur. For what we find in the place of the male in the beauty system formula as modified by Fonda, is not a new feminine consciousness, but an obvious male simulacrum: working out, muscle building. Moreover, the alleged new feminine consciousness is not identified merely with the male principle in general, but with a special version of it. It is an identification with the phallic substitutes of the powerless male, the working-class male: bulging muscles. To the extent that this new form of feminine beauty calls forth the substantial homosexual reserves in the general male population,[10] to the extent that it taps into male solidarity, it may serve as well or better than earlier ideals in bringing the sexes together at least for procreative purposes, now ironically under a homosexual sign.

Fonda's critique of the old beauty system is genuine. She fervently desires to be liberated from it, believes she has escaped it, and wants to help others. Commenting on her early vacuous and sexy roles she exclaims:

If I had only known what I was doing to myself. If I had only understood twenty years ago the futility, the alienation, the self-denigration of trying to fit oneself into a mold. It was as if I was thinking of myself as a product rather than a person.   (16)

The Beauty System

And on the extension of the system into the Third World, she remarks:

> A [Vietnamese] prostitute could increase her price with her American tricks if she conformed to the Western Playboy sexual standard. And these operations [eye rounding, breast and buttocks enlarging] weren't confined only to prostitutes. Many of them were done to women in "high society" such as the wives of Generals Thieu and Ky. These women literally had their faces and bodies Americanized. . . . The women of Vietnam had become victims of the same *Playboy* culture that had played havoc with me. (20)

One wants Fonda to succeed, if for no other reason than disgust for those groups and individuals who have made it their mission to attack her. But the particular way that she has struggled against the beauty system only succeeds in bringing the original contradiction to the surface where it is less obvious. She *becomes* the contradiction. She cannot see her approach to "beauty" as the ultimate logical extension of the cultural hegemony of the masculine gender as the only gender. As she strikes out against "trying to fit oneself into a mold," a serious revolutionary sentiment, she is evidently unaware that the mold she has made for her followers is harder and more permanent than any face make-up. She will eventually say:

> But something muscle-like does happen and I like it. Since you are reading this book you are probably like me and appreciate a woman's body on which the muscle cuts and contours are evident. This is what you get. (69)

And in the same book where she expresses hatred for thinking for herself as a "product," she makes herself into a product, literally: the "Jane Fonda" Workout Studios, Book, and Video. The limits of narcissism are reached in a photograph on page 20 depicting three Americanized Vietnamese prostitutes, intended to illustrate her criticism of the "*Playboy* sexual standard." The girls appear as a sad parody of the old beauty system. The one on the left has made herself up as an obvious copy of Jane Fonda.

CONCLUSION

In this paper the term "beauty system" has been used to refer to the diverse practices which are widely held to make a woman more attractive, *and* to the primary effect of these practices which is to harness the energy of the female libido, her desire for sex, to covering our culture's designation of "male" as the only gender category. Women must *pretend* to be women so that men can be thought of as *real*. The beauty system turns feminine desire against itself. Actual heterosexual relations are the first things to be sacrificed to the system. Beauty system arrangements were once rigorously gendered in the biological sense, but no longer. Biological women are now taking off their bras and make-up, wearing pants, developing muscles, and claiming to be "authentic." And biological males are wearing earrings, eyeliner, and so on. The secret of the mass appeal of allegedly ultra-macho stars such as Sylvester Stallone is they have learned to imitate the "sultry" or "hot" facial expression of a female who is signaling sexual openness. That the beauty system is no longer biologically gendered does not change its essential structure, of course.

All societies have deep cultural oppositions which can take the form of contradictions. Meaningfulness itself depends upon this. When analyzed, the feminine beauty complex reveals itself to be a deep structural contradiction covered by gender ideology. The beauty system is the only cultural complex designed to bring the sexes together, albeit only for procreative purposes, that is it is patterned female behavior intended to attract males. There is no elaborated corresponding set of male practices. Beauty ideology is a lived contradiction. Beauty practices and beliefs are experienced by both males and females as a coherent totality, as "shared meanings." Ultimately beauty practices and beliefs fragment human existence by turning all intentional acts against the self-interest of the actor. They drive the sexes apart and cut the woman off from men and the rest of society. The male gender remains the only marked gender, now ratified absolutely by equating "feminine" beauty with muscle. More important, the woman remains obsessively concerned with her physical *appearance* as the only basis she has for any claim she might wish to make as a woman, even claims she might wish to make for or against herself as a solitary woman, which is rapidly becoming the only "relationship" she is culturally allowed. She is beautiful. She is strong. She is independent.

Freudians and some feminists have made much of the way the Woman reveals the "truth" about civilization, that it was built upon male castration anxiety.[11] This revelation is effected via representation of the female sex as a "bleeding wound" in the place where the penis *should* be. What we have been stressing here is a simpler truth: namely that the myth of mutilation is a fine collective excuse, but even without injury, the male member is not an adequate base for civilization. Female insecurity which takes the form of "beauty" is only male insecurity displaced. This is the reason the real basis for it can never be found in the heart of the woman who experiences it.

EPIGRAPH

I already know a thing or two. I know it's not clothes that make women beautiful or otherwise, nor beauty care, nor expensive creams, nor the distinction or costliness of their finery. I know the problem lies elsewhere. I don't know where. I only know it isn't where women think. I look at the women in the streets of Saigon and upcountry. Some of them are very beautiful, very white, they take enormous care of their beauty here, especially upcountry. They don't do anything, just save themselves up, save themselves for Europe, for lovers, holidays in Italy, the long six-months leaves every three years, when at last they'll be able to talk about what it's like here, this peculiar colonial existence, the marvelous domestic service provided by the houseboys, the vegetation, the dances, the white villas, big enough to get lost in, occupied by officials in distant outposts. They wait, these women. They dress just for the sake of dressing. They look at themselves. In the shade of their villas, they look at themselves for later on, they dream of romance, they already have huge wardrobes full of more dresses then they know what to do with, added to one by one like time, like the long days of waiting. Some of them go mad. Some are deserted for a young maid who keeps her mouth shut. Ditched, You can hear the word hit them, hear the sound of the blow. Some kill themselves.

This self-betrayal of women always struck me as a mistake, an error.

You didn't have to attract desire. Either it was in the woman who aroused it or it didn't exist. Either it was there at first glance or else it had never been. It was instant knowledge of sexual relationship or it was nothing. That too I knew before I experienced it.   (Marguerite Duras, *The Lover*)

NOTES

* Financial support for preparation of this chapter was provided by the office of Jaime Rodriguez, Dean of Graduate Studies and Research, and by the Focused Research Program in Gender and Women's Studies, Academic Senate, the University of California, Irvine. The authors wish to give special thanks to Deborah S. Wilson and Asafa Jalata for their assistance in researching this paper.

1 This paper is a part of a series of analyses of systems of culture, especially on issues that frame the arrangement between the sexes, such as "beauty," "order," and "cleanliness," which the authors have undertaken in the past few years. See D. MacCannell and J. F. MacCannell (1982) *The Time of the Sign: A Semiotic Interpretation of Modern Culture*, Bloomington, Ind., Indiana University Press; J. F. MacCannell (1986) *Figuring Lacan: Criticism and the Cultural Unconscious*, London and Lincoln, Nebraska, Croom Helm and University of Nebraska Press; J. F. MacCannell (forthcoming), *Couplings: The Failures of Heterosexuality from Rousseau to Lacan*, Baltimore, Md, Johns Hopkins University Press; D. MacCannell (1973) "A note on hat-tipping," *Semiotica*, VII, 4, 300–12; D. MacCannell (1976) *The Tourist*, New York, Schocken; and his *American Mythologies* (in preparation).

2 See, for example, H. Grossett's "Is it true what they say about colored pussy?" and other selections in C. S. Vance (ed.) (1984) *Pleasure and Danger: Exploring Female Sexuality*, Boston, Mass., Routledge & Kegan Paul, 411–12 and *passim*.

3 E. Goffman (1979) *Gender Advertisements*, New York, Harper & Row, 8. See also his (1977) "The arrangement between the sexes," *Theory and Society*, 301–29.

4 The evidence used in the following is from observations and from several guide books to feminine beauty purchased in bulk at reasonable cost from used book shops in Southern California. Citations in brackets in the text refer to the following books, which range from the 1950s to the 1980s: L. Daché, *Lilly Daché's Glamour Book*, ed. D. R. Lewis (1956) Philadelphia and New York, J. B. Lippincott; E. King (1957) *Eleanore King's Guide to Glamor: Beauty, Poise and Charm in a Few Minutes a*

236

The Beauty System

Day, Englewood Cliffs, NJ, Prentice Hall; Princess Luciana Pignatelli (as told to J. Molli) (1970) *The Beautiful People's Beauty Book; How to Achieve the Look and Manner of the World's Most Attractive Women*, New York, McCall; *The Cosmo Girl's Guide to the New Etiquette* (1971) New York, Cosmopolitan Books; D. von Furstenberg (with E. Portrait) (1976) *Diane von Furstenberg's Book of Beauty: How to Become a More Attractive, Confident and Sensual Woman*, New York, Simon & Schuster; J. Fonda (1981) *Jane Fonda's Workout Book*, New York; Simon & Schuster; S. Brownmiller (1984) *On Femininity*, New York, Simon & Schuster.

5 The term "suture," the "joining of the inner lips of a wound . . . a line or seam . . . the conflux of the inner margins of elytra," *OED*, has disturbed several pre-publication readers of this chapter. We want to make clear that while this term does not reflect our personal sense of the vagina, it nicely conveys the cultural values which we wish to analyze. Its possibly negative connotation is appropriate to the cultural framing of the vagina as understood in this chapter: that is problematical, but not as negative as the "bleeding wound" of Freudians and some recent feminists. See, for example, Mulvey, cited in note 11.

6 See A. Wilden (1984) "Montage analytic and dialectic," *American Journal of Semiotics*, III, 1, 25–47, on forms of negation.

7 See, for example, a typical confession in R. T. Lakoff and R. L. Scherr (1984) *Face Value: The Politics of Beauty*, Boston, London, Melbourne, and Henley, Routledge & Kegan Paul, which opens with Ms Scherr's claim that the book was inspired by her having been dropped for a blonde.

8 Our argument is the positive side of the by now generally understood notion that in veiling the female pudenda "nothing" is being hidden, because it represents the "truth" of castration. In its practical consequence, however, "castration" by clothing is also the effective means of imputing objective reality to what is hidden underneath. This would explain why the general baring of female parts that is currently available (even traditional women's "covering" is often a diaphanous veil, made as if to be seen "through" to the lack underneath) still supports the myth of the superior "reality" of the masculine. Lynne Gilliland has pointed out that male dancers, in contrast to female strippers, *never* take it all off, whereas females are increasingly displayed in our culture without genital covering. This would make Roland Barthes's "Striptease" myth, wherein a rhinestone triangle still hides the naked truth, a passé form of revelation.

9 *The Sacramento Bee*, 3 February 1986, C5.

10 Jacques Lacan pointed out the monologic nature of human sexuality by calling it *hommosexuel*. Interestingly in *Pumping Iron II*, the docu-

drama about the female body-building contest in Las Vegas, it is the contestant who has most "masculinized" her display of gender that is depicted as having the tenderest relationship with her male coach.

11 See J. Derrida (1977) "The purveyor of truth", *Yale French Studies*, 67ff; as well as his other writings. See also L Mulvey (1975) "Visual pleasure and narrative cinema," *Screen*, 16, Autumn, 6–7, for a succinct summation of this position.

Index

Index

Index